EVO MORALES

EVO MORALES

THE EXTRAORDINARY RISE OF THE FIRST INDIGENOUS PRESIDENT OF BOLIVIA

Martín Sivak

palgrave
macmillan

EVO MORALES
Copyright © Debate, 2008.
English-language translation copyright © 2010 by Braden Marks.

All rights reserved.

First published in Argentina as *Jefazo. Retrato íntimo de Evo Morales* by Debate.

First published in English in 2010 by
PALGRAVE MACMILLAN®
in the United States—a division of St. Martin's Press LLC,
175 Fifth Avenue, New York, NY 10010.

Where this book is distributed in the UK, Europe and the rest of the world, this is by Palgrave Macmillan, a division of Macmillan Publishers Limited, registered in England, company number 785998, of Houndmills, Basingstoke, Hampshire RG21 6XS.

Palgrave Macmillan is the global academic imprint of the above companies and has companies and representatives throughout the world.

Palgrave® and Macmillan® are registered trademarks in the United States, the United Kingdom, Europe and other countries.

ISBN: 978–0–230–62305–7

Library of Congress Cataloging-in-Publication Data

Sivak, Martín, 1975–
    Evo Morales : the extraordinary rise of the first indigenous
president of Bolivia / by Martín Sivak.
        p. cm.
    ISBN 978–0–230–62305–7
    1. Morales Ayma, Evo, 1959– 2. Presidents—Bolivia—Biography.
3. Bolivia—Politics and government—2006– 4. Indigenous peoples—
Bolivia—Politics and government—21st century. I. Title.

F3327.M67S58 2010
984.05′2092—dc22   2010004269
[B]

A catalogue record of the book is available from the British Library.

Design by Newgen Imaging Systems (P) Ltd., Chennai, India.

First edition: July 2010

10 9 8 7 6 5 4 3 2 1

Printed in the United States of America.

CONTENTS

Chapter One

CIRCLING BOLIVIA
(JUNE 2006)

MONDAY, JUNE 12

Bolivian presidents govern from the Palacio Quemado (Burned Palace).

In 1875, dissenters of then-president Tomás Frías hurled flaming torches at the house of government from a neighboring cathedral, igniting a massive fire. The uprising was unsuccessful but even after the edifice was rebuilt, the name "Burned Palace" stuck, a fitting reminder of the volatile country Bolivia has become since its founding in 1825. Of its 83 governments, 36 didn't last for more than a year, 37 were de facto governments, and, to this day, no historian has managed to determine the exact number of coup d'etats and military uprisings.

Evo Morales Ayma came to the presidency after the first democratic revolution of the twenty-first century, a fact that has not been reflected in any modifications to the Burned Palace architecture or décor. None of its inhabitants seems to be bothered by the fact that its aesthetic remains almost entirely unchanged—not the palace staff members running around from 5:00 A.M. to midnight to keep up with a presidential agenda that changes every hour; not the women who traverse the hallways in traditional Bolivian attire, skirts with petticoats and miniature bowler hats; not the *campesinos*, small-scale agricultural producers who tread along the carpets and parquet.

A panorama of color leads the way to Morales. The Room of Mirrors, a large waiting room near the presidential office, is divided into two parts: one pink and the other gold. Amid cobwebs and a black piano that nobody ever plays are mirrors with gilded frames, a Persian carpet with earth tones, marble benches, and gray curtains with tassels. An electric heater radiates the warmth no longer provided by central heating.

Just outside Morales' office is a white foyer. The night when the writing of this book began, I stood there trying to discern the silhouettes moving around inside the main office through smoked glass. Once the president's men had exited through one of the doors, Evo stepped out into that white foyer to greet me.

"Hello, *Jefazo* [big boss]," he said.

In his own personal language, he uses "big boss" as a form of flattery and a sign of respect. But the real big boss, the one in charge, is him.

He greeted me, Bolivian style: for men, a handshake followed by a half hug.

"Thank you for everything. You've given me the support that has allowed me to be here. Thank you, my brother."

I got the sense that he'd repeated these sentences to many people many times since becoming president.

We originally met in Buenos Aires in August 1995, when he first rose to prominence as a popular *cocalero* (coca-leaf grower) union leader. In the almost 11 years that followed, I interviewed him for newspapers, magazines, and documentaries. His trust in me was based not only on the books I had published about former Bolivian dictator Hugo Banzer and the assassination of ex-Bolivian president Juan José Torres, but also on the conversations we'd had.

That night, he wore shiny black shoes, dark suit pants, and his signature *chompa*, a red, blue, and white sweater with a round neck, which made international news when he wore it to travel the world as president-elect in January 2006. The sweater took on a disproportionate symbolism because neither its color nor its material had any relevance to him, his presidency, or his supporters. By June, the neckline was already worn out.

When I walked into his office, he pointed and said, "Sit here, where I made the American Ambassador sit. He didn't realize he was sitting under the portrait of Che." Facing the image of Ernesto Guevara, on the opposite side of the room, hangs one of Evo. Both are made of coca leaves. Yet in that room, it's not the green of the coca leaves that stands out but the loud blue of the armchairs.

"How are relations with the United States?" I asked him.

"Serious. Some Marines came into the country disguised as students. I have confidential reports. I'll show them to you later."

His spokesperson, Alex Contreras, informed us that a dozen photographers were about to come into the office. They asked us to hug each other.

"Like we're in La Bombonera [the soccer stadium in Buenos Aires]," Evo said, and he told me about how he wanted to organize a rally there during his next trip to Argentina.

"I'm going to write a book about you," I told him. "I'll need to spend a lot of time interviewing you."

"Come travel around the country with me," he replied. "We can talk between the rallies and events. And you should come right now and watch my soccer team: We're playing against our miner *compañeros*."

Within a half hour, Evo was sporting a light blue uniform with his number 16 jersey. While he warmed up by flapping his arms, he made some signals. From the cement bleachers, about a hundred people followed his every gesture. He isn't very quick, but he kicks the ball skillfully and sometimes powerfully. That night he managed to score two goals, which he barely celebrated. His rivals, members of a mining cooperative, seemed more interested in greeting the president than the game itself. As a consequence they lost, 7 to 2.

By midnight, Morales was exhausted. The next day, he had to get up at 4:30 A.M. to fly to Quito, where he would take over as president of the Andean Community of Nations (CAN). While there, he would become upset with Peruvian President Alejandro Toledo.

"Listen, Evo, the CAN is not a union, and you're not going to teach me anything about economics," said Toledo when Morales brought up exclusion and poverty.

"But all you can teach us is what the World Bank says," Evo said.

"How can you say that to me?" Toledo became even more cross.

"It's true. After this, you'll go and work for the World Bank."

The meeting ended there.

From Tuesday to Wednesday Evo slept well, as he always does when he sleeps in the plains or the tropics.

WEDNESDAY, JUNE 14

At 5:03 A.M., a group of government ministers and vice ministers filled the small entrance lobby of the Burned Palace for a cabinet meeting with the president. But while they stood there trying to wake up, they found out that

Morales hadn't been able to leave Iquitos, in the Peruvian Amazon, because of fog. "We'll have the meeting anyway," said the meeting receptionist, a police-woman with curly red hair. That meant there was time to discuss a topic that affected them all equally but wasn't exactly business: how to get up at 4:30 A.M. A vice minister explained to another minister that, in order to wake up on time, he slept with the TV on and dozed until the alarm clock went off. They yawned as they moved about to keep warm. It was only 36 degrees Fahrenheit. About 15 soldiers came into the central hall tapping their feet and wearing red and white uniforms, white backpacks, and bayonets.

I went up to the bathroom on the third floor. There were certain objects that didn't have anything to do with the current government, such as the poster of the United States and Bolivian flags that read, "United in the War on Drug Trafficking," and others that did, such as the flags of Movement Towards Socialism (MAS) and carnival masks.

Tatiana, the president's personal assistant, told me there would be room for me on the plane with Morales to Villamontes in the Department of Tarija but not in the helicopter that would fly to La Higuera, the town where Che Guevara was assassinated.

"We'll coordinate," she added.

"We'll coordinate" means "We'll try to fix it." It should be followed with, "Although it may be difficult." In general, things don't work out as planned, but the enthusiasm put into trying is an integral part of what it means to be Bolivian.

At 5:45 A.M., Álvaro García Linera, vice president of the Republic, came into Tatiana's office looking stiff in a black suit without a tie and a gray raincoat. A tuft of straight gray hair falling over his forehead gave him the air of a middle-aged, laid-back skateboarder.

Tatiana passed him a call from the president. He still hadn't left the city of Iquitos in Peru.

"Biiiig Booooss," I heard.

"Hello, brother," the vice president responded. "The newspapers came out well: They gave good coverage of your trip.... Yes, there's still a conflict between those two miner groups. What we have to do is find some middle ground. Alright, brother, take care."

After hanging up, he told me that the president had asked for two things: that they bring him some jeans and tennis shoes, and that I travel in his airplane. Before heading down one of the halls, he asked Tatiana what decrees there were to sign. The plainness of the office suggested a post office or soccer team clubhouse, not the thousand square feet where the most important decisions of the state are made.

A little later, there was a change of plans with the air travel. Evo would travel in number 01 (the largest plane in the presidential fleet), but I wouldn't be able to join on the leg to El Alto, where they would fuel up. Álvaro and the other ministers would take plane 03. That meant I would fly, along with another 60 people, on the Hercules.

Hercules airplanes are the property of the Bolivian Aerial Transport fleet. One detail sets the Hercules apart from the others: The plane's back section is attached to the front and the wings by wires. On the way to the airport, a police major tried to explain that the Hercules planes are safe but then told a story to the contrary. "Ten years ago, one crashed into a river or lake just a few minutes after takeoff. An admiral swam up to the surface, but then dove back in to find his wallet. He must have been coming back from selling something or on his way to buy something. He had so much money that he gave each one of us on the rescue team two hundred dollars." His anecdote didn't help me forget my fear of flying on the Hercules.

The inside of the plane looked like a small metalworking factory with unreachable windows and three rows of benches. The air was the temperature of a refrigerator. The passengers (ministers, generals, colonels, intelligence agents, journalists, and a nurse) covered themselves with blankets until the engines turned it into an oven. Some members of the security team were carrying Styrofoam coolers.

"Is that armament, captain?" I asked the vice president's head security guard.

"No, it's for the fish that we're going to bring back from Tarija. On the way back, the plane will be full of that delicious fish."

Two hours later, the Hercules landed in the town of Villamontes. There was a lively turnout for the event. Schoolchildren wearing their blue and white uniforms, including two girls who looked like they were trying out high heels for the first time; teachers who scolded their talkative students; members of the military and police force; and MAS party supporters who said to the president, in signs and banners, "Thank you for returning our dignity to us," and bestowed Morales with letters, garland, fruit, fish, hats, flowers, photos, and even documents. In the president's box, soldiers and policemen sent text messages to unknown recipients; one minister nodded off while another walked around to keep from imitating his colleague. They had woken up at 4:30 A.M., and the midday heat had wiped them out. A bodyguard, identified by the inscription "Police" in English on his brown shirt and sporting a bulletproof vest, cleaned the president's glass with a thin cloth and then filled it with water.

"This is a civic ceremony," the presenter began. Evo doesn't like that definition: He thinks of civics as relating to provincial sentiments. Although in Bolivia informality is a characteristic of politics, from the first sentence uttered to its conclusion, the ceremony was impressively formal. In official functions, such as the one in Villamontes, the national anthem is sung, and every speaker salutes the important people in the president's box; there is an official presenter, an official musician, an official program, and an official feeling.

Circumstances don't always contribute to that feeling. Sometimes equipment fails, the electricity goes out, the schedule isn't followed, and the wardrobes are out of place. In Villamontes, the president was wearing a short-sleeve shirt, worn jeans with the back pocket coming unsewn, and blue tennis shoes.

Evo started off by talking about the Chaco War (1932–1935), in which Bolivia fought Paraguay. He evoked the memory of the fifty-two thousand Bolivians who died, one of whom was his uncle, Luis Morales. A good many of the families on the western side of the country lost someone, awakening a nationalist sentiment. Because Morales' speeches tend to cover many topics, he then went on to praise the heroes who were present, protected from the sun by the tent; he said that all public officials should learn the Guaraní, Quechua, or Aymara languages; and he promised to provide computers to schoolchildren.

On May 1 of that year, when he decreed that the hydrocarbon industry would be nationalized, the president ordered the armed forces to occupy the oil wells and plants of foreign companies operating in Bolivia. He wanted them to feel a part of the process and to begin to internalize a new enemy: transnational corporations.

The purpose of the ceremony was to pay tribute to the armed forces, and the president told of how he had been afraid of the lieutenants when he first got to the Burned Palace. "Now I trust them. I thank the Armed Forces for their participation in nationalizing the hydrocarbons." He closed with a shout, "Long live the Armed Forces!"

With that last shout, a military parade commenced that included combat divers and infantry soldiers camouflaged with branches who withstood the 110-degree heat. During the retreat from the parade, García Linera became a main attraction. Some girls from Villamontes who must have been younger than age 15 took pictures with him. "I think you're very good-looking but my mother likes you even more," said one of the Tarija girls who was still in primary school. The delegation's vehicles passed by many precariously built houses. Although gas lines run underground here, only 3 percent of those houses were connected.

When we got to the hangar on the Villamontes runway, for once Morales did not make the decision.

"Seven can't fly on the 03?" he asked the colonel in charge of the flight.

"Only six, Mr. President."

He announced that someone would have to stay on the ground. "I'll be flying as well as Álvaro, Juan Ramón [Quintana, minister of the presidency], Alex [Contreras, spokesperson], and the minister of health [Nila Heredia], who has to inaugurate a hospital. That leaves Janet [his assistant] and Martín [me]. What do we do?"

"We'll let them flip for it," García Linera proposed.

The vice president took a 50-cent coin out of his pocket. One side had the number and the phrase "Unity makes strength." The other side had the Bolivian Republic's coat of arms. He tossed the coin, and it fell back into his hand. I saw the number and breathed a sigh of relief: It was my ticket to La Higuera.

Morales is usually the one to make the decisions. During his first six months as president (that is, from the time he took office until this trip), he had passed the hydrocarbons nationalization decree, released an outline for agrarian reform, began the process of de-Americanizing Bolivia after more than half a century of dependence on the United States, sealed long-term alliances with Fidel Castro and Hugo Chávez, and settled the election of delegates to the Constituent Assembly by which means he proposed to refound the country.

The 03 has four beige faux leather seats facing each other, a fifth one by the windows, and a sixth, really just a half a seat, between the pilots, which is where the president sat. For takeoff he put on the same kind of Ray-Bans that Tom Cruise wore in *Top Gun*, but he did not allow any photos to be taken of him.

He enjoys himself on airplanes and helicopters, sometimes asking the pilots to perform acrobatic stunts. He laughs at his own jitters and the fear of the others.

"Shall we eat?" he asked after takeoff.

"There's food," Contreras said, "but there aren't any plates."

"We'll eat with our hands then," Evo said.

Contreras took yucca and potatoes out of a plastic bag, as well as a two-liter bottle of Coca Cola and a cardboard box filled with lukewarm pieces of rabbit, chicken, and goat. When we were about to start eating, the pilot remembered where he had saved some coffee saucers. We ate our lunch on those. Because Evo didn't have a table, the minister of the presidency cut up the rest of the goat on a metal tray and served some yucca and potatoes for him. The vice president took out a hot pepper, which he shared with the president.

They talked about the ceremony.

"I was moved by the speech of that last soldier," Álvaro said.

"A nationalist moment is coming. We need to set up the schools with some material about nationalism," Morales added. "I learned the history of Columbus, the Pinta, and the Santa Maria, but nothing about nationalism. It can't go on like that. Did you see how those girls sang the national anthem? Let's record a CD with them singing it."

He said that later that day he would receive documents proving that the Transredes oil company had financed some of the massive demonstrations organized by the elite of Santa Cruz (the richest department, the Bolivian term for state, in the country), demanding their autonomy from the central power. "That's how the Santa Cruz oligarchy runs," he burst out. Morales was already seeing that this region would become the stronghold of the most resistance to his government.

From a bed of clouds, he got excited with the idea that the area we were flying over could turn into a tourist destination. He stopped talking politics for a while and turned to a subject that entertains him: his marital status.

"This is a government for single people," he told me. "Every time I return from a trip, I'm afraid that Álvaro will have made a decree imposing a first lady."

"When we first met, you were planning to get married. What happened?" I asked.

"That's right. It was the only time that I came close to getting married. But my friend David [Choquehuanca, his chancellor] convinced me not to do it. I didn't get married, and now I don't think I ever will. Besides, I'm already married to Bolivia. Once I said to myself: 'So many people love me, but no woman wants me.' That was in the 1990s. I proposed marriage, and they would say to me, 'No, they're going to kill you, they're going to put you in jail.'"

"Who told you that?" I asked.

"Some of my girlfriends from the middle class, the professional class. And our female friends would also tell me, 'I would get married, but only if I could spend all my time with you.' And it is difficult. Imagine getting up at five o'clock every morning and leaving your wife there, abandoned in the bed."

The president's spokesman passed him some dental floss. Evo cut off a piece for himself and then passed it around. We all used the floss to get the meat scraps out from between our teeth, except for the vice president, who had brought a toothbrush.

"Álvaro," I asked him, "isn't it dangerous for you to fly with the president?"

"If they want to kill us, well, they'll kill us."

The ambassadors from Cuba and Venezuela, Rafael Dausá and Julio Montes, responsible for establishing cooperation between their countries and Bolivia, were awaiting the delegation. In that first stage, Cuba was helping with the construction of hospitals and ophthalmology clinics, contributing doctors and literacy tutors, and providing scholarships for five thousand students to go to the island every year to study. Venezuela announced that it would invest $1.5 billion in the hydrocarbons sector, that it had bought bonds, and that it would fund, among other things, the industrialization of coca leaf production. It also lent two of its helicopters and some airplanes for the president's trips abroad. Both countries would advise on matters of intelligence and security.

In addition to the ambassadors, there were about five thousand towns-people waiting. Some older women cried when the president passed by, and an MAS activist made eyes at García Linera. This revolution is emotional and libidinous.

The stage, constructed of pieces of fabric and wood, took up part of the town's main street. After the speeches, we heard a rap version of "Hasta Siempre" (the tribute to Che Guevara), and the delegation toured a hospital recently inaugurated thanks to funds from Havana. Later, in the dash to the helicopters—we were already two hours behind schedule—the minister of health was left on the ground.

From the sky, we could see the dense landscape that Guevara had once traversed. That's how this region of Bolivia is. Neither the state nor a strong president can cut through its obstinacy. The lack of resources to build roads and bridges has caused further fragmentation in a country already marked by it.

In a courtyard in La Higuera, the third and perhaps most solemn speaker of the day requested: "With conviction, we sing our national anthems." We were supposed to hear the Cuban anthem first, but instead we heard a recording of Cuban musician Silvio Rodríguez singing his hit song about a lost unicorn. Between the flags of Cuba and Venezuela, Cuban doctors and Venezuelan youth hummed along. Accompanying them from the stage was Camilo Guevara, the son of Che, who had his long hair pulled back in a ponytail.

García Linera, a professor of Sociology at the public University of La Paz, improvised a lecture on the figure being honored that day. "Che represents the spirit and passion of revolution in the twentieth century." He said that the war—Guevara's war—continued on but through different means. He turned to Evo and ventured, "Mr. President, without Che you would not be here today."

Daylight was fading in La Higuera. The event organizers brought out a cake with 78 candles. Everyone on the dimly lit stage sang "Happy Birthday" without the honoree present to blow out his candles and thank them.

In the middle of the applause, a bodyguard—and a player on the presidential soccer team—informed me that he would have to take my place on the helicopter so he could, I surmised, make it back in time for that night's soccer game. I refused, arguing weakly, "We can both go." I was convinced that, on these tours, missing the helicopter of history was not an option.

Without enough seats for both of us in the aircraft with Morales and his vice president, I would have to climb aboard the plane on which the head of security had invited García Linera to travel.

"No, I'm taking this one," Álvaro responded while urinating in an empty field.

Evo told us to run so we'd get there in time. We bushwacked through the mud, weeds, bushes, and trees trying to find where the second helicopter had landed. Once we made it, a well-informed Cuban announced that we were about to do something dangerous.

"What?" I asked.

"Ride in a helicopter at night in a mountainous region with low visibility."

After the 45-minute ride to the Viru-Viru airport in Santa Cruz, two small planes would carry the delegation to El Alto, and from there we would head straight to the La Paz Coliseum. This time, the soccer opponents were members of the crew for the morning show *El Mañanero*.

Evo asked me to referee the game. They even gave me a whistle, but I hardly used it. The players made all the calls themselves, from the goal kicks to the fouls. Someone called a hand ball that I hadn't seen, and a little later a heavyset man got a nod from Morales and replaced me without much formality.

At the end of the first half, the presidential team was beating the *Mañanero* crew, 5 to 0. During the break, Rafael Puente, vice minister of government, took Morales aside to explain that he had publicly announced that Carlos Sánchez Berzaín, the right-hand man of Gonzalo Sánchez de Lozada, Bolivian president from 1993 to 1997 and from 2002 to 2003, had secretly entered the country, but that he may have been mistaken. The second half of the game had become somewhat dull because the teams were so unevenly matched. However, when a cameraman came off the bench, he managed to make the crowd laugh by fouling Evo several times. Morales didn't complain: When he played military opponents, they always kicked him around much more.

After showering in the locker room, Evo came out with his hair wet and uncombed, wearing the green jersey of the Bolivian national soccer team. He looked worn out: In the past 15 hours, he had been in three different departments of the country, spending most of his time in airplanes or helicopters, and he had given four speeches.

"Get in the car," he ordered me.

He rolled down the window and Walter Chávez, one of his top advisors and the person in charge of communications, showed him a poster he'd prepared for the electoral campaign. The election for the delegates to the Constituent Assembly, who would reform the constitution and put forth a referendum that would define autonomy, the primary demand of the people of Santa Cruz, was just two weeks away. Both of these things would be put to a vote in the first six months of Morales' government.

"Go for it, big boss," he said to Chávez, and he told the driver to take him home.

The BMW 750 with tinted windows parked in front of the building where he sometimes sleeps on 20 de Octubre Street.

"What has been the biggest surprise since you came to the Palace?" I asked.

"The bureaucracy. I'm a prisoner to bureaucracy. I'm most worried about losing contact with the people, especially in La Paz, since it's easier on the inside of the country for us to hold events and rallies. Another thing is the security," he laughed as he said this. "But I'm getting used to it little by little."

"What's the decision-making process like for someone like you who has no experience with executive power?" I asked.

"Sometimes there's a Plan A, B, and C, and I decide. When I'm sure of something, I make the decision on my own."

"What decisions have you made on your own?"

"As military high command I made appointments that disregarded the usual order of promotions," Morales said. "There were some ministers who didn't want me to do that, and others who were afraid."

"Today I saw you with crowds of people, advisors and security. What happens when you're alone?"

"When I'm alone, I feel more inspired. Mostly at night. I sleep about two hours, and I wake up every ten or fifteen minutes. I don't even turn on the lights, but I'm thinking and ideas come to me," Evo stated.

"You once told me that when you wake up at night you pray to your parents. Do you still do that?" I asked.

"When there are serious problems, after resting for a little, like at one o'clock in the morning, I pray to my parents, I believe in my parents, I return to my homeland."

A few minutes before 1 A.M., he got out of the BMW and went off to sleep or pray.

THURSDAY, JUNE 15

On national holidays, La Paz doesn't seem like itself—it's silent. There aren't any horns honking or voices of the children, who work on the buses, opening and closing the doors and outshouting each other as they compete for passengers.

Around midday, the president ordered a soup that he couldn't eat because he had to rush off to the military airport in El Alto. Airplane 01, upholstered in burgundy with matching carpet, brown leather trim, and room for six people, has one inconvenience: There isn't a bathroom. Nevertheless, before taking off, the flight crew served him tangerines and Coca-Cola to mitigate his hunger. Morales slept until we landed at the Rural Area Mobile Patrol Unit (UMOPAR) headquarters in the tropical area of El Chapare. It was in this region of coca leaf cultivation that Evo carved out his identity as a union leader. It's his territory.

From the headquarters he went to a small restaurant where the cooks came out to hug him. Seated at the white, plastic tables covered with red tablecloths and surrounded by desserts, sodas, and wooden screens dividing the patrons from one another, Evo ordered fish soup for some and fried fish with yucca and potatoes for others.

He told of how earlier that morning he'd offered the position of vice minister of sports to Milton Melgar (a former soccer player from the Bolivian national soccer team) to replace one of the three vice ministers he had fired because of supposed acts of corruption.

"Will he play on your team?" I asked.

"Of course. If he accepts, he'll start Monday and play on Wednesday. We have a difficult game."

He announced that the Latin American television network, Telesur, would begin to broadcast high school games live in El Chapare.

"Last week some young people selling empanadas asked me about the high school games and not about government," Morales said. "To me, the best way to involve people is through sports, especially in a poor country like Bolivia. Some schools have complained that there are students as old as twenty-two participating in the games. But if that's what it takes to get those youngsters to go back to school, then it's worth it. Now we just have to incorporate math into the equation."

While stirring boiled yucca with his spoon, he ordered more soup. Delfín Olivera, in charge of easing relations between the military and the *campesinos*, told him that a new union was being formed. "Set up a private meeting, I'd like to get to know them," he directed. Olivera said that getting the *campesinos* to trust the military was turning out to be a rather difficult task. At the head of the table, a military colonel spoke to him as a fellow military member: "Mr. President, last week there were two DEA [Drug Enforcement Administration] helicopters running tests."

"Tests for what?" he interrogated.

"The factory that makes those helicopters suggested that all their machines be inspected," said the colonel.

Evo reminisced about the carefree life in El Chapare. "It sure would be nice to play some racquetball and take a nap," he said after learning that he'd have to travel to Yapancani in Santa Cruz.

"Do you like flying in helicopters?" I asked later, as the blades turned.

"No, but I have to," Evo said.

Because we took off with the door open, the wind in the president's hair gave him a punk-rock look. After a little while, we could see Yapacani from the air. A crowd of people were surrounded by different shades of green.

"Did you prepare your speech?" I asked.

"I just talk about what comes to me," he said. After checking to see how many of his supporters there were, he let out an "Ooo-ooo."

Morales conceives of politics as a show of strength in the form of rallies. They convey the extent of the leader's authority. He said, "If they see you all alone, the empire or international organizations, they're going to impose their own policies."

The president wanted to show the elite of the city of Santa Cruz, 75 miles away, just how many thousands of people were with him. The helicopter landed on an uneven field, where 40 soldiers were barely able to contain Evo's supporters.

The group representing the elite of that region, the Pro–Santa Cruz Committee, which has influence over a good part of the population of the department, had asked Morales to define his stance on autonomy that week, and he responded at the Yapacani rally: "They just want autonomy so that people from Oruro will need a passport to get into Santa Cruz." He then clarified that he would vote "No" on autonomy despite having expressed the contrary during the first months of his term.

During his speech, Evo looked at the four bullet points he had scribbled down on a piece of paper: the history of the MAS, Nationalization, Unity, and the Constituent Assembly. Instead he focused on the upcoming war: the war for land. Although the 1952 Revolution began a process of agrarian reform, Hugo Banzer's 1971–1978 dictatorship distributed more than 74,000 acres to a handful of people in Santa Cruz and Beni, and the practice of concentrating large amounts of land in a few hands continued for years.

The Santa Cruz elite wanted the Prefecture (the governance run by the Pro–Santa Cruz Committee) to establish and distribute small, unfarmed plots of land. Morales, however, promised that the national government would be in charge of the program.

After the ceremony, some Andean women who had never abandoned their traditional skirts, even down in the hot plains, adorned the president with braided coca leaf garlands and crowned him with a leather hat with three branches. Drops of sweat fell down his forehead. A couple of *campesinos* fainted from the intense sun.

In the helicopter, Evo realized that he had once again left the minister of health on the ground. It happened during the final rush through the thousands of people jostling to touch him. The minister had to return by car.

The person in charge of the La Paz airport VIP area received the president, saying, "All clear." That is the phrase that a Bolivian president hears the most. They say it to him when he enters the house of government, a military house, or when he boards a plane.

"Where are we headed, Mr. President?" the escort inside the presidential BMW asked.

"To Alfa 330," he answered with a laugh, using the codeword for the San Jorge presidential residence.

The escort reported that there was some new intelligence: A group from the Sin Techo (Homeless) movement had tried to take over Morales' property in Cochabamba.

"Were they armed?" he asked.

"No, they only had machetes. Some *campesino* leaders restrained them, and there were no confrontations. The situation, Mr. President, is under control."

Within a minute, the president fell asleep clutching the door handle.

San Jorge is the residence of Bolivian heads of state. The first floor has a minimalist ambiance without a single feature to make a president feel at home or even like a president. Sánchez de Lozada invested thousands of dollars into the house to make it feel like his own, but then he had to leave both San Jorge and the presidency, when the people of El Alto and La Paz revolted in October 2003. The first-floor dining room is accented with burgundy curtains, a flat-screen television, faded pink chairs, a bronze coffee table, and an official photo of the new head of state.

Upon entering, Evo collapsed on the sofa.

"Is the soup ready?" he asked the house waiter who had come to set the table.

"Still," she replied. In Bolivia, "still" means "not yet."

"But I asked for it from El Alto," he complained.

He grabbed the remote control, spread open his legs, and stretched out. He flipped through a World Cup soccer game in Germany, a segment about Tom Cruise, and a runway show on Fashion TV, stopping finally at CNN in English.

"I'd like to be able to understand. It's important," he said.

His assistant, Janet, came in, but he kept his eyes on the screen.

"Any news, boss?" he inquired.

"[Minister of Water Abel] Mamani requested an urgent meeting," Janet said.

"Schedule him for five [in the morning]."

"What else?"

"Nothing," his assistant answered.

"What about Álvaro?"

"He's at home."

"Call him."

Evo added strips of *locoto*, a spicy green pepper, to his beef soup. It was his dinner, but it could have just as well been his breakfast. His meals and his schedule are the same every day of the year. "I don't know what it means to take a vacation; it's not part of my culture. The last time I took one was four years ago."

"You haven't had a day off either?" I asked.

"No," he replied. "It's just that I don't know how to do it. I can't go a day without doing what I do: meeting with people, visiting communities, conversing with my supporters, discussing things with the ministers. You know how I am. I've always been like this, even before I was president."

"Don't you get tired?" I asked.

"Yes, sometimes. Today I woke up at five and had to sleep two more hours. I fall asleep on airplanes before takeoff. Even on helicopters with all that noise."

Evo has within him a tremendous willingness to devote himself entirely to his role, to make up for the weaknesses of the administration and his own limitations by working tirelessly.

While eating his soup, Morales was distracted by a report about the Brazilian soccer player Ronaldo in the middle of World Cup fever.

"Lula [the Brazilian president] said that he'd gotten a little fat, and Ronaldo responded by saying that at least he didn't drink alcohol," I told him, in reference to Lula's supposed alcoholism reported by the *New York Times*.

"Last time I saw Lula he looked a little run-down. The presidency wears you out. I had my last night of drinking before I assumed office. I won't drink like that for five years."

Janet brought him a cell phone. "It's Álvaro," she said.

"Did you call him, or did he call?" he asked.

"He called," Janet replied.

After they hung up, I turned on my tape recorder and had the same problem as always. In interviews, Evo becomes more formal, changes the tone of his voice, and structures his speech using the same sentences he says in his public addresses.

"Yesterday you held a military ceremony and tribute to Che Guevara, who fought against the Bolivian military. How are you going to get the Armed Forces and Guevarism to coexist under your government?" I asked.

"There are Guevarists in the Armed Forces," Morales said. "In those days, the military couldn't understand Guevarism. Now the Armed Forces support this democratic process of profound changes. Che came looking for change and when the military stood in his way, he fought it. Many groups of the Bolivian left didn't have a clear position or ideology; even the *campesino* movement betrayed him. The only difference between now and then is the armed struggle. We're still standing up for the liberation of the people, but democratically and peacefully."

"In 1995, you told me that the people in El Chapare were on their way to becoming another Chiapas [referring to the Mexican Zapatista uprising of 1994] and that there was a possibility of a civil war," I queried further. "Have you prepared yourself for that war?"

"It would be very stupid of me to tell you these things, *compañero*. This political movement we've organized has curbed any armed confrontation. The union battle has allowed us to come to the government through a peaceful means," Evo responded.

He left the room to meet with a deputy. When he came back, he said that he didn't feel at home in the residence, that he doesn't have any privacy, and that they monitor everyone who comes or goes. His initial plan to live there with the leaders of the Houses of Deputies and Senators and García Linera, and to work with them 24 hours a day, never came to fruition. Only Edmundo Novillo, number one in the House of Deputies, resides there. That night, like the one before it, the president would sleep in his apartment on 20 de Octubre Street.

SATURDAY, JUNE 17

While Alex Contreras was eating the official Palace breakfast—papaya juice, coffee with milk, and bread with butter and peach jam—his cell phone rang.

"What do you mean they already left, comrade?" he asked.

He hung up and said, "They've left us. We have to hurry to the airport."

Contreras never changes his calm tone of voice, generally using the word "comrade."

"Let's go, Boss, step on it or we're going to miss the helicopter," he said to the taxi driver, who seemed to be moving in slow motion. A few security motorcycles were sent ahead to clear traffic. The spokesman told me that a few months before, to avoid missing a plane, he'd ridden on the back of a security motorcycle and made it just in time. We, too, made it just in time.

In the helicopter, the Cuban ambassador told the president that, the night before, Fidel Castro had seen footage of Guevara's birthday ceremony and had described it as "the swearing-in of La Higuera." He also said that the Cuban leader had a surprise waiting for him.

"Tell me, big boss," Morales requested.

"He might come to Bolivia."

By midday, the weather was splendid. From where the helicopter took off, the color of the houses made El Alto look like a city built out of mud and bricks. Twenty years before, there were only six housing developments clinging to a few factories, but by 2000, the city had acquired 800,000 inhabitants. The increase in poverty in rural areas meant that El Alto grew exponentially from internal migration, although the city now struggles with poverty. In 2001, 53 percent of the city's people didn't have drinking water, and the average daily income per family was $2. Even so, the wealthy of bordering La Paz have lost their advantage for two reasons. They no longer control La Paz, and the people of El Alto have become a powerful social force capable of paralyzing the political capital of the country and bringing down the government, as occurred with that of Sánchez de Lozada.

We traveled to Los Yungas, another coca farming region. From the helicopter, we could see a road that was only wide enough for one and a half cars but where two regularly pass. Contreras said that a vehicle falls over the edge once a week. The *campesino* roadblocks are often effective there: They scatter the route with rocks and then hide in the mountains. When people come to unblock the road, they throw stones and sticks at them. This can go on for weeks. Their strength and ability to mobilize could eventually impact Morales' government, which established that each family could only cultivate 1,600 square yards of coca. Many coca farmers from Los Yungas did not sympathize with that limitation.

From the sky, we didn't see any villages until, on the side of a hill amid mountains and coca farms, we could make out a crowd of people waiting for the president in the small town of Irupana. Because the helicopter couldn't land there, it began to circle wildly around, looking for a place to alight where it wouldn't crush anyone. In my notebook, I tried to describe, in vain, the passengers' frightened faces. I was thinking about presidential funerals and other things like that when the helicopter finally managed to touch down in a soccer field.

From the trailer of an old truck, the presenter, a bit hoarse from having entertained the crowd, shouted: "The *cocalero* president has arrived. He plants coca just like us. He's our brother."

At the ceremony, a plan to industrialize coca leaf production, with the initial support of a million Venezuelan dollars, was inaugurated. The first performance of the afternoon was delayed because one of the musicians of Los Yungueñitos, a band from the region, burst into tears after greeting Evo. He cried and cried until the presenter asked him to stop crying and play. Two women convinced the guest of honor to dance to the music of the Andean flutes, pan pipes, and cymbals.

The electricity went out shortly thereafter. "We're having technical difficulties," the presenter announced. An avalanche of people appeared on the right side of the stage, waiting for the performance. "We're making a bad impression on our president," he lamented. While the technical problems were being resolved, Morales was given letters, documents, garlands, small treats, and posters decorated with coca leaf details. At one point, he went up to talk to a young woman holding a flag.

"What's your name?" he asked her.

"Milka," she replied.

"How old are you?"

"Seventeen."

"Where are you from?"

"I'm from Irupana. And you?"

"I'm from Oruro," the president answered.

The return of electricity forced him to address the crowd.

I'm getting a little jealous. With this many people, you all are going to beat El Chapare. One of my *compañeras* here just said to me, "We've fought together" and started to cry. And she's right about that. Sometimes it was you all who started the marches. And other times we started them. Coca awoke this political instrument. Cocaine continues to be a problem for the United States, not for us. And coca continues to be a pretext for subjugating us. In Iraq, they went in for oil. Here, for coca. Industrialized coca, at first, isn't going to make us money, but we have to have patience. We've made shampoo with coca. My hair felt a little strange, but my housemate told me that it can keep one's hair from falling out [laughter]. She set off to get some coca shampoo, and I went with her [more laughter]. She's not my girlfriend: I'm still single. I'm just campaigning a little. We need to ration coca crops [some whistles]. When production is regulated, the product costs more. My recommendation is not an imposition. The union must ration per family and per person.

The stands were packed for the post-rally soccer game. Evo's team brought out two large bags of balls and kicked them up in the air. Their opponents were the members of a Los Yungas team, with the exception of Clemente Mamani, the mayor, who was wandering aimlessly around the field. His teammates wanted to take him out, but the president insisted that he play the whole game. The first half ended 4 to 2 in favor of the locals. The game seemed to be cinched until Second Lieutenant Vega came in and scored four goals from the most unexpected positions.

A little while later, on the same field, a table was set up with products from the region: yucca, peanuts, bread, squash, wild pig, chicken, cheese, plantains, bananas, eggs, dried potatoes, and other vegetables. We ate while the crowd watched us. Then children and the elderly advanced upon the tables, as the soldiers asked them to come one at a time and reprimanded the older folks who tried to hide peeled eggs and pieces of pork in their hats.

Going from the mountains to the High Plateau of El Alto makes for a noteworthy experience. From the midst of the highest peaks, one suddenly comes upon a flat plain. A few miles from the airport, Evo asked the pilot to do a couple of loops.

That night, and for the first and only time that week, I would get to fly on a commercial aircraft.

The inside of the VIP lounge of Aerosur Airlines is like an austere living room in different shades of purple, green, and white. A World Cup soccer game between the Czech Republic and Ghana was broadcast on the television. At halftime, an ad for Podemos (the primary opposition party) denounced the Chávez-ization of Bolivia and claimed that the country would change everything up to its flag.

"Do you see this?" the president asked me. "They don't even make any kind of proposal. It's all Chávez, Chávez, Chávez [Hugo]. Put me in touch with Walter Chávez."

"Walter, I was watching sports this afternoon, and all I saw was publicity for Tuto [Quiroga, head of Podemos]. Fix that, brother. Fix it, soon. It won't do for the MAS to be without publicity."

The flight attendant, also dressed in purple, green, and white, offered him coffee and juice.

"From your hands, even poison," he said to her before choosing the first option.

From the first seat in the first-class section of the plane, he talked about the rally in Irupana. "Two weeks ago they were threatening with a roadblock, but they haven't blockaded anything." Surgically enhanced flight attendants, with whom Morales did not flirt, served cold meat with salad.

"Did you believe what I said about my housemate and the shampoo?" he asked me.

"No, it seemed like you were talking about a girlfriend," I replied.

"[Laughing] Why doesn't anybody believe me? I'll introduce you to her: she's my housemate," he insisted.

"Do you honestly enjoy it when airplanes and helicopters do tricks in the air?" I asked him.

"Of course, we'll do some tomorrow. Fidel told us that we need to see a psychiatrist for what we do in airplanes," Evo responded.

In the Cochabamba airport, some friends and union leaders were waiting for him.

"Hello, big boss," he said to one of them.

SUNDAY, JUNE 18

Morales arranged to meet me in the office where he carries out his duties as the highest authority of the committee of the Six Federations of the Tropics of Cochabamba (the *cocalero* unions). At 4:50 A.M., singing drunks and others who were chasing down their alcohol with hamburgers were still walking down the streets. He showed up without any traces of his position as president: no official car, bodyguards, ministers, officials, or advisors. He was accompanied by a group of *cocalero* leaders. Some of them were speaking Quechua and chewing coca leaves. Evo, for his part, does not usually chew coca leaves.

His office is located in an old house with peeling paint, its windows protected by thick, black bars. Bare light bulbs hang from the ceiling. The walls are covered in newspaper clippings and photos of Morales the union leader and Morales the president.

"Why do you keep your union position?" I asked him.

"My *compañeros* asked me to. Plus, that's what makes our movement different. It's a movement based on social movements, and as leaders we should keep in touch with our supporters. I don't want to govern from the Palace. I feel more like a leader of unions or social movements. I don't feel so much like I'm the president. Only when people call me 'Presi' or Mr. President. I don't like it when they call me that. I like it more when they call me Evo or *Compañero* Evo," Morales replied.

"Your name and photos are everywhere," I said. "Aren't you afraid that power will become too personalized in you?"

"In Latin America, unfortunately, I've seen that political movements become focused on certain people. It's my responsibility to offer a guarantee. There will no longer exist leaders drunk on power or despotism. That's why I ask my *compañeros* to correct me if I make a mistake. How many times have I made mistakes? And then the social movements come to me and say, 'What's going on, *Compañero* Evo? Some policies need to be corrected.'"

"And what were some of your mistakes?" I asked.

"No major failures. Some procedures and some supreme decrees, for example, that didn't quite conform to the rules," Morales said.

"What do you have the most to learn about?"

"I haven't yet mastered economic matters. For me every day is an educational experience. Before it was through the unions, the conferences, the marches, the rallies. Now it's the Palace. It's one thing to have a title and another to know something."

"What would you like your children to study?" I asked.

"I can't say, Brother. I want for them to have social conscience and intellectual capacity."

"There are parents, for instance, who want their children to be lawyers," I commented.

"Not me. I'd actually like to eradicate all the law schools as a matter of public health. I see the judicial system we have in Sucre as a faithful model of colonialism," Evo responded.

A dozen people were waiting for Morales at the entrance of his office. He let most of them in for breakfast. Celima Torrico, a union leader with braids reaching down to her behind (and who was named minister of justice in January 2007), had prepared rabbit stew with potatoes, onions, and beans.

While they ate, Morales resolved the issues of his *compañeros*. One of them said he didn't have enough money to pay for the transportation of the demonstrators that day. Evo pointed to the closet. "In there you'll find *Somos MAS* T-shirts [a play on words that, using the abbreviation for *Movement Toward Socialism*, literally translates to: 'We are MORE']. Sell them for five pesos [$0.62] in the market, and use that money for gas," Evo ordered.

Another leader said he was worried because some of the MAS candidates didn't even know how to say his name.

"There isn't time to replace them. Talk to them and help them," he said dryly.

He complained to the women about the food in La Paz.

"It's all hot pepper," he lamented.

He said to me, "Don't write that."

Celima gave me a suspicious look but for a different reason.

"Do you know how to eat a rabbit?" she asked me when she saw the animal almost intact. Everyone else was eating the rabbit with their hands and adding large amounts of spice.

Evo took his T-shirt off in the office. Janet handed him a black turtleneck.

"Isn't this a woman's shirt?" he inquired as he put it on, exposing his bare chest to everyone. He recalled a friend of his from El Chapare with whom he used to swim naked in the river. When they got undressed, his friend would stand like a soldier and look at the sky to show he wasn't peeping.

A third union leader complained that all the signs featured pictures of the president. "We need to show our candidates," he said. He was wearing a wool hat—the kind that some backpackers wear as a badge of honor to confirm their passage through the rugged terrain of Bolivia—sandals with alpaca socks, and had a huge wad of coca leaves in his cheek. Another person commented that some of the candidates had become overconfident and needed a wake-up call.

When leaving the office, Morales was talking on the phone with a *compañera*. He asked her: "Is there *desayuno* or *desayuna*?" (*Desayuno* means breakfast; *desayuna,* the feminine form of the word, would indicate that he was referring to a woman rather than food.)

It's a recurring joke of his.

Evo asked his assistant to buy the daily papers at a traffic light. He saw a picture of himself with Che's son. "He's nothing like his father. Much more calm."

He then read Bill Clinton's words in support of his government.

"Now Podemos is going to say 'Just Say No to Clinton,'" Contreras said, and everyone laughed.

"I like being the copilot on the small planes," the president said, changing the subject. "During the electoral campaign I thought several times that I should learn to fly just in case one of the pilots has a heart attack or something. Would you prefer not writing your book to going up in the helicopter?" he asked me.

Before climbing aboard, he listed who would be in the delegation: "Álvaro, Alex, Janet, Hernán [another assistant], Martín, and me. Rebeca [Delgado, a MAS candidate for the Constituent Assembly] and Margarita [Terán, a *cocalera* union leader] can board later." Several of them laughed.

"You aren't taking me seriously. What happened to presidential authority?" he asked.

They were laughing about Margarita, who also happened to be the president's ex-girlfriend.

It was green around Cochabamba, but we could also see the pale yellows from the recent drought. Clouds and fog blanketed Colomi, our first destination, making it impossible to land. But Evo insisted to the pilots that there was a place to touch down.

"There," he said, pointing out a barely distinguishable patch of land.

Dodging power lines, we landed next to some rural dwellings. The people gathered around with their chickens and other animals. Two little boys shouted, "Evo, Evo."

"Did I wake you all up with the helicopter?" he asked them.

In Aguirre, a small group of houses without drinking water, barter is the most common form of commerce, and cell phones don't work. As he passed by the buildings made of mud and brick, Evo recalled that he'd slept in one of them during a march from El Chapare to La Paz. It was cold, so they warmed up with soup and blankets.

People in Colomi live off potatoes and river trout. The traditional drink is *guindol*, made from fermented cherries.

"The solution to this cold is *guindol*, my *compañero*," the president explained.

At the entrance to the town at the side of the road, there is a shed made of iron and sheet metal that serves as Colomi's market. A truck was waiting there to take the president to the soccer field where the event would take place. Security remained in the hands of the men and women of the Union Police (PS). A Cochabamban man with big sideburns and a moustache carried a wooden rifle and never left Evo's side, not even while he was on the stage. This was not an accident: The president had said that he would defend the revolution with arms just a week before.

A woman wearing the native hoop skirt and wool socks, and carrying her baby in woven cloth on her back, served *guindol* in mini glass jars. "You're going to get me drunk," he said to her. The liquor warmed his body, which was covered by confetti and adorned with five garlands. This is a welcoming ritual in Bolivia, indicating that the guest has arrived.

Although García Linera managed to conceal all of the *guindol* that he'd been drinking during his speech, he forgot his agnosticism onstage. The vice president said that up high was God, and a little bit below him was the constituent assembly and a little bit below that, the government.

Meanwhile, the president told me that I should drink 12 *guindols*. He then reminisced to the ten thousand people present that he'd been to Colomi hundreds of times for marches and demonstrations. One of those times they had taken an off-road shortcut up through the mountains, but then the clouds lowered unexpectedly, and they ended up wandering around in circles, their guide unable to find the way out. He emphasized that the people there knew him well, that they had seen him a little bit drunk on *guindol*, and that they had seen him cry, recalling his sorrows and lost loved ones.

The delegation ate lunch at La Guinda, a restaurant with a dining room split into two floors. Before sitting down at the L-shaped table, Evo thanked the MAS leaders: "What a big rally, *compañeros*. I was only expecting a thousand people because I know how hard it is to gather together at seven o'clock in the morning on a Sunday in the cold and fog. For our government big rallies are important."

They toasted with *guindol* and ate fried trout with rice, yucca, and salad. The people who really knew how to eat the fish left the spine intact. From his seat on the upper level, Morales urged "bottoms up" to the tables below. "Drink until you've had twelve, Brother," he shouted to me when it was my turn. He scolded the vice president for drinking Fanta with his fish. "Keep on drinking the *guindol*, *compañero*."

As best I could, I made it to the René Barrientos Base, where the Venezuelan helicopter was waiting. García Linera requested a short horse ride. He rode around the perimeter of the field at a gentle trot.

After takeoff, they opened one more bottle, and we took sips from the cap. Hernán, Evo's assistant, spilled a little bit of *guindol* every time it was his turn and didn't worry about the flammable content. "Relax, it doesn't have alcohol in it," he lied to me.

The president requested a last round, and then the euphoria and happiness came to an end. He was leaving the cold weather behind and still had three rallies to go to with speeches to deliver, anthems to sing, garlands, and hugs. The *guindol* had run its course for everyone except for me: I was the only one still tipsy.

Morales changed out of his turtleneck and into a short-sleeve shirt. In Shinaota, the next destination, it was already 95 degrees. "The Americans," he explained, "consider this place to be the world capital of cocaine." Once there, the people came out of their houses to meet him. "I'm the accordion player's daughter," a little girl said to him. The stage, in the shade, faced the main road of Shinaota. The coca farmers who had gathered there had the sun shining in their faces. Some of them, Alex Contreras let slip, were too confident of a victory in the national election on July 2. But there was no doubt as to who would win the elections there or even that MAS would get more than 90 percent of the votes. In one community, an investigation was launched because one person voted for Podemos in the presidential election. They wanted to find out who had done it.

"We've made it to the Palace," Evo reminded them in his speech, "gathering the dead and the wounded. We've made it to the Palace marching, rallying. We've moved forward."

He uses that expression a lot: "Move forward." Politics, for Morales, is quantified in steps forward and backward. Those steps forward are illustrated by mobilizations, marches, and elections.

In his speech, he recalled how, many years ago, he used to walk all the way to the union office. "Back then, there wasn't much funding because there was a lot of coca, but the price was low. If there is going to be a lot of production, there isn't going to be a good price."

In closing, he said that he had been invited to watch the World Cup final.

"Do you want me to go?" he asked.

"Nooo," they answered.

Evo followed the same paved road to Chimoré. There were fewer people than expected. He cursed at someone on his cell phone. A *cocalero* wearing an UMOPAR hat and Ray-Ban sunglasses, gaunt and skeletal, was acting as head of security. Sugar cane stalks marked off the perimeter of where the coca workers stood. They served grapefruit juice. The president requested a moment of silence in honor of Casimiro Huanta, a union leader assassinated in 2001. The shouts of some children playing with a ball interrupted the quiet.

After the ceremony, Morales went to the UMOPAR headquarters in Chimoré. Rebeca Delgado (a MAS candidate for the Constituent Assembly and former lawyer for coca cultivators accused of drug trafficking) talked about how every time she'd gone to speak with those who had been arrested she clutched onto her purse with both hands. "I was afraid someone would plant cocaine on me." She rarely dealt with the local authorities. "I had to talk to the DEA. Many of them didn't understand Spanish. When a coca stomper was injured, I had to struggle with paramedics who said they preferred English." The UMOPAR headquarters, she said, was run as an extension of the U.S. embassy and not of the Bolivian state.

No one knew exactly where the next rally was. "We'll see it from the sky, Boss," Evo said to one of the pilots. In the low flight over the plain, he contemplated the palm trees, coca farms, streams, villages, ponds, and houses. He seemed like a cartographer checking to make sure that everything below was in order and in its rightful place. Moving around the helicopter, he named the little towns and some of the families who lived in them. He also pointed out the location of San Francisco, where he has his plot of land. "It's right near a stream." A friend worked on his land. It isn't unusual for *cocaleros* to farm the land of others and give half of the earnings to the owner. Normally this is because they don't have the $5,000 that a little plot would cost.

He arrived at the last and biggest rally of the day at 4:40 P.M. Half of the crowd was waiting for him on the bleachers of the soccer field when the helicopter landed. Watching the helicopter land had become a spectacle that didn't end until the engine was turned off. The other half congregated on the main street, facing the president's box. The Union Police, carrying clubs and with UP identification on hand, ensured that nothing unforeseen would happen.

The ceremony ended at nightfall. In the caravan moving at walking pace, a braided UP woman yelled to the president, "I'm single, too."

At the restaurant, cooks wearing facemasks and gloves served a fried fish dish with rice and fried yucca. Afterward, they gave the president a wild pig from the region as a gift.

Felipa, a veteran leader of the *cocalero* movement, sat down across from Evo. "She's an older woman who acts like a young lady," he said by way of introduction.

Felipa said that many families with the last name Morales had named their sons Evo in recent months.

"One of them died," she said and brought about a momentary silence.

"What did he die from?" the president asked.

"He had a fever."

At the beginning of the twenty-first century, out of every 1,000 children born in Bolivia, 54 die.

Evo praised the corpulent coca farmer who handled security for the event. "I want you to become the Union Police Commander," he said to him in his usual way of congratulating his people and keeping their hopes up about possible future promotions.

It had been the last rally of this tour. The Revolution, despite a certain personalization in the figure of Morales, is embodied by these *campesinos*. They have fought to live well, to defend and sell their coca, to eat three times a day, and to allow their children to go to school so that someday they can get to the city, which is synonymous with progress. These people's lives were at stake in every roadblock, every night spent waiting for UMOPAR agents to arrive, or in the early hours of the morning, blind from beer. Evo believes that his ability to remain in power is connected to what these *campesinos* do for the Revolution: this strange, epic, imperfect, barefoot revolution.

Because it wasn't possible to fly to La Paz that night, the delegation discussed where they would sleep. Rebeca Delgado suggested her six-person cabin. "There's no electricity, but we could buy fuel for the lamp," she explained.

"The seven of us will fit," the president ventured. His vice president said he needed to read some documents.

"We should look for some gasoline then," Delgado concluded.

"We'll sleep in the cabin, and then we won't have to pay for a hotel," Evo insisted. He would have saved about $25.

When they realized that the gas station was closed, there was no other option but to travel to a hotel in Villa Tunari for $4 a room without bedside tables or a television.

A deputy asked Janet whether the president would need a bodyguard at the hotel door.

"Of course," she answered.

At sunrise, Hernán said that Morales wanted another shirt to replace the one he had stained the day before at the last ceremony.

"Well, there aren't any," Janet replied.

"The store opens at seven," the hotel's one employee reported.

"We don't have time," said the vice president.

Janet found a blue soccer jersey that had been given to the president as a gift in Colomi. They ironed it quickly.

At 6:00 A.M. on the dot, Evo came out of his room in a good mood.

"How are you, Bosses? Who partied last night?" he joked.

"Any news from La Paz?" García Linera asked him.

"No, there's a little issue here. A group of *campesino* leaders have come to me with a problem they're having with a council member. I'm going to talk to him."

Evo canceled the meeting with the government ministers. "But I want to be there for Milton [Melgar]'s swearing in," he said.

Seated in the dining room at the headquarters in Chimoré, in which ten of three hundred UMOPAR agents were eating, he ordered hoof soup. He described it as "the Viagra of the Amazonas region."

A colonel said that the soup helps his subordinates to last all day. They leave at 5:00 A.M. and don't come back until 3:00 P.M.

Morales said that most of the arrested coca-leaf growers were once brought to these headquarters. "They had us cooped up in here for days," he recalled as he fished a potato out of his soup. "I'll tell you more about it on the airplane."

He called the minister of public works and services, Salvador Ric, who was in charge of the event in Santa Cruz that afternoon.

"Big boss, we have an intelligence report that says they might try to cause some trouble at the ceremony. We have to be careful. Let's do it at three o'clock and not at two."

The air force colonel informed him that the plane was ready.

"How many can fit?" the vice president asked.

"Six."

"Martín, comrade, you've been saved. There's room for you," Contreras said.

From the runway, we got a better view of the UMOPAR base. It has white houses with air conditioning, other smaller houses with wood trim, a television satellite, and radio towers; it also has a control tower with seemingly endless metal bars, four parked helicopters, and a military seal with two rifles and a skeleton wearing a military cap with the UMOPAR motto written across: "Only those who are willing to die for a noble ideal deserve to live."

On the plane, Morales recounted his past on that base:

I was confined down there. They set a trap for us. It was a meeting organized by a *campesino* leader with allegiances to the National Revolutionary Movement (MNR). They brought me there in handcuffs. We were in a car listening to a soccer game, Bolivia against Brazil, or some other important team when they said, "Breaking news, coca farmer union leader arrested." They drove me to Santa Cruz without anything to eat. A girlfriend of mine had invited me to a graduation but I couldn't go.

He remembered Luis Caballero, commander of UMOPAR, as "the most sadistic one." Before falling asleep, and in a whisper, he said that the United States was still in control of the runway from which we had just taken off.

Evo woke up at the airport in El Alto. It was the last of 17 flights in that hectic week. When the airplane stopped in front of the VIP lounge, he could see the 20 uniformed agents and members of the security team who were awaiting the *cocalero* leader to return him to the world of presidents, official cars, bulletproof vests, the San Jorge residence, and "all clears." He was in this new and unexpected world to change everything that he could about it or to return to El Chapare or Orinoca.

Chapter Two

FROM THE ANDEAN HIGHLANDS TO THE TROPICS (1959–1995)

Dionisio Morales Choque chose a first name for his son, "Evaristo," from the *Bristol Almanac*, which advertised Murray & Lanman soaps, scented lotions, and remedies for broken capillaries. Then he hesitated. He had considered "Eva" if the baby were a girl, and so he finally settled on the strange name that resulted from swapping the "a" with an "o." "Evo, with three letters and no more," he said. And so Evaristo became Evo. Many years later, the president would ask himself why his parents hadn't just called him Adam.

On October 26, 1959, Aunt Luisa, the local healer of the Isallavi community, assisted in the birth of Juan Evo Morales Ayma, saving him from an early death. His mother, María Ayma Mamani, began to bleed heavily during labor, and Dionisio raced to the nearby town of Orinoca in the Sud Carangas Province of the Department of Oruro in search of a midwife, but he never found one. There was no hospital nor was there any kind of medical help in Orinoca. The neighbors pooled together herbs that the healer applied to María's fragile body soaked in her own blood. Someone ran out to Lake Poopó to get water.

The aunt's weak voice was heard amid the shouts of the woman giving birth: "Maybe you're craving something and that's why the little babe can't be born."

"I saw bread baking, and I wanted some."

They made a tortilla with flour and alcohol. María tasted it, and after a little while her son was born over sheared sheep's leather because she didn't want to dirty the few clothes that they had.

From the start, Evo was marked as a survivor. Four of his seven siblings died, one at birth and the other three—Luis, Eduvé, and Reina—from curable diseases.

The health policies of the 1952 Revolution, which also brought universal suffrage, nationalization of the mining industry, and agrarian reform, never made their way out to those confines. Neither did electricity, gas, or drinking water.

The first word that Evo pronounced was *tamta*, which means ball in Aymara. He played with different types of balls: first made of wool, then of cloth. While his llamas grazed in the hills, he dribbled around them in zig zags. The yareta plants and wild grass served as a goal post. Clubs, his dog, observed his progress.

His first protest, when he could barely walk, was against his mother. Because the *wath'ia* (food cooked in the earth) was taking a long time, he took advantage of a moment of inattention and tried to grab the pot. But he burned his elbow and his ears; he still has the scars. María hardly scolded her favorite son. "We have to look after Evito," she always insisted. Faced with any illness, she could cure it with herbs, and when he was burning up with a fever, she put coca with sugar under his armpit.

His oldest sister, Esther, would have been called Estefanía, but their father also changed her name at the last moment. She was often left in charge of her younger siblings, Evo and Hugo, and the animals. They would fill their bellies with toasted corn, sometimes *lagua* (cornmeal porridge), and *chuño* (dried potatoes). María was often explicit with her daughter about their financial situation: "We must live off what we have. If we have it we make it, if we don't have it we don't make it." María had experienced that reality firsthand when she was working as a housemaid in Oruro and had to be satisfied with breadcrumbs because her employers didn't feed her.

The Morales family spent one winter in Orinoca subsisting off only a single sack of corn. They ate corn for breakfast, lunch, and dinner. When it ran out, Dionisio and Evo brought about 50 male llamas to the town of Independencia. They walked for three weeks in the rain and cold to trade them for corn, salt, and dried meats.

Like all the little kids in that region, Evo became a worker the day he began to walk. At five years old, he was already given the responsibility of herding llamas. Some commentators would later attach an almost biblical weight to his role as a shepherd, seeing it as a harbinger of his destiny to become a leader.

For days and days, he walked from Oruro to Cochabamba with his flock, his father by his side. Only the buses of the Danubio and Nobleza lines interrupted the silence of those infrequently traveled roads. The passengers threw orange peels out the windows that he would catch and chew on. He longed to someday go up into one of those fleets and contemplate the landscape in rapid motion.

In Isallavi, the Morales family lived in an adobe house with a straw roof. It was no more than a ten-by-thirteen-foot room that served as the bedroom, kitchen, and dining room. They had their corral off to the side. The dirt floor was not just the result of poverty and lack of materials. The Aymara communities prefer direct contact with the land, Mother Earth, which they call the *Pachamama*, and they avoid intermediaries, such as cement and even furniture. At dawn, Dionisio would make his offering to the *Pachamama*; María would also make a ritual *ch'alla* offering with alcohol and coca leaves so that they would have a good day.

As part of his education, Evo had to memorize three rules of conduct: *ama sua* (don't be a thief), *ama quella* (don't be lazy), and *ama llulla* (don't be a liar). The fourth he added in later: *ama llunk'u* (don't be servile).

Although the primary language of the people of Orinoca was Aymara, they were also familiar with Spanish and Quechua, the languages of the communities that lived in the valley below. As the years went by, Evo opted for Spanish because, in his words, it allowed him to "centralize communication." Certain political rivals would later criticize his inability to give speeches in Aymara or Quechua.

To get to the school in Calavilca, Evo walked three miles along a narrow horse path. In that little hut, lost amid the bleak upland plateau and the wild grass, he received a basic, rural education. For him and his classmates, the world ended right there. The name of their country, *Bolivia*, sounded to them like something from another planet. He didn't have an idea of coexistence among Bolivians. He thought that humans and animals shared a life of subsistence. When they made him draw a donkey in the first grade and he painted it red, yellow, and green, the colors of his country's flag, his classmates made fun of the sketch for the whole year. He admired his math teacher, Justiniano

López, even though it bothered him when he scolded them for eating onions. "That's for the privacy of the home," he protested. At that time, the boys wore wide-leg pants, and López complained, "What nice pants and manes of hair, but your kitchens are full of soot." Over the years, Evo reevaluated everything his teacher did to draw their attention to their poverty.

At six years old, he moved with part of his family to Calilegua, in the Argentinean province of Jujuy, where Dionisio worked in the sugar harvest. Because Evo's arms weren't strong enough to cut sugar cane with an axe and peel it, he sold ice cream. "*Picolé, picolé*," he shouted in the fields of sugar cane workers. At first, the Argentines didn't understand him because in Aymara *picolé* means popsicle.

In Calilegua, the Morales family hardly had anything to eat, and for months they got by with noodle tostado and tea. There, Evo attended school, but to do his homework he propped up his books on adobe blocks and kneeled on a sheep's leather hide to read and write. Because his family spoke in Aymara, Evo didn't understand the lessons, and, after a little while, the family cut short his studies.

Upon returning to Orinoca, he again pursued his schooling. He would often spend the night in the community where the school was, which represented a feat of conquered freedom. There, he learned to cook corn soup, quinoa, and wheat with beef jerky.

At 13 years old, Evo organized something for the first time in his life: the community soccer team. They called themselves "The Fraternity," and he made himself team captain. Three years later, they elected him to be the training coach of the whole region. With the wool of the llamas that he sheared and the foxes that he hunted, he bought balls and jerseys. As he coached, he heard his father and other neighbors saying that he would make a good manager, a good leader. He was ashamed to ask what the words "manager" and "leader" meant. He was only trying to be like Carlos Aragonés, a forward on the Bolivian soccer team who held the spotlight for 15 years.

When he moved to Oruro to continue studying, Evo tried out to play for the San José team, but didn't make the cut. He began high school at the Marcos Beltrán Ávila School near the cemetery. In Evo's hometown, his favorite indulgence had been to kill a chicken to eat for a family party, but in Oruro he tried out the urban novelties: letting his hair grow long and hanging out with friends.

To finance his studies, Evo worked as a baker and brick layer. He would get up at 2:00 A.M. to make bread and then attend classes in the afternoon.

He didn't stand out: In the third year, of the maximum 70 points, he got his best grades in geography (53), civics (52), and history and English (51), and his worst grades in physics (37) and chemistry (39). He improved in the fourth year: 41 in physics and 52 in philosophy. Since he got help from his classmates because he was working so much at his two jobs, he prefers to say that he only got through the third year and that he's not really a graduate.

In contrast, he proudly tells about having been a trumpet player in the Oruro Imperial Band. His father had taught him the art of tuning up his lips, and he bought wind instruments for his community with the money that his mother had saved. In school, Evo perfected his technique. He liked to play traditional Andean folk dances for the performers in the carnivals and get all of the costumed people to dance. Thanks to the Imperial Band, he got to know the mining centers of Potosí.

Evo would have liked to work as a journalist. As the years went on, he became convinced that the reporters were informed about what was happening in Bolivia.

He was obliged to register for the draft, and in 1978, he entered the 4th Ingavi Cavalry Regiment in the Miraflores general headquarters, the heart of military power. During this time, the Armed Forces dominated politics: They had already been governing from the Burned Palace for 14 years. The president was Hugo Banzer, the Bolivian dictator who stayed in power the longest (1971–1978) and who, later as an elected president (1997–2001), would find a bitter enemy in Morales.

Alongside the other soldiers, Evo held back a march of coca workers in Coripata, Los Yungas. There was one death: "Little soldiers, you have gotten out of hand," one of their superiors reproached them. A color photo from 1978 shows him very skinny, with the white helmet and gray uniform of the military police.

After the draft, he went back to work with his family, but Orinoca had become hostile to them. In 1980, the communities suffered through the *El Niño* storm cycle, which killed 70 percent of agricultural production and half of their animals. One winter's day, Morales and a group of youths began to harvest the potatoes, but a frost fell during the night and ruined the crops. They were left without the means to obtain food or money.

His mother cried for an entire day. His father, during a night of drinking, decided to move his family to Los Yungas. "We'll never prosper here," he concluded.

The Morales family walked for a week to Los Yungas, but they didn't buy any land because the prices were beyond their means.

The second destination was El Chapare. In Port San Francisco, they reserved about 25 acres located over the road. Casiano Ayma, Evo's maternal uncle and a teacher in Orinoca, loaned Dionisio the money to pay for the lot. On the second trip to El Chapare, they almost lost everything. By mistake, someone took the suitcase with the money, which was under Evo's care at some point. The land cost about $5,000, the value of four or five power saws. Dionisio paid Casiano back in llamas.

And so the Morales family left the Andean Highlands and moved to the tropics.

On the morning of November 23, 2006, Evo visited Orinoca as president to deliver the Juancito Pinto vouchers, an aid of $25 for each schoolchild.

At dawn, he had been with the Patacamaya tank regiment in the La Paz plateau, where he harangued the troops, fired from a tank against a hill, and laughed when it was verified that his marksmanship had retained a certain dignity.

From the helicopter, the way to Orinoca looks like a dry plain, with streams that don't bring anything in or take anything out. At that altitude, the plateau is an immense brown patch broken only by the shadows of a few clouds and dirty water that will vanish at any moment. Thirty minutes of flying had passed without the president distinguishing a single person. "Do you see how there's nothing?" he asked to emphasize that he came from that nothing.

With the music of a military band in the background, the town received him in full. The children, made protagonists by their receipt of the Juancito Pinto vouchers, wore blue and green cardigans. As the president crossed the narrow dirt streets, they all asked him the same thing:

"What did you come for, *tío* [uncle]?"

For the children, he was still "*tío*"—a member of the family of Orinoca, the most important and the most popular.

Orinoca is a town of about 2,000 inhabitants, 3,000 fewer than there were at the beginning of the 1980s, when the president's family emigrated. In the last 25 years, there has been a diaspora toward the sugar harvest of north Argentina, Cochabamba, and El Chapare. Those who stayed continue to endure the eight cold months of the year and remain dedicated to llamas and potatoes.

Buildings in Orinoca are constructed of dirt mixed with grasses, stone, and water; they are short, as if everything in the plateau were flattened to fit the bodies of its inhabitants. Stones abound. They can be seen in the buildings, on top of the roofs of the houses to keep them from flying off, and in the streets, waiting to be relocated. A whitewashed church, brand-new electric power lines, a soccer field, a small square, and the emerald green town hall moderate the arid landscape.

In Orinoca, the Movement Towards Socialism (MAS) won almost the entirety of the votes in the presidential election. According to its leaders, they didn't make it to 100 percent only because a few old men and women got confused and submitted the ballots for other parties that they thought looked similar to those of the MAS.

Morales, dressed in a brown chamois leather jacket, white shirt, and dark pants, went up to the stage of wooden tables and saw posters that were familiar to him: "Technology and Practical Knowledge Workshop" and "Self-expression Workshop." In front, a group of women laid out a blanket on the ground, over which they dropped coca leaves. Another group put down coal that emitted a dark smoke. They thanked the *Pachamama*.

The event began with a musical number. The students who were dancing had parts of their feet and legs uncovered, exposing white stripes of skin that the cold and dryness had inscribed. They wore hats, colorful clothes and socks with sandals, and played a song dedicated to their grandparents who had traveled the valley with llamas in search of corn and flour. When they returned, the community would welcome them with that song.

In his speech, the president promised that the Juancito Pinto voucher was a product of the money raised from the nationalization of the oil and gas plants. He recalled the clay chairs in the school and also that in fourth and fifth grade he planted his first pine trees.

"The money that you're receiving is not mine, nor does it belong to the government. Careful, children, that your parents don't take it away for beer or anything else because this money is for you. One child bought himself a pregnant sow. What a visionary!"

In the classroom of the school, Morales ate a lunch of llama with potatoes and quinoa-cola to drink. There wasn't any silverware, but there was toilet paper with which to clean up. Evo sat with army officials and other leaders so that they could plan the reconstruction of schools. The Venezuelan pilots challenged them to a soccer game. "We'll play for the helicopter," he answered them.

A very hunched-over old lady entered the room and gave him four eggs, and when she spoke something into his ear, Evo's face transformed. Someone explained that those eggs were her only goods.

I asked Morales to show me the house in which he had grown up. Although there are hardly any locks or keys in Orinoca, his door was wedged shut. "They locked you out, president," a friend of his father's said to him, and many of them laughed. The chief of army, General Freddy Berzatti, asked a boy who wore the jersey of the German soccer team, a maroon sweater, and a baseball hat, to climb through a crack in the window. "What are they going to give me?" the boy asked slyly. Berzatti helped him get in through the window. Technically speaking, this was an illegal break-in committed by the chief of army.

Inside, the low ceiling, a sagging cloth, looked ready to fall down. There were two beds, a mattress, and posters of soccer players and sports stars and one of an intruder: the political leader Jerges Justiniano. "This was one of the best little houses in town—the number of llamas my father sold to build it!" Evo said and accepted the invitation to have a beer in the threshold of his property. The people of the town came closer and asked him for photos. "One photo for one llama," he joked while he hugged the shoulders of the boy who had cleared away the entry.

"How do you feel in here, President?" asked a general.

"Like nothing's changed. Like how I always felt."

"How many of you lived here?" one union leader inquired.

"Just me and my little brothers and sisters, particularly me and Hugo."

He asked his neighbor to take care of his house and to never take down the posters. He told them that on Mondays, when he was 16 years old and living in Oruro, he wouldn't eat breakfast so that he could buy the sports supplement of the daily paper *Hoy*, which he was collecting.

While they were looking for a trumpet so that he could play, the president reminisced about his time with the Imperial Band: "When I joined the band I didn't drink beer. But since they paid me in beer I would bring it to the little tent where they sold it for two pesos and they gave me one peso. At night the musicians would get drunk."

There wasn't any time for the concert, however. Something was going on in El Chapare that he had to attend to urgently.

Originally populated by indigenous jungle Yuracareans and blessed by three Jesuit missions at the end of the eighteenth century, El Chapare is a tropical and subtropical region of 15,000 square miles in the center of the country. In 1953, the National Revolution began to slowly colonize El Chapare, a process that deepened with the expansion of coca leaf cultivation in the 1970s and exploded in the middle of the next decade.

When the Morales family arrived in 1981, the price of the leaf experienced an increase that lasted for five more years. As a result, El Chapare went from a population of around 40,000 inhabitants to 215,000 seven years later. Until 1988, 88 percent of the colonizers had one plot, 10 percent had two plots, and the rest had three or more. For this large majority of small landowners, the advantage to coca in relation to other crops was that it could be cultivated up to four times a year, and the yields are high: One load of coca leaves (roughly 100 pounds) is equivalent to 15,000 oranges.

The Morales family settled down in Villa 14 de Septiembre, a town composed of 30 log shacks without doors or windows and with some improvised sheds that served as bars. The road dead ended at a nameless river through which log canoes replete with coca, yucca, papaya, and banana would travel.

The everyday routine changed for Evo. At first he thought he could live off a fruit diet. He had orange juice for breakfast, and the rest of the day he ate papaya and banana. After a few days, he began to feel dizzy and started to cook rice and yucca and hunt *jochi* (a rabbit-sized jungle rodent). His hands became rough from using the machete so much, and he felt like they would burst. The ancient planters told him that they were crying blood tears.

He integrated himself with the community through soccer. The Sunday of his debut—he still remembers the cap and sneakers that he wore—he made several goals and turned out to be the best player on the field. The locals began to want to play with him, to ask him about his life and how long he planned to stay. He founded his team, New Horizon, which emerged as the champion of the August 2nd Central Tournament. One of the decisive games almost ended in blows after a landowner with approximately 2,500 acres tripped him.

Shortly thereafter, he joined the union. In each town in El Chapare, the syndicate, which fulfills whatever functions the state does not, constructed the roads, the school, and the soccer field. Evo was named the Secretary of Sports for the August 2nd Headquarters of the San Francisco Syndicate. They called him "the young ball player," especially the women, because he brought a ball to every get-together or meeting to play during the recess. Responsible for organizing the tournaments, he invited miners from nearby with whom they would cook and often end up dancing, smashed from the beer and pure alcohol they drank after playing.

The death of Dionisio in 1983 forced Evo to reduce the number of hours he dedicated to the syndicate. From then on until 1985, he concentrated more on his plot of land, traveling to Orinoca every so often to attend to some of his father's outstanding businesses.

That year he began to make coca production his priority, giving up on the rice—it offered little profit—and bananas, which he requested from the Murillo syndicate. Foot by foot he would work on his plot with the day laborers until nightfall. Dionisio had instilled in him the belief that stopping during the day was lazy. One permitted distraction was fishing, but it never went well for Evo. Instead of fish, he caught rays or turtles.

That private world of near subsistence had to coexist with the threatening world outside. A foundational event in his relationship to politics occurred in 1981. Drunk soldiers murdered a *campesino* because he wouldn't agree to incriminate himself as a drug trafficker. They beat him, sprayed him with gasoline, and burned him alive. Evo felt that death in his bones. He began to meet up with a group of young people who called themselves the Juvenile Center.

General Luis García Meza had risen to power after a coup d'état in July 1980. He counted on the support and advice of the Argentinean dictatorship, and he brought a group of officials dedicated to cocaine trafficking into the Burned Palace. The last name of one of his secretaries proved to be indicative: Ariel Coca was discovered with a small plane full of cocaine.

When international pressure for the denunciation of drug trafficking became intolerable—the U.S. Department of State declared that "for the first time, the mafia has purchased a government"—García Meza gave one of his maxims to the country:

"Bolivia can survive off potato starch and jerky."

He lasted three months in the Burned Palace.

The legacy of that ferocious dictatorship ended the military rule that, with interludes of power on the right and left, and even some short-lived civil governments, had dominated politics since the 1964 coup d'etat against the National Revolutionary Movement (MNR).

In 1982, the left-wing Democratic Popular Union (UDP), led by Hernán Siles Suazo, initiated the democratization of the country. But he couldn't hold back the economic crisis: It imploded, bringing a hyperinflation to Bolivia of 1,282 percent in 1984 and 8,767 percent in 1985. Siles attempted to stop it with gradualist methods and a de-dollarization, but he found himself spread beyond his means with the economic crisis, pressure from the Bolivian Worker's Center (COB), and conflicts in the government coalition. The administration left other astonishing figures: It had gone through seven cabinets and 80 ministers in less than three years.

In August 1985, the MNR introduced, in the midst of hyperinflation and the political crisis, some major adjustments. Víctor Paz Estenssoro, the leader of the 1952 Revolution, proclaimed: "Bolivia is dying on us." To prevent the country from dying, he imposed Supreme Decree 21.060, a packet of measures of neoliberal orientation, backed by the United States, that included reduction of government, fiscal adjustment, liberalization of the economy, and an opening up to foreign businesses, which would later participate in the privatization of state companies.

Although he managed to stop the hyperinflation, it had brutal consequences. Unemployment rose to 25 percent, and by 1991, eighty thousand jobs had been lost, among them those of twenty-three thousand miners in the state companies. That catastrophe symbolized the end of the state born of the 1952 Revolution: From then on, the miners would no longer be the head of social struggles. Many of them, in the wake of the economic crisis and the decline in the prices of minerals, moved to El Chapare and reinvented themselves. They would come to represent around 10 percent of coca farmers. Slowly, these new *cocaleros* united with the oldest ones from the tropics of Cochabamba to make Los Yungas a center of prime importance.

During the 1980s, the Washington agenda didn't limit itself to Decree 21.060. Above all else, they made the fight against drug trafficking their top priority. The increase in cocaine demand in Europe and the United States caused a production boom in Bolivia. (In the late 1980s, U.S. citizens snorted $20 billion worth of cocaine into their noses.)

The United States called for the eradication of the coca leaf crops and led a militarization of El Chapare that ignored the National Congress by effectively taking control of the territory and deploying the different security forces there according to their whim. President George H. W. Bush expressed the spirit of this crusade: "The logic is simple. The fastest and cheapest way to eradicate narcotic trafficking is at its source....We need to do away with the plantations where they grow and eliminate the laboratories." In 1992, 72 percent of U.S. foreign aid was tied up in the war on drugs.

To varying degrees, the Bolivian government at the time accepted the impositions of Washington. Decree 21.060 required foreign aid, and the foreign aid was dependent on the accomplishment of the eradication goals.

In turn, the *cocaleros* living off coca leaf cultivation began a sustained fight against eradication in the mid-1980s through a repertoire that included roadblocks, marches, hunger strikes, and confrontations with the military.

Law 1008, which was propelled by Washington in 1987, defined the legal and illegal zones for cultivation. That law located El Chapare as one of the "surplus zones" and demanded that the coca fields be supplemented with alternative crops. The compensation of up to $2,500 for each eradicated acre that the Bolivian government offered—by means of U.S. aid—didn't manage to diminish the *cocalero* movement.

National sovereignty, the ancestral relationship with the coca leaf, and the right to defend their most profitable means of subsistence, grew firm and the fight in El Chapare became profoundly anti-United States. "*Causachun coca! Wañuchun yanquis!* (Long live coca! Death to the Yankees!)" became the battle cry. It was the same cry Morales would make, in front of the press, the night of December 18, 2005, when he learned that he had received more than 50 percent of votes for the presidency.

In the 1980s, the relationship between the United States and Bolivia was defined by events in El Chapare, and as coca continued to occupy a primary place on the national agenda, Evo climbed up the union ladder. After being General Secretary (1982–1983) and Secretary of Records (1984–1985) of the San Francisco Syndicate, he assumed the role of General Secretary of the August 2nd Headquarters in 1985. In 1988, he was elected as the Executive Secretary of the Federation of the Tropics.

He had already founded the Broad Front of Anti-imperialist Masses (FAMA) with his colleagues. The origin of the name reveals how much they discussed political identity in the tropical labor unions. At first they named it the Broad Front of Anti-imperialist Bases (FABA), but one of the leaders suggested that they take out the word "anti-imperialist" because it sounded "very political." But it ended up as FAB, the same acronym as the Air Forces of Bolivia, so they had to restore the original version.

FAMA lost its first election in 1986. Evo perceived that the age of the leaders of his group was an issue; they were seen as such youngsters. Nonetheless, he didn't try to hide his jealousy or rivalry with older union members who perceived him as a threat.

When he won his seat in Congress in July 1988, he decided to dedicate himself entirely to the union. He often repeated the principles defined by his new mantra, "to be honest and direct with his constituents and at the front of all marches and rallies."

He thus grew up in the school of *campesino* unionism. It's his political origin, and for many years he understood politics as a sum of assemblies, negotiations with politicians and officials, and fights in the streets and roads.

Morales always threw himself directly into the fray. In 1984, he was involved in the first roadblock that resulted in death: Three *campesinos* were murdered near the Peruvian border. In May 1987, another five died blocking the way in protest of the Triennial Plan (a plan instigated by Washington, forcing a reduction of coca over the course of three years). According to the *campesino* unions, Rural Area Mobile Patrol Unit (UMOPAR) and Drug Enforcement Administration (DEA) agents were responsible for the 1988 Villa Tunari massacre, in which 11 coca farmers were murdered. Those killed were protesting the use of herbicides in crop eradication.

On the one-year anniversary of the massacre, Morales spoke at a commemorative ceremony. The next day he was beaten up by a group of UMOPAR agents who, thinking he was dead, threw his body in the mountains. An archive photo shows him on a stretcher, seemingly beyond recovery.

Filemón Escobar influenced Evo in a decisive way at that time. An ex-miner leader and Trotskyite, Filemón had learned to respect the coca leaf during the 20 years that he spent in the tunnels. Before going into the mine, he would chew on coca leaves with his fellow workers to strengthen and protect himself. A pioneer among mining leaders, he would frequently travel to El Chapare after the structural reforms of 1985 to promote the political defense of the coca leaf. He gave about 300 seminars in which he trained hundreds of *campesino* leaders politically and ideologically. "I gave it to them straight," he remembers. Filemón saw a firm leader in Evo and one loyal to the coca leaf. "The coca leaf," he would lecture, "has the same value to us as does the host for Catholics. It is our relationship to the *Pachamama* (mother earth)."

According to Escobar, there was a "fierce" line of *cocaleros* with rifles at their disposal who had received military training during the draft. "Evo," he recalled in an interview for this book, "was a fierce little thing and he wanted to stick it to *gringos*. One time he told me that he wasn't interested in elections and that El Chapare had the conditions for a guerrilla group. We argued a lot and I told him that he was a spoiled child." In fact, Morales never opted for the armed struggle, even though it came up as a latent possibility in interviews and speeches at the time.

Instead he—like a good many of his *compañeros*—relied on organization. They would come to have around 700 syndicates divided into 27 rural centers and organized around 6 federations financed by union members.

The syndicate controlled everything: from protest assignments—some of them had to work while others maintained the roadblocks—to income, to the dry law—they weren't allowed to sell corn liquor during roadblocks—and even marriage trouble. "I was the union leader," Morales told García Linera in an interview for *Sociology of the Social Movements*, "but I resolved a few marriage problems. Lawyers complained that we were affecting their interest, what they make off divorce cases! [...] If the husband made a mistake, sanction; for the wife, sanction, generally communal work." In the case of a serious offense, they would, and still do, tie the offender to the *Palo Santo*, a tree with carnivorous ants.

Paid just enough by the federation to—in his words—eat and walk, Morales received people in a little room, furnished with an old typewriter, a telephone, three little tables, a dozen chairs, and posters and signs on the walls, but it suffered from one absence: the big map of El Chapare that they had to return because the union wasn't able to make the payments on it. In that room in 1991, journalist Martín Caparrós asked him what happened to the coca leaves that were turned into cocaine.

"We produce our coca, we bring it to the main markets, we sell it and that's where our responsibility ends."

The greatest benefactors of the business didn't live in El Chapare. In the mid-1990s, a harvester earned $2.50 per day, and a coca stomper earned $4. The families that owned two acres could make up to $2,000 a year. But the biggest business was left for others: A crop worth $1,500 in El Chapare, once crystallized in Japan, would go up to $120,000.

In 1993, the United States relaunched its offensive. During a visit to Bolivia, drug czar Lee Brown declared that "the war should be against the hive, not the bees." The hive was the *cocaleros*. He arranged an agreement that committed Bolivia to eradicating 12,500 acres of coca by March 31 of the following year in exchange for aid in the amount of $20 million. President Gonzalo Sánchez de Lozada, who was involved in drafting Decree 21.060, was a wealthy business miner who spoke a choppy Spanish that sounded similar to that of many U.S. ambassadors. He proved to be a good ally to Washington.

In that context, Morales announced that committees dedicated to preventing eradication would be reinstated. "If the government doesn't lift the forced eradication, all sixty thousand of us producers are going to go into hiding to confront it," he threatened.

In August 1994, Morales was arrested. He was traveling next to photographer José Luis Quintana on a bus to El Chapare when civil agents boarded. "Fucking Indian," they yelled as they beat him. They brought him to Cochabamba in a pick-up truck with tinted windows. Quintana had the exclusive, and his daily paper *Hoy* featured the news of the illegal arrest on the front cover. Since then, Evo calls him when there is news or to invite him to have a few beers with him.

One of Evo's skills has always been his ability to establish a personal rapport with journalists and photographers. In addition to his friendly style, he was able to articulate his opinions with simplicity, and in a way that made good headlines. Consequently, he began to construct himself as a character in the media. "I am afraid for my life," he said before starting a dry hunger strike in jail.

Evo was accused of sedition and organizing irregular groups. His neighbors from Villa 14 de Septiembre went into hiding because the "lions" (a nickname for UMOPAR agents) were going house by house looking for them. While waiting for his liberation, they planned a major roadblock in secrecy.

A milestone in the history of the *cocalero* movement took place the day after Morales' arrest, August 29. The march "for life, coca and national sovereignty" that covered the 360 miles that separate Villa Tunari, in El Chapare, from La Paz was begun.

Followed by helicopters and unlicensed vehicles, around 3,000 *campesinos* initiated the march. For the most part, they walked in lines and ate potatoes or corn that they boiled and heated up wherever they could. They carried chamomile and *paico* leaf for stomachaches, and took alfalfa for strength. To maintain a good pace, they took *k'auke* breaks (coca chewing sit-ins), healing their knees with *chillka* leaves. As the days progressed, they began to suffer from symptoms of exertion: bloodied and blistered feet, diarrhea, and vomiting. There were further moments of concern. One group of marchers became ill when arriving in the town of Inquivisi because of the candies and river water sweetened with sugar they'd consumed.

Another group was almost carried away by the current when crossing the La Paz River with water above their waists. In Santa Rosa, the cold forced everyone to seek refuge between the headstones of the cemetery.

They also had internal feuds to settle. Non-*cocaleros* questioned the predominant place of the *cocaleros*. They complained about receiving fewer resources and demanded that the fight for land possession be prioritized on the agenda.

Freed from prison on September 7, Morales joined up with the march. Five days later, he participated in a debate with the minister of government, Germán Quiroga, in *De Cerca* (Close Up), the political program hosted by Carlos Mesa, who would later become president.

"The public can plainly see," Evo said, "that they are trying to eliminate Evo Morales and his supporters, I imagine by the recommendation of the American Embassy."

He had created an effective style of speaking of Evo Morales in the third person. In that debate, moreover, he came off as competent and clear. When the minister maintained that 66 percent of the coca of El Chapare found its way to narcotics trafficking, Evo responded:

Say I give you all of the coca in El Chapare, do you think that's going to eliminate the market in the United States? If we finish with coca in El Chapare, the illegal problem will move into Los Yungas and later we'll say that ninety percent of the coca of Los Yungas goes to drug-trafficking. El Chapare is run by the DEA and the American Embassy.

After 22 days, on September 19, the marchers arrived in the political capital of the country, and the residents of La Paz could see that they weren't just phantoms, as the government had been suggesting that whole week. "With guns, or bombs, this protest will not calm!" they shouted. "With bombs, with gas, the march is in La Paz!" They left graffiti that has survived the passage of time and painting over of walls: "Gringos: eradicate your noses."

The march managed to bring national attention to the coca issue, which had previously seemed to be confined to El Chapare. It also brought Morales' leadership to the national stage. "We Aymaras and Quechuas," he said, "are the expression and voice of so many races and this expression is beginning to shine and to change like the color of the coca leaf: now it is red and brilliant. And that is why we, too, have begun to shine at the national level." A Bolivian news agency chose him as the person of the year.

But that didn't give Morales immunity. In April 1995, he was arrested during a sting operation that, allegedly, prevented a coup that was planned from the shores of Lake Titicaca involving unseemly groups affiliated with Colombian guerillas and Peru's Shining Path. It was actually just a meeting of the Andean Council of Coca Producers, chaired by Morales. They held him in nearby Tiquina, where the soldiers treated him well. They did, however, torture two of his associates, demanding that they accuse Evo of links to drug trafficking to end their torment. They didn't comply.

A day later, Morales was taken to the Special Judicial Police (PTJ) of La Paz to negotiate with a junior secretary of state. They offered him his freedom in exchange for his support of a coca eradication plan. He didn't accept. The minister of government, Carlos Sánchez Berzaín, threatened him by saying that there was a DEA plane waiting to remove him from Bolivia.

Juan del Granado, president of the Congressional Commission of Human Rights, visited him in his cell and calmed him down.

"They're bullshitting you. There's nothing to this. They can't remove you from the country, it's just blackmail, it's a lie," del Granado told him, and he gave him a blanket.

The former congressman would recall how the worry began to fall away from Evo's eyes. He had been imagining himself in a U.S. prison. Instead, they confined him in the Beni Prison along with eight *cocalero* leaders.

A few weeks later, free again, Morales traveled to Argentina.

"**I**'m Evo," he said.

I met Morales on the first Friday of August 1995. When he introduced himself, he only had one concern: to get the cold out of his bones. He tried to warm up with a simple technique, tapping his feet against the floor, rubbing his hands against his pants, and putting his head in his chest, just as swimmers do before diving head first into the water. He came from the tropics.

The morning we met, I was alone in a classroom in the Department of Philosophy and Literature at the University of Buenos Aires, without central heat or any other means to raise the temperature. Evo didn't look any different from the hundreds of thousands of Bolivian farmers and construction workers who go to Argentina to work for a dollarized wage that they sent back to their country.

But Evo was included on the list of invitees to the seminar "Perspectives of Liberation in Latin America," together with Brazilian theologian Frei Betto, Nicaraguan commander Omar Cabezas, Chilean theorist Martha Harnecker, and Argentine writers David Viñas and Osvaldo Bayer, among others.

Evo wore gray pants, a blue sweater with a red line across the chest, and a black windbreaker. Nobody paid any attention to him or the way he was dressed. One year after an uprising in Chiapas (a southern region in Mexico), led by the Zapatista Army of National Liberation (EZLN), the focus of the seminar was the Zapatistas.

Evo was keeping an eye on El Chapare. Some of his *compañeros* had been hospitalized after resisting the removal of a roadblock. A state of siege was established in Bolivia. After having to make so many calls to give instructions about how to keep the struggle going, he went through his provisions for the trip.

"I don't even have enough for Marcos (of the Zapatistas) books that I want to take back to my *compañeros*. Would you be able to help me out and get them to give them to me for free?" he asked me after the interview in the classroom.

My position as a correspondent to the La Paz–based paper *Hoy* didn't exactly allow me to help.

"They call him Evo?" asked the book vendor from whom I requested a few books free of charge.

"Yes, that's what they call him," I answered.

"I don't believe you. Give me five pesos for two books," he said.

In two minutes, I came back with him.

"Hello, I am Evo," he stated.

Reluctantly, the book vendor gave him two books. I proposed that we go to the downtown bookstores because there would be more books about Zapatistas and we would be able to take some of them. He told me that he didn't steal. I told him that we would just borrow them and then return them later. "Let me think about that," he said.

He said there was something he didn't like about himself: "I am not fit to read books or documents."

He then told me he was thinking of getting married that winter. "I'd like a liberation theology priest to perform the ceremony on a coca plantation." He omitted the name of his fiancée: "She's afraid of the DEA. It's more her family's fear, they've all decided against me because her father was a big MNR activist who was greatly persecuted. When they hear it's Evo, damn, they get spooked," he said.

When we spoke of politics—the dominant topic of the meeting—he insisted that he was not a politician but rather a union leader. Nonetheless, he already saw that it was necessary to create his own party. He and his *compañeros* were discussing the possibility of his running in the 1997 elections, and they planned to collect signatures in the following months.

"There is a national sector of Political Instrument, called Assembly for the Sovereignty of the Peoples (ASP), that is formulating statutes and programs. It would be like a party but with one tactical part and another strategic," Evo said.

"Could you explain the difference for me?" I asked.

"We'll go over that another time."

By the afternoon, he told me that he wanted to do a second interview to tell me things that he hadn't told me in the deserted classroom.

"I don't think we're very far away from what's happening in Chiapas to be reproduced in Bolivia. If the government continues to assault us, El Chapare is going to burst: We're close to civil war. I would be very interested to meet the Zapatistas leader, Marcos," Evo said.

"Do you see the possibility of an armed uprising as unlikely?" I asked.

"I don't know. The bases will decide," he said.

Once more he flirted with the idea of an insurrection.

"I am tempted," he said, "to declare Fidel Castro the commander-in-chief of liberation forces in Latin America. There may be many leaders, but I better stop myself there because we are always accused of being subversive."

After finishing the second part of the interview, I asked him what had moved him to make such statements. He laughed and his eyes sparkled.

"You have no idea what's going to happen with what I've told you," he said.

"That bad?" I asked.

"Wait and see."

The daily paper *Hoy* belonged to businessman Samuel Doria Medina, leader of the Leftist Revolutionary Movement (MIR), which didn't have anything to do with movements or leftism or even revolution. With the worst of intentions, that interview was put on the front page.

"It wouldn't take that much for the Chiapas phenomenon to happen in Bolivia."

"Evo seeks summit with Subcomandante Marcos."

"Confessions of an unknown Evo Morales."

Sánchez de Lozada's government used the interview with me to accuse him of being a violent terrorist. They spent years branding him as a drug trafficker, narcotics guerilla, and an accomplice to the drug barons. Morales' next step, while he continued dodging the DEA and even bullets, was to immerse himself in the muck of politics.

Chapter Three

THE TRICONTINENTAL TOUR (NOVEMBER–DECEMBER 2006)

Evo Morales is sleeping with his hands resting on his abdomen. A blanket warms his legs, and a carefree expression gives him the air of an adolescent. Exceptionally, nothing seems to disturb him, neither the flashes of lightning shaking the Caribbean Sea below nor the hurricane winds blowing the seven-seater plane from side to side. He seems to be delighting in a peace that is not his.

Morales wakes up abruptly. His eyes, narrow from exhaustion, are bloodshot. His body stoops forward clumsily, but his straight hair sticks up.

He looks to his side and says to me, "I had a dream."

This is important to him, for his destiny as president, and possibly for the political forces that govern from the sky, the jungle, and the Burned Palace.

"The DEA was trying to scare me off. Out there, in the mountains," he said.

It's 3:25 A.M. in Nigeria, the country we left behind a few hours ago; 10:25 P.M. the day before in Cuba, the next destination of the tour; and 10:25 P.M. in Bolivia, according to the blue watch that—no matter what country he's in—Evo keeps set to the time of his home.

Juan Ramón Quintana, an ex-military man, sociologist, and minister of the presidency, asks him, "And where were they chasing you off to in the dream?"

The president closes his eyes and attempts to recover those lost images. Finally, he has to give up.

"It was the DEA, it was the gringos. But I don't remember anything else," he stated.

For him, those dreams are usually premonitory signs that he should pay attention to in the same way he listens to the suggestions of advisors or the proposals of unions. In June 2006, the day he met with the then-ambassador of the United States in Bolivia, David Greenlee, he dreamt that Fidel Castro fell down while he was walking with him through the streets of Orinoca. When he woke up, he called the Cuban Ambassador, Rafael Dausá, concerned for the health of the commander. The diplomat calmed him down: "Fidel is very well, Evo. Relax."

Weeks later, on July 31, the Cuban government made Castro's illness public and announced that they would delegate his role to his brother, Raúl Castro. On September 7, Morales traveled to Havana to meet with Fidel for two hours, and he gave him a wooden Indian figurine as a gift. "He was pretty sick," he tells us on our flight to Cuba, where Castro's eightieth birthday celebration is set to take place and be recorded. Almost an official farewell.

Morales compares this December 1, 2006, visit with his first trip to Havana, in 1992, when he was participating in a conference. To him, Havana tastes of Tropicola soda and pool water. Those were the liquids that kept him on his feet when he finished with that event.

An unknown *cocalero* leader, he came to the island with a one-way ticket, a single dollar, the promise that his return would be paid for, and a fervent desire to meet Castro. He saw him for the first time in the Palace of Conventions, and he realized that he wanted to speak with that same intonation, to be able to link sentences together for hours. He attempted to greet him but didn't have any luck. He registered himself on the list of speakers and waited two days. However, in the moment of truth, his ideas became clouded and he delivered a confusing and erratic three-minute speech. He hadn't recovered from this disappointment when the practical problems surfaced. There wasn't any money for his return. Until they could manage to get him a seat on a flight to Peru, he survived off Tropicola and pool water.

Once in Lima he exchanged his dollar for Peruvian *soles* to speak with Juan Rojas, a Peruvian *campesino* leader, who loaned him $100 so he could make his way back to Bolivia. He was a day and a half late to a *campesino* gathering because the roads were flooded with rain.

"All that to meet Fidel," Morales concludes as the plane nears the red carpet and the interminable Cuban receiving line prepares to welcome its beloved son.

The tricontinental tour began a week earlier in the city of Santa Cruz de la Sierra. To join the delegation, I had to present myself at the Burned Palace on Saturday at 11:00 A.M. with a passport and proof of the yellow fever vaccine. But Friday at 9:00 P.M., the president's secretary explained that we should get to the El Alto airport immediately because we would be flying on a commercial flight to Santa Cruz to take the tour plane the next day. The delegation included the presidential escort, Major of the Air Force, Jaime Zabala; the bodyguard, Police Captain Raúl Tejerina Coro; the assistant to the president, Nelly Vázquez; and the reporter from the national Channel 7, Irguen Pasten Bráñez.

The next day, in the Santa Cruz Viru-Viru Airport, the aide gave a sign of alarm. "That plane seems small," he determined when the Falcon of the Venezuelan state oil company PDVSA appeared somewhat diminished next to a 747.

The Falcon, valued at around $25 million, boasted such classy details as a dark wood trim, matching faux leather seats, wine glasses displayed in a glass case, and a plasma screen television.

"Eight people will fit in there," the pilot assured.

"But there are ten of us," I answered.

"But only eight will board," he said, closing the debate.

"Shhhhhhhhoot. I'll call La Paz," Zabala worried.

La Paz told him that a plane for 12 people had been requested from Caracas.

"Nobody tells me anything," the pilot went on. "They just gave me these orders. I have to go from here to Rotterdam [Holland], even though I still don't know the layovers, and on the way back we go to Nigeria and Caracas."

"But the last country of the tour is Cuba," I added.

"I can't land in Cuba with this plane. It's registered in the United States," he countered.

In short, there were several problems. The most urgent one was to reduce the delegation from ten to eight. This situation was fit for a reality-TV contest: La Paz, via a governmental voice, would inform Zabala, and then he would say who could board the Falcon. We were sitting in a van, suffering from the midday heat of the Bolivian east. The suitcases were sitting to the side of the little stairs, next to the gifts that the president would present in Rotterdam: shawls of vicuna wool for the Dutch-Argentine princess Máxima Zorreguieta and for Queen Beatrix.

Zabala issued the verdict as to who would remain on the ground.

"Nelly, okay, and who else? Martín?"

Nelly gave the camera to the aide and instructed him to give Morales two Maca pills every day; the pills are a natural energizer used by some athletes to improve their performance and by some nonathletes to improve their sexual stamina or to keep from feeling tired during the day.

The Caribbean pilot, meanwhile, continued to be baffled by the Bolivian delegation. When Zabala informed him that they would arrive in Santa Cruz on Tuesday and would remain a few hours only to change course to Nigeria, he almost lost it.

"I cannot. According to regulations, after flying 15 hours, I have to rest 24. If we arrive on Tuesday, we can't head back until Wednesday morning."

He couldn't manage to reconcile the world of aviation academy rules and protocol manuals with the peculiar practices of the Bolivian president.

After arriving in the small aircraft from La Paz, Evo requested that we speak in the Falcon.

"Brother, there was some confusion. But you will travel to Nigeria with us later on."

My friend Maggy came with her son to pick me up and take me to a public pool in the outskirts of Santa Cruz de la Sierra. We spent the afternoon in the water among people drinking beer, children scorched by the harmful sun, grass roofs, hamburgers that took too long to grill, inexorably ravenous mosquitoes, and water slides. It was an abrupt social descent—from the possibility of brushing shoulders with Dutch Royalty, I went to splash about with the Santa Cruz middle class. Inside those swimming pools, warmed by the sun and children's pee, I thought about the ordered chaos that surrounds Morales. When it comes to the question of state efficiency, a desirable thing for a transoceanic tour, it should be qualified with an irrefutable fact. Despite much improvisation, changing of plans, and lack of seats on airplanes, the machinery of the state is capable of movement.

The president was back in La Paz by Tuesday to receive marchers who had walked for several days to demand the end of the large rural estates and a more equitable distribution of land. In response to part of that demand, the government drafted modifications to the National Institute of Agrarian Reform (INRA) law that were approved by the house of deputies but held back by the opposing majority in the Senate. Their strategy consisted of avoiding meetings on the subject and denying the president authorization to remain absent from the country for more than five days. Hence, Morales had to return from Holland to Bolivia instead of traveling directly to Nigeria.

Tuesday couldn't have gone better for him. He met with the marchers, and then two substitute senators from the opposition decided to give quorum to the government, and by nightfall the new law was approved. At 10 P.M., when he should have been leaving for Africa, all of the *campesinos* that would fit into the Burned Palace were celebrating and awaiting a speech.

The members of the transcontinental delegation (Zabala, Tejerina, Noah Friedman-Rudovsky, the president's photographer) were also awaiting Evo's speech but in a tiny room in the Viru-Viru Airport. When Zabala felt like all the air had been used up, he asked a soldier, who had been trying unsuccessfully to tune into the speech, to leave the room.

There were other Bolivians, intending to immigrate to Spain, walking around the terminal. That week, LAB, a Bolivian airline, had an offer to reimburse 50 percent of the ticket value to those who were unable to get through customs in Madrid. Tickets were sold out until April 1, 2007, when the requirement for visas to enter Spain would go into effect. In another room of the airport, those returning from Madrid who didn't know how to read or write had to ask the literate passengers to fill out their customs forms while airport officials looked the other way.

Applause, shouts, and a prevailing chant erupted from the television: "The people, united, will never be defeated." Some farmers displayed their land possession paperwork. Alejandro Almaraz, the vice minister of land, mentioned the three people who had died that week during the march to La Paz. One of them was struck by lightning.

"Long live the agrarian revolution!" shouted Almaraz.

If the president invited a future minister or a minister he wanted to reward onto his plane, I would have to go back to swim in the public pool. Zavala's phone conversations with his superiors multiplied my fears. He reported to a colonel that there had been a misunderstanding with the pilots: They thought they were supposed to fly to Lagos and not to Abuja, the present-day capital of Nigeria. It was telling how his body stiffened when speaking with the colonel and even more so with the general.

Evo announced that on that historic night they had put an end to the large rural estates in Bolivia:

The fight for territory is the fight of our ancestors and we are absolute owners of this noble land. For more than five hundred years they subjugated our land. The distribution of land is part of a program of agrarian reform [...] I couldn't accompany you in this march. I have seen you from the plane. I'm coming from the outside and now I must go back out again. But it isn't just to parade around. It is to do things for Bolivia. Yesterday we were in Holland...twenty meetings.

One of my acquaintances in the little room said there had actually only been 19 meetings, but another reminded him that the twentieth had been with a Bolivian businessman with investments in Holland.

"They have accused us," continued the president, "of paying the opposing senators [in order to achieve the approval of the law]. We will never pay."

The delegation argued over which day to stamp Morales' passport. Noah suggested Tuesday in case the senate didn't give authorization to be absent for more than five days. "The stamp is from Wednesday, and it can't be rescinded on a president's passport," Zabala answered at 1:00 A.M.

In the palace, they were shouting, "Evo, Evo" when we finally received an instruction: "To the plane."

Morales arrived at the Viru-Viru runway in a euphoric state.

"I still can't believe what happened, boss, what you missed," he told me, already seated in the French-registered Falcon, which replaced the one that had taken him to Holland. It was older, less comfortable, and longer, but it was also safer. It had three engines.

The president smiled his white smile with metallic details, which remained frozen on his face for a while.

"And how did it happen?" I asked.

"This has been an important day. I was thinking about issuing a decree to change the law, but this morning the senators of Podemos began to call to say that they wanted to join up," Morales stated.

"And they spoke to you?" I asked.

"No, with Álvaro [García Linera]. I had five decrees already prepared, which were the foundation for the law that was finally passed. But I was hesitant," Morales explained.

The minister of the presidency, Juan Ramón Quintana, with short dark hair and round-framed glasses, explained that the decree could have had constitutional obstacles and done political harm to the government. He recounted how Senator Mario Vargas, of Podemos, took the first step. He wanted something for his region, the Amazon.

"The Vargases," he continued, "are seven brothers with various economic exploits in that region."

"But all the Vargases exploit the human being," Morales added.

Fatigue soon began to defeat him. With his hands over his belly, Evo rested his feet on the empty seat across from him. When the plane taxied in the direction of the Atlantic, he closed his eyes.

Facing each other in the other pair of seats, Quintana and I coordinated the awkward mechanics of crossing our legs with the ultimate goal of snoozing until the first layover. I could see the red light of the plane's wing out the window, already moving at 600 miles per hour.

When he awoke in Fortaleza (Brazil), Evo was still euphoric, as if his rest hadn't interrupted anything. He said that he hadn't been able to sleep, that he kept thinking about the ceremony at the Palace and that he remembered a quote from the leader Felipe Quispe: "There was the smell of Indians in the Palace."

In the VIP room of the airport, he had a coffee and began to give instructions by phone. "Big boss, we've got to get the Constituent [Assembly] in order." He knew that the previous night's blow had helped him to crush the opposition. He didn't have any interest in there being an interlocutor because he didn't respect them. "They only attack my government, they don't recognize anything positive in me," he stated.

On the plane, they served cheese and pastrami sandwiches, which Morales washed down with a diet Coca-Cola. The chat, from Fortaleza to Nigeria, would go from politics to his childhood and from his childhood to his dreams. Every so often, we'd be interrupted by an urgent call.

He talked about the *lik'ichiri*, a possible cause of the death of his father, Dionisio, in 1983. The *lik'ichiri* extracts the fat from the body and weakens it. In its classical and colonial version, it was represented as a priest who attacked the Indians, taking their fat from them to make church bells. The myth was modernized in the second half of the twentieth century, when the fat could also be served as fuel for planes or to pay the external debt.

The president had had a dream that he believes served as a symbol of Dionisio's death in El Chapare. A plane fell from above the Orinoca soccer field, composed of dry dirt and a few ailing goal posts. Nevertheless, he woke up in a great mood. He sang and whistled at sunrise. After preparing his breakfast and lunch, he lay down to rest, something that he generally didn't allow himself.

That afternoon, he sent his brother, Hugo, out to buy a few things in Cochabamba. After awhile, Hugo's wife came into the house looking upset. Morales thought Hugo had had an accident.

"Father died," she informed him.

At first, Evo thought she meant her father, and he told her it was okay to cry. "Your father died," she responded. Shortly thereafter, Morales met with the farmhands to tell them. He couldn't attend the burial of Dionisio, however, nor that of his mother in 1992, because he was in Canada at the time.

The image of the plane falling was, for the president, a legacy from his father. One night Dionisio had a dream that a vehicle was prowling about his house, and he interpreted that death was prowling around the family. The next day, a relative passed away.

In the Falcon, Morales expressed heartfelt and meandering memories of his father. He recalled his sad drunkenness on pure alcohol, sometimes tinged with cinnamon, or his weeping when he gathered his children and made them cry, recalling how much he had been made to suffer from poverty.

Evo never knew his father's birthday, but he did know that Dionisio was only 16 or 17 years old and still fairly immature when he met María Ayma, who was 15 or so years older than him. When he started to see her as an old woman, Dionisio told his children that she had once been young and pretty. One of his best anecdotes recounted the time that they were bringing animals from Orinoca to sell in other communities when he lost his nephew Asensio, who they then rediscovered, many years later, married and with kids.

Later, while he was eating a ham and cheese omelet and bread and butter, Evo anticipated that his meeting with Libyan President Muammar Gaddafi, in Nigeria, would make world news.

"It won't harm you?" I asked.

"No," he replied.

"He's much better with the United States," I suggested.

"Yes, but without taking down his flags," Evo responded.

"The Iranian president [Mahmud] Ahmadinejad, now he is more complicated," I stated.

"I have had contacts with him," Evo said.

I brought my index finger to my lips, and told him, "Shhhh." Evo repeated the gesture and laughed.

"We need," the president went on, "Gaddafi's cooperation with $50 million and credits. We should already have a work committee."

The creation of committees is pure Morales.

The conversation then turned to Argentina. Evo was surprised to hear that Néstor Kirchner, the Argentine president, had sent his representatives to vote for the privatization of the state petroleum business when he was a governor, as well as other irrefutable facts that proved that Kirchner had a not-so-progressive past behind him. He was also amazed to learn the extent to which people govern with polls in mind in Argentina.

"We do it more the opposite," Quintana said.

"One a year," Morales added.

He then changed the subject to Diego Armando Maradona, the soccer player, as an almost obligatory stopover in the chat about Argentina.

"I want him to come play in El Chapare in the celebration for the first-year government," stated Evo.

A while later, after several failed attempts, he got the airplane telephone to work.

"Big boss, what are they saying on ERBOL, Panamericana, and FIDES?" he asked in reference to three of the most important radio stations in Bolivia.

Morales explained that García Linera would receive mayors in La Paz. They told him about the ladies in Santa Cruz who had burned the *Wiphala*, the seven-color rainbow flag of indigenous Andeans, and he requested a radio spot about it. "We have to resolve the issue of the two-thirds this week," he said, determined to make the most of his good moment. Various sectors of the opposition were demanding—with picket protests—that the new constitution be approved only with a two-thirds vote by the constituents, and not with the simple majority the government desired.

Minutes later, the plane landed in Abuja and the Bolivian delegation walked down the steps and onto a red carpet. The representative of the president of Nigeria said to me, "Welcome, minister."

Abuja was the headquarters for the first South—South meeting of the presidents of Africa and South America, instigated primarily by Brazilian president Luiz Inácio Lula da Silva on the other side of the Atlantic. In summits of high politics, they also debate over subjects that aren't high politics. My first mission on Nigerian soil is a good example.

The president's only guard, Captain Tejerina, forgot the passports on the plane, but by the time he realized his error, the Falcon had already disappeared. A second setback had to do with his firearm. When I went with him to declare it, a Nigerian in a bright red tunic and sandals informed him that he could only enter the country with one 16-bullet magazine and that the other magazine had to remain in custody or on the plane. Tejerina opted for the latter.

"How will you know that he's left the bullets?" I asked.

"A witness will accompany you and take a photo," the Nigerian stated.

This first mission was accomplished in its totality: Tejerina found the Falcon, complete with the wings and passports, and the witness photographer shot testimony of the event.

Bolivian delegations have a peculiarity. They are so sparse that local governments will triple or quadruple their support personnel. When Morales went to Santiago, Chile, for Michelle Bachelet's inauguration, the Chilean government was alarmed because he came accompanied only by his chief of security, and supplemented that with six guards. In Nigeria, the guards and officials who joined us tripled the six-person delegation.

The summit organizers reserved a presidential suite in the Hilton Hotel for Morales, which included three rooms, a five-foot-tall porter dressed in a white tailcoat, and a Bolivian flag. To save money, the president decided we would all share the rooms of his suite. I had the luck of sleeping in the same bed as Minister Quintana.

At 9:00 p.m., Evo went down to eat at a restaurant serving local cuisine when one of Gaddafi's men introduced himself.

"Leader," he said in Spanish, "is very interested in meeting with President Morales tonight."

At first, the meeting was going to be in the Bolivian presidential suite, then at the official dinner. Later on, Evo confirmed that it would take place in that restaurant, but then they went back to the first plan. Finally, once he returned to his room, he was notified that it would take place in the Libyan embassy, after the dinner and sometime after midnight. In the midst of the confusion, Gaddafi's Spanish-speaking advisor assured Morales that they would definitely have the meeting: "*Líder* says that protocol isn't necessary between revolutionaries."

At dinner, Angélica Navarro, the Bolivian ambassador in Geneva, related that Libya had sent a South–South cooperation document to the summit, which brought up the topics of security and defense. She doubted that Gaddafi would ask for explicit support from Evo in that document.

Líder no longer led the pan-Arabism and pan-Africanism movement that, in 1977, forecast the arrival of a socialist, popular, and national "State of the Masses," a third track between capitalism and Marxism. In 1980, Gaddafi broke with the United States after the North American embassy in Tripoli was raided. In 1986, Washington dropped bombs over several Libyan cities as well as the presidential palace. One of Gaddafi's daughters was killed. Relations worsened when the African government assumed civil responsibility for the bombing of a PanAm plane in

Lockerbie, Scotland, in 1988, and committed to indemnifying the families of the 270 people killed. Their anti-U.S. rhetoric ended in the mid-1990s: The insurgency of radical Islamic groups caused Tripoli to seek an understanding with Washington to neutralize them. In May 2006, the Bush administration announced that it would reopen its Libyan embassy after almost 25 years, and he spoke highly of Gaddafi's forces in the fight against terrorism. He did not praise Libyan oil in the context of high prices and scarce supply.

In a campaign tent, pitched in the patio of the Libyan embassy, Gaddafi received his guests. Among green drapery with camel details, a television tuned to a news channel, fluorescent lights, and coffee tables, a cast-iron chair flanked by two fans stood out as the place where *Líder* thought and aired out his ideas. Of the guards, the most conspicuous one was sticking out his butt, had a blatantly dyed moustache, and a military cap on.

Gaddafi was wearing a reddish beret and a brown shawl, and his hair was dyed black. He awaited us while sitting in a Chesterton armchair. When he got out of the car, Morales already almost had his arm out.

"A pleasure to meet you," the Bolivian chief of state said.

Evo had already been to Tripoli when they invited him to receive the Gaddafi Human Rights Prize, an award of $50,000, but he didn't meet with *Líder*.

Sitting down, Gaddafi told of how he rejoiced at the arrival of left-wing governments and the rejection of neoliberalism in Latin America. "Let's give thanks to God for that," he requested. There were little pillows at their feet for praying.

"Thanks very much," answered Morales.

"No country can fight alone," Gaddafi continued. "Now is the time for regional integration."

Líder made them bring out a world map that had different-colored regions instead of countries. He gesticulated exuberantly while drawing diamond shapes and emulating prayer, but seemed distant. He rarely looked his guest in the eyes.

He proposed a treaty with the countries of the South Atlantic: "A zone of stability, peace, and disarmament. A zone without a foreign base." He didn't mention the United States, although the idea of a foreign base brought an echo of his more radical youth.

"Libya is at Bolivia's disposition," he concluded, and they agreed that a commission would work toward the improvement of bilateral relations. They said goodbye exuberantly.

In the Hilton suite, at 1:00 A.M., there was an evaluation of the meeting. Making the encounter public that same night could provoke undesirable headlines in the Bolivian press, such as "Morales came to Nigeria to meet with Gaddafi," and would consequently distort the meaning of his participation in the summit.

Evo asked where the attending journalists were from, and Noah answered that they were all members of the Libyan official press. While watching a Barcelona soccer game on the plasma television out of the corner of his eye, he came to a conclusion. "I don't need to hide whom I meet with. We're going to disseminate the information now."

A different spin occurred to him.

"Bolivia wants to export its democratic and cultural revolution to Africa."

Morales is, in fact, critical of some African countries: They govern their native peoples, but the status quo has changed very little. He believes that he can be the spokesman for the current group of decolonizers in Africa and America, who come to power to demonstrate the diversity of the country as well as to implement deeper transformations.

The meeting concluded, and I assumed a new role, reporter for the Bolivian Information Agency (ABI). I sent the first newswire at 4:30 A.M.:

> (ABI) Abuja, Nigeria. President Evo Morales arrived Wednesday night to Nigeria, where he will be one of the principal speakers of the first African-American summit....

The minister of the presidency was snoring when I came into the room. It wasn't until three hours later that Morales asked for the Bolivian daily papers and a coffee. He had spent almost the entire night talking on the phone from his bed.

Chaos now made up part of the summit. The night before, a couple of guards had gotten into a fist fight in one of the elevators; at sunrise, in the door to the conference room, a fat, bald security guard, wet with perspiration, struggled for 40 minutes with journalists and guests, to whom he yelled, "Move back, move back." No one could get through their agenda, the press conferences ran over, and none of the documents arrived on time.

Evo saw the disorganization and thought obsessively about the following week's Cochabamba summit week, in which he would receive many presidents. He asked Quintana to set everything up in Cochabamba after the tour to guarantee that it would go smoothly. "It needs to be run with

military discipline," he said, calling to mind the minister of the presidency's
army background.

He became excited, imagining how it could be. "There have to be people
in the streets applauding the presidents and children with flags from all of
the countries. The presidents should attend the ceremony in the stadium
and we have to make Cristina [Fernández de Kirchner] wear a traditional
Bolivian skirt."

"Cristina dresses in haute couture," I told him.

From where he sat eating three fried eggs, he saw Lula coming into the
Hilton lobby with a group of officials. He was in a wheelchair because he'd
injured himself playing soccer. At the summit, the Brazilian president had
kept his speech vague and general.

Evo spoke after Lula and Gaddafi. He compared decolonization, which
for him involved pitting the law against the large rural estates, to the "colo-
nized" form of government of the old regime. "Before, the IMF and the
World Bank imposed policies in English and Bolivian politicians were
the ones left with the task of translating them." Marco Aurelio García, a
Brazilian foreign affairs advisor and former campaign manager of the presidential election that Lula had just won, slept soundly while Morales spoke.

During lunch in the suite, Evo said that they needed to organize a press
conference. It's a fallback for him: When there is no agenda or meetings
planned, or when he wants to solidify his position on something, he calls
for one.

Ecuadorian journalists dominated the conference, but I interrupted
them to urge the Africans, and a Japanese man who hardly knew of Bolivia's
existence but impressed everyone with his eagerness to know, to ask questions of the president.

I was supposed to be the interpreter for an interview with the Nigerian
state-owned television station and also with Al Jazeera, but the latter was
canceled at the last minute. When the reporter from the local channel told
me that his viewing audience averaged around 36 million, I got nervous.
That would be like all of Argentina suffering through my English. They
suffered for 15 minutes.

At 5:00 P.M., I was again in the middle of major politics: I helped the
chief executive officer of the Hilton realize his dream of taking a photo
with the president. In contrast, Evo's ultimate desire was to buy handmade
Nigerian crafts to bring back to his friends. Because the prices at the hotel
frightened him, he moved on to a market at the suggestion of one of the

bellhops. But it didn't turn out to be the right place either: They sold blenders at suspiciously low prices, popsicles by the dozen, and cell phones with expiration dates. After three minutes, he was already on his way back to the airport.

Sitting in a yellow leather chair over a red carpet, he awaited the Falcon's turn for departure from a VIP room without windows. The room even had golden chairs and handcrafted cabinets. The television was permanently tuned to CNN International.

Other presidents, also waiting for their authorization to leave, came in and out of the VIP room. First was Blaisé Compaoré, the leader of Burkina Faso, a landlocked country in which illiteracy rates for women are up to 84 percent and the GDP is $1,300 per capita, half that of Bolivia. Compaoré wore a black suit and a sky blue shirt without a tie, and gold jewelry shone from some of his fingers and his left wrist. He asked Morales about the flight schedule from Nigeria to Bolivia, the Spanish language, and the other languages spoken in Bolivia.

"Tell me about Burkina Faso. What's your main industry?" Evo asked.

"Cotton."

As small talk quickly dwindled, the president's eyes drifted to the news channel. They both yawned at the same time.

With crossed arms and legs, Morales complained about the delay with a verb that he has made his own: "They've blockaded us, big boss."

He then said that he wanted to make an effort to visit a place in Havana that he'd never been to, the Tropicana cabaret.

Bharrat Jagdeo, the president of Guyana, walked into the VIP lounge. I returned to the role of interpreter. Subtly, Jagdeo insinuated that he had spent months trying to get into contact with Evo but that the Bolivian Foreign Ministry hadn't been very friendly. He told of his problems in Washington and the difficulty he'd had with multilateral credit organizations. "I want to improve relations between our countries, and that is why I want to come to Cochabamba," he said. But there wasn't time for that because they were interrupted by three announcements: The pilots of the Falcon hadn't managed to get decent catering, a storm was brewing in the Caribbean skies, and take-off would be in ten minutes.

During the first layover in Cape Verde, Morales announced, "I'm going to remove [Minister of Education Félix] Patzi."

From Cape Verde to Martinique, I ran the tape recorder for an interview for the Argentine edition of *Newsweek* magazine. When I finished, Morales complained that I'd asked questions about anti-Chilean sentiments in the Bolivian army. "You know where we stand."

"Evo, I ask and you answer whatever you want," I countered.

Quintana acknowledged that those sentiments did still exist among some soldiers, and he suggested it was one of the things to work on with the armed forces.

I requested another hour to interview him for this book.

"What topics are left?" asked the minister of the presidency.

"Women," Morales answered.

"Let's talk about the women that were sent to spy on you and betray you," I suggested.

Quintana said that some were underage. Morales talked about the various ways that the opposition had tried to get rid of him, from the beatings to the attempts to plant drugs on him.

The first big assault, on October 29, 1989, was one day before the ceremony commemorating the Villa Tunari massacre. Up to that point, it was the biggest audience of his career at 30,000 people.

"I was out celebrating when the UMOPAR agents fell upon me. They punched and kicked me with relish. As they were beating me up, I asked them how much the gringos were paying them. I couldn't defecate for days, and half of my body was immobilized," Morales said.

At that point, corruption in Cochabamba increased due to the liquid funds circulating among drug traffickers and law enforcement fighting against them.

Evo recalled other confrontations, such as when he was attacked and slashed with a machete or when a crazy person tried to provoke him. "We're not vengeful people," he said in reference to the ones who once beat and tortured him and yet still belonged to the security forces.

"Why do you think they never killed you?" I asked him.

The minister of the presidency answered that Carlos Sánchez Berzaín, the ex-right-hand man of Sánchez de Lozada, didn't do it because he knew the risks of a populous outcry.

"'Tuto' Quiroga, on the other hand, was much more willing to carry out the U.S. embassy's dirty work, and he would have done away with the president if he'd had the chance," said the minister of the presidency.

Evo gave silent approval to this theory. Then he told of how they attempted to plant drugs on him. During a trip to Mexico, someone tried to put drugs in his luggage. Another time, during a layover in Lima on the way back from Europe, they lost his suitcase. "I swore at them," he recalled. "I swore at them like I'd never sworn. I was a parliament member, and I yelled at them, demanding that they make my suitcase appear. Since then, I only travel with one bag, and I don't check it."

All the attempts by lawyers, priests, and political leaders to buy him off have failed. He has always seen money as a wicked thing. He doesn't desire it or even want to touch it. His vices before taking office—or, better said, the ways he enjoyed himself—included some partying, playing sports (racquetball or soccer games), and his Friday nights spent as a bachelor.

He jumped from talking about those pleasures to the church. He told about the time a priest offered to be the one to marry him.

"I'm only Catholic to go to weddings," he replied, laughing.

I asked him whether he believed in God.

"I believe in the land. In my father and my mother. In the Cuchi-Cuchi. And today is the celebration of the Cuchi-Cuchi," he replied.

"The hill, Cuchi-Cuchi?" I asked.

"Look into it. You want everything chewed up for you, boss," Evo responded.

He woke from his nap radiant and happy.

"I've been awake for the interview since five," he told me.

He said that promising information continued to arrive from Bolivia and that the opposition still hadn't recovered from the impact of the agrarian reform law modifications. Strangely, he didn't get any bad news at that time. Instead, he received it all at once upon returning to his country.

After being asleep for five minutes, he was startled awake by a dream.

"The DEA was chasing me again," he described. "Out there, all throughout the mountains."

There were orange flashes of lightning in the sky when the Falcon landed in Havana. The long caravan traveled from the airport to the city in the faint light of dawn. There were only a few people outside waiting for the early buses and even fewer driving cars that were in the throes of midlife crises.

The place where they put up the Bolivian delegation, *El Laguito* (Little Lake), owes its name to the man-made lake that occupies the main part of the property. In addition, *El Laguito* boasts several houses, palm trees, streams with bridges, BMWs and Mercedes Benzes, flamingos, ducks, coconuts, birds and aviaries, and gardens with state-of-the-art lawn mowers. It's there where they host the most distinguished guests of the Cuban government.

The stone house assigned to Morales and his entourage had more than enough rooms and a team of cooks and servants on staff 24 hours a day. He ate in a long dining room with bulky furniture. The cooks already knew what he liked and had fish soup waiting for him.

Evo spoke of the 22 hours he'd spent in Holland that week. In The Hague, he had to remind one of the 18 judges of the first International Criminal Court, René Blattman, where he'd come from. Blattman had also served as the Bolivian minister of justice under Sánchez de Lozada, which Morales repeated to him a total of six times. He likes to scrutinize the backgrounds of certain men and women in politics, referring to them as either résumés or criminal records, depending on what he thinks of the person in question. He told of how the Shell executives he met presented themselves as being open to negotiating. They assured him that the company wanted to invest but that the long-term commitments concerned them.

He also recounted his failed meeting with Princess Máxima Zorreguieta. The princess, who advised the United Nations (UN) in microfinance, which she defines as "an opportunity to depart from poverty," explained to Morales that the most important thing was the "culture of payment" and a low interest rate. The president responded that neither of those things constituted a problem for Bolivia. Every time he tried to broach other topics, the princess reiterated her distrust of Bolivia's culture of payment. By the rules of the throne, Noah would have to wait 24 hours to be allowed to print the photo he'd taken of the president next to the princess. "They were so stiff and rigid that I couldn't get a single decent photo," the journalist said.

Queen Beatrix received the president coldly and only asked procedural questions.

"The king and queen of Spain were very different," Evo said, dunking his spoon into a third bowl of soup. "He told me that he could mediate between Bush and me, and that he would command a mission."

But he did cause one upset with the monarch for his Montevideo speech, especially with regard to what he said about Bolivian immigrants in Spain. "Calm down, Evo," Juan Carlos said to him afterward in one of the hallways of the summit.

After breakfast, Morales visited Club Havana. He wanted to check on his gift for Castro: a cake made of coca flour, adorned in cream with drawings of coca leaves. The bakers, Rolando and Luisa, had traveled to Havana early to prepare it. The owner of an El Alto bakery, Rolando, utilizes the coca leaf to make creams, shampoos, baked goods, and other things, although he doesn't take it as far as Patzi, the minister of education, who insisted that one could use it to manufacture thin condoms.

With bottle-cap glasses and a ball of coca leaves in his left cheek, Rolando begged Evo to make sure there would be a picture of him with Fidel and the cake, which would improve his résumé. He explained that he got to where he was because of a mention in a Reuters wire. "I owe Reuters nearly everything."

The president went for a walk on Club's beach to see the ocean more closely and to feel the water on his feet. A couple of tourists checked him out and then asked about the man wearing pants and a short-sleeved shirt. Morales looked out at the horizon and asked, "Which way is Miami?"

"There, straight ahead, 90 miles," answered the Cuban ambassador to Bolivia.

When returning to El Laguito, the van driver gestured to an adolescent boy wearing an orange T-shirt fishing in the lake: "That's Elián González."

Gonzalez's case had gained mythological proportions in 1999. A ship-wrecked Cuban boy had washed up alone on Miami shores because his mother and her boyfriend, who were traveling in an aluminum boat, had drowned. He was returned to the island and his father by the U.S. government despite the protests of Cuban exiles in Florida.

Evo had lunch in the dining room with the band Arawi and Juan Enrique Jurado, singer and MAS delegate to the Constituent Assembly. He described the celebration of the Six Federations of the Tropics of Cochabamba for them. All of the members donate half of their Christmas bonuses for food and drinks. In the middle of the night, most of them have to make sure that their wives get back home, but the festivities continue until sunrise. In 2005, the year they celebrated their victory in the presidential elections, the party lasted until 7:00 A.M. They ended up having beer and fish soup for breakfast by a stream in El Chapare whose name nobody can remember.

That afternoon, Havana was dominated by the event: "Memory and Future: Cuba and Fidel. A hug from Guayasamín for Fidel." In the Friedrich Engels room of the Carl Marx Theater, longtime Cuban revolutionaries mingled with newer Latin American versions. Ignacio Ramonet presented his book, *Fidel Castro: My Life. A Spoken Autobiography*. It was actually the third edition of a long interview with the leader of the revolution, corrected by Fidel and published by the Cuban state. The oil painting by Ecuadorian painter Oswaldo Guayasamín, depicting a somewhat somber Castro, was also on display. Then the speeches began.

From Haiti, President René Préval said he hoped Fidel would serve for many more years. Venezuelan minister Nicolás Maduro committed a gaffe, saying: "Farewell, Commander." Daniel Ortega, president-elect of Nicaragua, spoke cautiously. "Fidel has been a source of inspiration. He has taught us to fight. And as a gift for him, we now have the victory of the FSLN (Sandinista National Liberation Front)." To prop up his 2006 presidential campaign, he started a Christian discourse about love and peace, and he chose a member of the right wing as his running mate.

The Bolivian president, the most applauded of the night, was received with a standing ovation and the shouts of "Evo-Evo." He improvised atop the platform. "Surprised by the human quality of Fidel," he said in his style of formulating sentences with undefined verbs. He spoke of the fight against imperialism and about how several Latin American and African countries were joining together. "And why shouldn't some from the Middle East join up too in order to put a stop to North American imperialism once and for all?" That comment earned him an informal complaint from the U.S. embassy in La Paz.

Later on, Morales attended a cocktail hour for special guests, and in the next room a weak and ill Castro received him for a few minutes.

Throughout their many encounters since that first visit in 1992, with the taste of Tropicola in his mouth, Evo has been able to develop a relationship with Castro almost like that of father and son. One coincidence helped: The president of Bolivia was born in 1959, the same year of the Cuban Revolution.

The primary advice that Fidel gave him—or what Morales remembers as the most important—was in Havana in 2003: "Don't do what we have done. Make your revolution a democratic one. We're in different times now, and the people want profound changes without war." They were meeting in his office, surrounded by the busts of José Martí and Abraham Lincoln, an oil painting of Camilo Cienfuegos, and an autographed photo of Ernest Hemingway.

Evo, who had flirted with the idea of an armed fight, made these words almost his own: The revolution would be with votes or not at all.

"If I become president someday and the U.S. blocks us economically, what should I do?" he asked Castro in 2004.

"You don't have anything to be afraid of. Bolivia is not an island like Cuba. It has neighboring countries and natural riches that it ought to mine and learn to make the most of. There is Lula, Kirchner, Chávez, Cuba. We didn't have any of that, not even the Soviet Union in the end," Castro said.

In April 2005, Evo traveled to Havana for knee surgery. After the operation, the Cubans insisted that he stay and rest after the years of stress he'd put on it. Because Chávez visited Havana on April 29, Fidel requested that the three of them appear together in a photo of "the axis of evil."

"When I heard him," Morales would recall, "I forgot to pick up my crutches, and I walked right over to him. The doctors stood there looking surprised. It seemed like a biblical command: 'Evo, rise and walk.'"

The weekend before the hydrocarbon nationalization decree of May 1, 2006, the Bolivian president met with the two of them in Havana again in a summit for the Bolivarian Alliance for the Peoples of Our America (ALBA). Evo hadn't told Chávez about the nationalization in advance, but he had mentioned it to Castro. "I couldn't hide it from him," Morales explained.

"Why don't you wait to do it until after the start of the constituent assembly?" asked Fidel by way of suggestion.

But Morales made his own decision and did it before.

Amid his recollections of their relationship, there was a tender one. Castro fell asleep early one morning while accompanying him from the hotel to the airport. "It made me feel like hugging him," he told me on December 1, thus concluding this particular collection of anecdotes.

At 7:00 A.M. the next morning, he arrived at the Plaza de la Revolución for the civic military procession, the final and most massive of the ceremonies in honor of Fidel's eightieth birthday.

The crowd, although made up of both committed political supporters and others not so committed, shared one certainty: At any moment, Castro would appear to say goodbye. In addition, 500 journalists and 2,000 delegates from 82 countries suspected the same thing and traveled in especially for the occasion.

The cast of characters seemed to be seated according to a hierarchical structure: In the center box were Raúl Castro, Evo, Daniel Ortega, Gabriel García Márquez, Ignacio Ramonet, and a few other celebrities. One rung down, in a sort of semicircle, were the most distinguished members of the Armed Forces and the Cuban Communist Party. The special invitees were on a third level, such as actor Gérard Depardieu and filmmaker Pino Solanas, among others. In front of the boxes, separated by 50 meters of asphalt where the parade of tanks and people passed by, were photos of Marx and Lenin. An imposing mural said: "Militarily, this country is invulnerable." On another mural, Fidel appeared with his rifle in hand, surrounded by arms, helicopters, big tanks, small tanks, and the text: "These things will never again yield before the Empire."

On December 2, in addition to Castro's birthday, the people were celebrating the fiftieth anniversary of the founding of the army and their disembarking from the *Granma*, the boat that brought Fidel and another 80 members of the 26th of July Movement from Mexico for their expedition.

The first speaker, a 15-year-old student, said that it was a day "to pledge infinite fidelity." In her conclusion, which she read confidently, she praised "Raúl's advice, Che's fearlessness, and Fidel's charisma." Raúl spoke afterward, providing evidence that his strength must be his advice. When he finished, leaning away from the microphone, he addressed the leaders of the second box: "What a message we're sending to the Yankees!" The crowd shook their little Cuban flags in such a way that they sounded like fans and applause.

The military procession included fighter planes, infantry troops, helicopters, and more. García Márquez asked Raúl technical questions. In his turn, Raúl spoke with Morales, who wasn't waving the little flag with quite the same enthusiasm as Ramonet.

After the weaponry, children with blue T-shirts walked by, creating the visual effect of the sea. Over them sailed the *Granma*, or rather her imitation. For nearly two hours, hundreds of thousands of people paraded past. "Fidel, your 80 years are ours too," affirmed a poster. "We must move forward as we did in the Sierras [a key guerrilla terrain during the Revolution]. Firmly and without stopping," demanded another. A first-level Cuban official commented: "We haven't yet realized that he is mortal, and we're not prepared for him to disappear."

To the side of the Bolivian delegation's microphone, Gérard Depardieu, wearing Adidas gym pants and a white shirt, smoked and chatted with someone in French.

Upon returning to El Laguito, Evo went straight to the private dining room for his fish soup. He talked about the evening show at the El Nacional hotel, which he'd attended after the night's cocktail hour. He liked the mojitos and the dancers.

He looked at Noah's photos and selected some of them for street posters.

"I'm ready to go back, big boss," he said.

"Why's that?" I asked.

"Well, I'm just lazing around. All I did today was go to the parade," he replied.

"They should have brought you your phones," I said to him, but he didn't seem to like my comment.

"You don't enjoy these tours?" I asked.

"No, not really. I like to go, attend the conference, and come right back. If not, well, I feel like I'm just lazing around," he responded.

He'd only slept two hours, spending almost the whole night speaking with Bolivia. He called leaders and officials. He wanted to know why the Juancito Pinto voucher had relaxed some of the *cocaleros*. "The president will discipline them," Quintana promised.

Evo said that he'd just seen a million people pass before him, in reference to the procession.

"It takes 46 years of revolution for that to happen," the minister of the presidency observed.

Evo liked the martial form of the civic military procession. He believes in organization and mobilization, and he aspires to see it done with ponchos, suits, and olive green uniforms all together in Bolivia.

In addition to his political and ideological affinities with Castro and Chávez, he feels a respect for them that he only reserves for those capable of moving hundreds of thousands of people. "That's it, boss—the people mobilized."

He moved onto the rule of proportions. If there were a million people in Havana, then there should be 800,000 in Cochabamba. Nobody mobilizes that number in Bolivia. He bet that he could gather 60,000 people in the Cochabamba stadium, where he would conclude his presidential summit.

"For the celebration of the first year of government, we should be able to bring out 100,000. We'll bring out 20,000 *cocaleros*: I'll be in charge of that."

He had scheduled a meeting with the chancellors of Venezuela and Cuba and Cuban vice president Carlos Laje for noon that day. "It has to be fast. I want to get back to La Paz as soon as I can." He got angry when a public servant couldn't find a phone number. "Get creative, sister," he ordered.

García Linera called urgently to inform him that they'd have to approve the contracts with the oil companies by Sunday morning.

"Get it done, big boss," he ordered again.

Instead of going back in the Falcon with the president, they assigned me a seat on a bigger plane that would take the delegation that had arrived first. I went to Old Havana with Maya Nemtala, the chief advisor of the ministry of the presidency, and the chauffeur said that he would come for us at 4:15 P.M. I sat down in a bar: It was the first time that I had left the presidential agenda in five days.

The chauffeur never came, so we took a taxi to El Laguito. "The plane left," said a Bolivian consul at 5:00 P.M. He explained that after the president took off, they alerted him that the Camastrón—our plane—would leave at 5:00 P.M. and not at 7:00 P.M. as originally planned. The Venezuelan pilots claimed that the aircraft couldn't fly at night, but the real reason was that they had to be free as early as possible because there were only a few hours until the presidential elections in their country.

Armando, a Cuban official, explained why the chauffeur hadn't come by to look for us: "He runs on orders, and the order was just that." So they only picked up the 12 Bolivian musicians who were supposed to fly with us. They had to prioritize who was more important over who was less important, meaning Maya and me. The Burned Palace received a distorted version of events from one of the president's secretaries: "They were wandering around and missed the flight." I now understood how certain internal disputes worked.

The summit of South American presidents was about to begin. Morales had to host his first international meeting since coming to office, as well as fight against the most severe internal conflict yet. A significant portion of the country was rising up in demand of departmental autonomy and the two-thirds approval for the Constituent Assembly. The heart of the protest was centered in Santa Cruz, the original headquarters for the summit until the president decided to move it to Cochabamba. In the days before it, he feared the worst.

"The opposition wants to call off the summit," Evo told me hours before the first presidents were to arrive. He walked around his room, minimally furnished with just a Formica table, four chairs upholstered in synthetic leather, a bed, a few shabby dressers, and a television set. It had been a tense morning. He got angry with Kirchner, among others, because the Argentine president wouldn't agree to travel to Cochabamba.

The biggest storm in the city's history was closer to calling off the summit than the opposition was. On Thursday, 8 percent of the rain that falls in an entire year had fallen. Four people died, and the city was left in shambles. Some of the rooms had flooded in Hotel Portales, where they would put up a majority of the delegations.

Evo saw a message from the beyond in that storm.

In the here and now, I ended up trapped in downtown Cochabamba. I was walking with the water up to my knees, and I began to feel the freezing cold in my calves. I saw the employees of a funeral home securing the coffins to keep the storm from breaking them loose and carrying away the dead. One corpse had sailed 128 feet in a coffin. Lost in a street without electricity, some people shouted at me from a hair and makeup salon: "Young man, come in here or you'll freeze or be electrocuted." Frightened teenagers stood inside. They brought over a table with a sewing machine that was still emanating heat to warm my legs.

Meanwhile, the east was boiling over. Between Thursday and Friday, five attacks occurred. One of them was a shooting at the Center for Legal and Social Studies (CEJIS), a nongovernmental organization sympathetic to the government. Seven hundred people were on a hunger strike, a group of university students had taken over the tax offices, and marginalized groups threatened to declare independence. But the escalation did have one setback for the opposition. In the middle of the hunger strike, the Podemos senators were filmed with plates of chicken leftovers.

"Four regions call council meetings to solidify their road to autonomy," headlined *La Razón* on December 9. That afternoon, hours before the beginning of the summit, thousands of Santa Cruz residents gathered in the central plaza of their city, insulting Morales and shouting "independence." From his house, the president hardly paid them any attention. He spoke for a little while with García Linera. The vice president had stayed behind in La Paz to reach an agreement so that the August 6, 2007 version could be considered a draft constitution.

The presidents began to arrive that afternoon.

Delivering his welcome speech in the Liberty Auditorium of the Greater State of Cochabamba, Evo spoke of the novelty of combining the presidential and social summits without any participants clashing or competing against each other. He was also trying to address the Bolivian public, which was why he mentioned opportunists and greedy people. He was thinking of Santa Cruz and its allies, but he didn't make that point explicit.

In the auditorium, an unexpected conflict did arise between Evo's and Chávez's security teams. Although each president could enter the place with five people, the Venezuelan guards—all 25 of them—wanted to be the exception, and a Bolivian police captain tried to impede them. The tension grew until they nearly came to blows. "We're in Bolivia," he yelled at them, and they stood at attention.

Morales later pacified a more complicated conflict between Chávez and Peruvian president Alan García. It all began with Venezuela's open support of García's primary electoral rival, ex-colonel Ollanta Humala, the leader of the Peruvian nationalist movement, which venerated the Andean past and the resistance against Chile during the War of the Pacific. In a meeting alone with Evo, Chávez accepted the armistice with García. However, to Evo's surprise, he pounded the table several times with his fist and said that he would hit it awhile until his fury abated.

"Alan García, from now on you are my friend," he said to him hours later in the presidential plenary session. There, the Peruvian took pleasure in speaking to his colleagues as an ex-Leftist. He admonished himself for fighting against imperialism in the 1980s, as if that were a sin of youth rectified by a maturity that had now made him understand how the real world works.

Lula arrived in Cochabamba as the great reconciler. In his previous meeting with the host, he stressed the democratic conduct in all of the elections during an imminently electoral year without going into what each result would mean. During his speech, he said something odd: "I got into the cabin of the plane and realized that Bolivia is situated exactly in the center of South America. Let's create a South American Parliament in Cochabamba."

Morales watched for that headline.

Unlike Lula's conciliatory tones, Chávez brought his warlike spirit. He kissed the key of Cochabamba as someone kisses a crucifix, he gave his opinions about the internal matters of Bolivia (he said that the setting reminded him of the months prior to the coup against him), and during the sessions he criticized the Andean Community of Nations (CAN), Mercosur, and even the Union of South American Nations. "So many meetings, so many summits, but we're still not clear on where we're headed.[...] From summit to summit and the people go from abyss to abyss." He proposed that the South American Union call itself *Unisur*, and he said that the presidents needed to take political Viagra.

Lula and even Evo attempted to contain him. "CAN and Mercosur are effective instruments," Morales said in the session in which he had to act as both moderator and host. Perhaps a little inhibited, he gave the floor to the participants, calling them *compañero* or *compañera* before giving their title or name. But in the press conference, he began to shine again. "Two thirds of the presidents have arrived, and I am content," he said, alluding to the two-thirds majority, one of the demands of the opposition.

That afternoon, in the Félix Capriles Stadium, he felt an enormous wave of relief at the sight of 50,000 people in the stands: He'd been waiting for that moment during the entire tricontinental tour. Seated in plastic chairs on the turf, there were around 2,000 delegates participating in the social summit.

Chávez promised that he wouldn't talk too much, which he didn't quite fulfill: "They want to burn Bolivia down." Bolivian government officials calculated a potential ad for the opposition in every sentence. The Venezuelan president recalled that, after giving his speech in the 1999 Iberian-American Summit, he received a note from Fidel that said, "I feel like I'm no longer the only devil."

"The devilhood," he said in the stadium, "continues to grow: Evo, Daniel Ortega, Rafael Correa [president-elect of Ecuador]. Someday the American empire will be a paper tiger, and we will be a tiger of steel."

Evo spoke of Bolivia and of the constant conspiracies since he assumed the presidency. He said that one conspiracy included rumors of García Linera's supposed plan to take over the presidency. "When we read it, we laughed. We're a team, a white bull and a black bull. I'm not used to the gossip. It doesn't exist in the social movements."

After Morales made a swift exit, the Argentine songwriter Piero hugged Daniel Ortega for several minutes. "We're definitely changing," Piero announced, already aboard the "Evomobile." He debuted a song about Bolivia that touched on the subjects of the sea, the Wiphala flag, and other standard Bolivian themes.

There wasn't time for an evaluation of the world tour or the Cochabamba Summit.

"They're coming after me," Evo told me before boarding the small plane.

A dream similar to the one he had on the way to Cuba about the DEA forecast another persecution.

"They're coming after me, and I have to defend myself. They think that I don't know who Katari was," he warned.

Chapter Four

COCALERO
(1995–2003)

Twelve thousand eight hundred feet above sea level, the Aymaras once contemplated the ashy earthen walls of the extensive valley below where La Paz lay. La Paz was a small group of adobe and stone houses and defense walls that made up the commercial link between Cusco and Potosí.

That view began to change at the end of the eighteenth century with the revolts in the high Andean plains, the valleys, and the coast that brought about the Bourbon reforms. The beginning of a new kind of absolutism of the Spanish throne, these reforms sought to redirect colonial power and included unpopular measures, such as tax increases. Echoing from those revolts, in the words of historian Sinclair Thomson, the most powerful anticolonial movement in the history of Spanish domain in the Americas took place.

The Insurrection of 1781 extended throughout the Andean south, but the most radical zone was in the Aymara territory of La Paz. In its two phases, the siege of the city lasted for 184 days and was led by a communal leader, Tupac Katari ("Resplendent Serpent" in English).

During the uprising, Katari proclaimed that the Aymaras would become the absolute keepers of the land and their wealth. His consort, Bartolina Sisa, remarked that the combatants foretold of a time in which "only the Indians would rule."

The siege of La Paz ended when Spanish forces sent from Buenos Aires, the capital of the new vice royalty, carved up Katari in the name of God and the king. His right arm was put on display in Ayoayo, his left arm in

Achacachi, his right leg in Chulumani, and his left leg in Caquiavari, each a separate Highland village.

None of the Aymaras, Quechuas, or any of the other indigenous groups living in what is today Bolivia held official roles, and they were never acknowledged by the governing elite—exclusively of European descent—as the ones truly deserving of the emancipation from Spain's dominion, which led to the founding in 1825 of the only American country to pay tribute to Simón Bolivar in its name.

The marginalization of Bolivia's indigenous groups was repeated in the central event of twentieth-century Bolivia, the 1952 National Revolution. Despite the fact that the revolution brought universal suffrage and expanded political participation to Bolivia, in the 50 years that followed, not a single *campesino* or force otherwise identified as an indigenous group had electoral success.

Unlike institutional politics—political parties, elections, and legislative battles—*campesinos* and indigenous groups organized themselves into communities, *ayllus* (traditional Indian units) and syndicates. A product of perpetual institutional exclusion, they've expressed themselves like all popular sectors in Bolivia, in the streets, sidewalks, and blockades.

Evo Morales was also afraid of that curse word: "politics." In 1995, he didn't consider himself a politician, and he was fearful of getting into politics, as if it were a prison from which he wouldn't be able to escape later. "They'll see me," he said, "as a villain, a bum, a crook."

On October 12, 1992, the only session of the Assembly of Native Populations took place. The "political instrument" option (a euphemism for political party) was debated because of the limitations that the political struggle had already demonstrated. Having thought about this much already, Morales explained the problem. When they reached agreements with the government, they suffered because they had no party through which to enforce them. So the idea of having a "political instrument" came back, right before their eyes, as the best means to complement the *campesino* union mobilization. For their part, the radical Katarists postulated the self-determination of the indigenous people and their refusal to participate in any way under the laws of the state, which they continued to see as colonial and colonizing.

Morales' position received the support of the majority in the Trade Union Confederation of Bolivian Campesinos (CSUTCB) in 1994. In his first electoral experience, the municipal elections of the following year, *cocaleros* and other *campesino* groups strongly supported the Assembly for the Sovereignty of the People (ASP) led by Alejo Véliz. They obtained good results, especially in Cochabamba. They won ten municipalities and 49 town council seats. "We want to vote for ourselves," declared Morales, who had refused candidacy to be mayor, to explain the positive electoral performance.

In 1996, Morales reached his ultimate goal in *campesino* syndicalism, to chair the Committee of the Six Federations of the Tropics of Cochabamba. He held that position for ten years, even after becoming president. In June, he made public his aspiration to manage the Bolivian Worker's Center (COB). With the crises of the mining and manufacturing sectors, he called for more *campesino* presence in the organization.

Months later, the MNR offered to integrate him into their presidential ticket with Juan Carlos Durán, the successor of Gonzalo "Goni" Sánchez de Lozada, for the 1997 elections. He declined the offer, as he had done with others.

"I am not a traitor like Víctor," he responded to Goni's emissary.

Víctor Hugo Cárdenas is an Aymara and Katarist leader and was Sánchez de Lozada's vice president (1993–1997). He is a good example of the multiple interpretations that have been made of Katari.

At a *campesino* conference in 1997, it was proposed that Morales present himself as a presidential candidate. The offer troubled him. He thought they were making fun of him, and he didn't sleep for a few nights. When told of the offer and his refusal in an assembly of *cocaleros*, one leader attacked him, saying that he had said no because he already had under-the-table agreements with the traditional political parties. Those loyal to Evo threatened to beat the accuser, and some of his female supporters started to cry.

Evo agreed to run for Congress. In alliance with United Left, he was elected to represent El Chapare District 27 with a record 70.1 percent of the votes.

The 1997 election held special significance for Bolivia and Latin America: It was the first time an ex-dictator from the 1970s returned to the presidency by way of the popular vote. In a coup in August 1971, Hugo Banzer Suárez buried one of the most important left-wing projects of the twentieth century in Bolivia and ruled with fire and brimstone until 1978. To protect himself from those who wanted to prosecute him for his role as dictator—led by Marcelo Quiroga Santa Cruz, who would have taken him to prison for his crimes of corruption and plundering of the country—he created his own party, the Nationalist Democratic Action (ADN). After the restoration of democracy in 1982, Banzer's party would alternate in power, together with Sánchez de Lozada's MNR and Jaime Paz Zamora's Leftist Revolutionary Movement (MIR). This successful game of balances and alliances received the name, not always pejoratively, of "pact-democracy." By virtue of these agreements, the neoliberal consensus dominated, bringing about Supreme Decree 21.060 and an alliance with the United States.

Banzer was a man of the United States. Educated in the School of the Americas, his coup, like that of Pinochet, counted on Washington's support and advice, as well as financial assistance and arms. An unclassified document from the State Department, dated in 1976, gives a hint of the intensity of the relationship: "He knows and likes the United States, and he has strayed from his own path several times to demonstrate his adherence to the leadership of the U.S. in this hemisphere and around the globe."

By 1997, Banzer had traded his military coats for gray suits. He now preferred saccharine words over his legendary maxim: "To the friend, everything; to the indifferent, nothing; and to the enemy, the club." But he continued to follow the path marked out by U.S. interests. He made the driving notion of Washington his own—with communism dead, drug trafficking now constituted the greatest threat to Bolivia and to the Western world. He must have received a pardon from above; despite evidence pointing toward his own involvement with drug trafficking and that of many members of his party, Banzer continued to be a great ally to the U.S. government on that issue.

When he assumed the presidency, the ADN leader carried forward the Dignity Plan, devised in the United States, which, with the motto "Zero Coca," proposed the eradication of 117,500 acres supposedly dedicated to the cultivation of coca, as well as the relocation of between 5,000 and 20,000 El Chapare families to "human resettlement zones."

From the bench, Evo characterized Banzer as "the worst politician in Bolivian history." He focused his efforts on defending the coca leaf, denouncing forced eradication, and showing support to the union movement. When he was in La Paz, he lived in a small apartment with the other four United Left deputies. They maintained the *campesino* lifestyle through their schedules and meals. In October 1997, they celebrated Evo's thirty-eighth birthday with a party in the apartment, complete with musicians playing the traditional *charango* guitars. They gave him a silk tie that he never wore.

Evo struggled with his new life in the legislature. During those first months, he reported to Congress every Monday at dawn, but he soon learned that nobody worked on that day of the week. Some legislators wouldn't even arrive until the following afternoon with their suitcases in tow, having recently landed in La Paz. On Wednesdays, he attended the Committee for Human Rights. The week ended with the Thursday session, to which a majority of the deputies brought their luggage so they could fly out that same night. "I felt like some schoolboy," Evo recalled years later. Although he didn't wish to establish personal connections with his peers, he did begin to imitate their routine after awhile. He paid more attention to El Chapare than the House: "They blockade me."

Because the Dignity Plan sought to eradicate the *campesino* protests—and not just their coca crops—Evo led a new march on foot in 1998 that united El Chapare with La Paz over the course of 23 days. Ambassador Donna Hrinak set the official tone by classifying it as a "drug march." The minister of government, Guido Nayar, wouldn't agree to have a debate with Morales. Banzer's officials were generally friendly with Ambassador Hrinak: On her birthday, some of them accepted her invitation to drive around La Paz by motorcycle.

In the four years of Banzer's government, which were marked by the chaos of the mega-coalition he created, including economic stagnation, corruption, and nepotism scandals, Morales became a permanent official target. He was the perfect and long-wished-for enemy.

They accused Evo of being a drug trafficker, of being the main link, the closest ally, the primary chancellor to drug trafficking, of maintaining relationships with the narcotics guerillas, of being the godfather of chemical traffickers. They brought him before the courts on charges of assassination, instigating crime, being responsible for disappearances, armed alliance, claiming to represent the rights of the people, belonging to a criminal organization, making attacks against transportation and public service, and destroying goods of the state. They accused him of owning 500 acres, of owning 150 acres, of being financed by guerrillas and foreign governments, driving drunk, being the dictator of El Chapare, being the king of El Chapare, taking pleasure trips to Europe, and notating addresses from Colombian guerrillas in his agenda. They made fun of him publicly, saying that he didn't know how to add. They mocked the way he spoke and what he said when he did speak. They gave him—through the president of private businesses—a Bible and a constitution to civilize him, and they scheduled meetings to do business with him in rooms with crucifixes.

Morales endured the attacks, and his figure grew in stature. His followers' unconditional support made him stronger, within and outside of El Chapare. He blamed the government and U.S. embassy for the personal attacks, the death of 30 *cocaleros*, and the Zero Coca plan. He proclaimed that they would resist eradication in arms. "If Banzer doesn't want coca, there will be an armed fight," he declared in October 2000.

The Banzer government wanted to expel Evo from the House for disrespect and sedition. He wasn't forgiven for linking the president with drug trafficking. "Civil death" was publicly proposed by the party of government, and a minister demanded that Morales retract his statement. "Why don't you retract your grandmother," Evo responded. The government requested that Morales be placed on "definitive leave" from parliament.

At the end of his term, Banzer announced that he had met the Dignity Plan's eradication goals and that only 1,500 acres of coca were left. The *campesino* syndicates responded by covering the roads of El Chapare with coca leaves. They wanted to demonstrate that, regardless of eradication, they would continue cultivating coca.

In addition to the resistance of the *cocaleros* and Morales, Banzer faced two other crises brought on by street politics: the War of Water and the uprising of the Andean Highland Plateau led by Felipe "El Malku" Quispe.

The War of Water began when the World Bank dissuaded the government from building an aqueduct that would make it possible to address the increase in water demand in Cochabamba and instead proposed the privatization of the water industry. The transnational company benefitted by the concession, Tunari Waters, arranged an increase in prices at the beginning of 2000. Factory workers, students, other workers, neighbors, and *campesinos* united and gathered around the Coalition for the Defense of Water and Life to protest against the hike. Morales brought many thousands of *cocaleros*. One of them said to him: "In Chapare, bullets fly and in Cochabamba, tear gas."

The protest wouldn't be stopped by Banzer's dispatch of 1,200 soldiers, the conditions of the site, the 175 wounded, or even the six deaths. The War of Water ended with an unexpected result: Tunari Waters lost the governmental concession in April 2000, and a cooperative took charge of the sale and distribution of water. Comuna, a group that included Álvaro

García Linera, among other intellectuals, characterized the successes of Cochabamba in the title of his book, *The Return of Plebeian Bolivia.*

For the first time a collective that combined regular assemblies with the struggle in the streets had reversed capitalizations or privatizations. It also brought to light a topic that would dominate the Bolivian agenda in coming years: the recovery of natural resources in a country with a deep-seated memory of plundering.

The successes in Cochabamba and a police riot made Banzer think about resigning from the presidency. His government had also suffered on a minor scale due to an internal problem. His wife, Yolanda Prada, had found a Viagra pill in the presidential residence and mounted a small scandal.

In September of that year, a new uprising starring Felipe Quispe took place. Evoking the Katari's siege, Quispe called for blockades and marches throughout La Paz. The insurgents maintained that they shouldn't pay for water or land and that they wouldn't stop planting coca. Banzer faced a complex spectacle. The inability of Morales, Quispe, and Oscar Olivera, a factory leader who emerged during the War of Water, to develop a common project, however, may have been what saved the government. The competition and rivalry between Morales and Quispe would deepen over the years.

Once the social unrest had eased, Quispe received me with a vigorous handshake at 6:00 A.M. one Sunday in August 2001. His eyes communicated a certain sternness. García Linera, his army companion from the Tupac Katari Guerilla Army (EGTK), with whom he'd shared a prison cell between 1992 and 1997, was also present. Between long silences and mistrustful scrutiny, Quispe oscillated between the possibility of an armed insurrection and his responsibility as a *campesino* leader. He promised that the next meeting would occur in the Burned Palace, where, in addition to enacting a series of nationalizations and expropriations, he would replace the ministry of Campesino Affaires with one of White Affaires and create a reservation for whites in La Paz. Katari was the model and example to follow.

"We are in the time of the *Pachakuti*," he said. "The stones will reveal unexpected things, and the rivers will sing once again."

In that same conversation, "Malku" Quispe criticized Morales' inability to speak Quechua or Aymara and discredited him as an opportunist and traitor, surrounded by white-*mestizo* advisors.

After Banzer resigned in August 2001 due to terminal cancer, Jorge "Tuto" Quiroga assumed the presidency. A University of Texas–educated engineer with the air of a technocrat, Quiroga had Washington's continued support because the U.S. government saw him as a champion in the fight against corruption and the best ally to lead the war against drug trafficking and the coca leaf.

The new president repaid their sympathies. At the beginning of the "War on Terror" launched by the Bush administration after the September 11 terrorist attacks, Quiroga made ten antiterrorist agreements into laws. Declassified files from U.S. State Department documents reveal the numerous congratulations he received for that feat during his official visit to Washington in December 2001.

With the support of the embassy and the prevailing parties, he proposed the expulsion of Morales from Congress one month later. They accused him of being responsible for the deaths of two police officers during a conflict that resulted in the closing of the coca market in Sacaba, near Cochabamba. Five *campesinos* and four members of the security forces were killed.

The accusation was based on press clips in which Morales called to "set fire to El Chapare" (the verb in Spanish, *incendiar*, refers to radical mobilization of a population—in this case, the *cocaleros*). In his defense, Evo clarified that what he'd said was that the country would burn with anger if the government didn't repeal the decree closing the market. He wasn't granted two of his rights under the Ethical Code of the House of Deputies: five days for the accused to present his defense before trial (Morales was given 24 hours) and 16 days for the process of expulsion (in this case, it was cut to 2 days).

Aware of the weakness of the accusation—clippings from daily papers don't constitute proof—Quiroga put his confidence in a dossier that supposedly contained conclusive proof against Morales, which the U.S. government had promised him.

In the middle of the brief trial, a top Bolivian official paid a visit to the U.S. Embassy Deputy Chief of Mission Patrick Duddy. He brought a bag with him that he hoped to fill with folders, documents, and possibly even videos so that he could return to the president's office victoriously.

"Of course, you know that this meeting is confidential," Duddy said.

The Bolivian official didn't believe that *cocaleros*, as Evo had claimed, had managed to infiltrate the embassy, but he still tried to portray the meeting as secret. He grew more and more impatient until he finally saw the documentation that would forever frustrate him: a memo written in English that mentioned Morales' visits to Fidel Castro and hinted at his supposed relations with the Colombian FARC (Revolutionary Armed Forces of Colombia), as well as his stay in Libya to receive a prize.

The official dialed Quiroga's number as he left the embassy.

"We've got nothing, Tuto," he warned.

A report based on newspaper clippings—the government was too ashamed to use the dossier—nonetheless resulted in Morales' expulsion as a congressman. One hundred forty deputies from the traditional parties voted in favor: the MNR, ADN, MIR, New Republican Force (NFR), and Civic Solidarity Association (UCS).

"This was a trial against Aymaras and Quechuas, and the corrupt drug traffickers who threw me out each got $1,300 to vote against me," Evo proclaimed at the start of a hunger strike inside the Congress building. Taped up above the mattress where he slept at the time was a sign demanding that Congress shut down.

Although he lost the expulsion trial, it would bring Evo unexpected benefits soon after. His excommunication from a rather discredited institution warped by discredited politics would ultimately contribute to the growth of MAS in the electoral campaign that was about to begin.

U.S. Ambassador Manuel Rocha attempted to shore up support for the presidential candidacy of Sánchez de Lozada in the June 30 elections. Rocha came from Buenos Aires, where he had been in charge of business affairs. When he arrived in La Paz, he surprised businessmen, politicians, and journalists with his lectures about what Bolivia should or should not do. In meetings with Sánchez de Lozada and his team, Rocha demonstrated his unconcealed support.

The U.S. aura surrounding the Sánchez de Lozada campaign was supplemented by Greenberg Quinlan Rosner, a U.S. consulting firm that counts Nelson Mandela and Tony Blair among its clients. The MNR candidate would pay $2 million out of pocket, while the party would contribute that same sum for further campaign expenses.

The documentary *Our Brand Is Crisis* shows how the consultants came up with a winning idea in the beginning: Only Sánchez de Lozada could pull the country out of the economic crisis. The presence of the U.S. team required constant translation during meetings with the locals. The experienced politicians, primarily Carlos "The Fox" Sánchez Berzaín, disagreed with the consultants' proposal to bring forth a "negative campaign against Manfred."

NFR candidate Manfred Reyes Villa came to lead the polls with 35 percent of the projected votes. An ex-army captain and Cochabamba mayor, Villa's weak points included the exponential growth of his patrimony and his relationship with Reverend Sun Myung Moon of the Unification Church. They didn't skimp on big resources for the "negative campaign."

Evo, in contrast, never worried about Goni Sánchez de Lozada or Manfred, not even when the polls showed that support for his own candidacy had risen from 6 or 8 percent to 14 percent two weeks before the election.

During those days, Ambassador Rocha had lunch with Sánchez de Lozada, Sánchez Berzaín, and Carlos Mesa, the vice presidential candidate. Rocha surprised Mesa: "He's just one more on the team," he thought. At that lunch in Sánchez Berzaín's house, the ambassador let it slip that the enemy was Evo, not Manfred: "Morales is a potentially significant political enemy. We might regret it if we let him grow too much."

Although Manfred Reyes Villa awoke a certain sympathy in Rocha, the ambassador considered him to be inferior to Goni and thought that his business dealings made him vulnerable. Manfred did everything humanly possible to seduce him. Ricardo Paz, his campaign strategist, who also had good ties with the embassy, explained to State Department officials that Manfred could guarantee the gradual change the country needed, but he quickly discovered that it would be difficult to "de-Gonify" Rocha.

When Manfred met with the ambassador, he emphasized that he was just as trustworthy as Goni and would respect the status quo. He also explained that he was linked to the United States in a special way. In addition to his properties and investments, his children lived there, and he enjoyed belonging to the club of upwardly mobile Bolivians in Florida. Certain traditional politicians generally lose any sense of shame when they cross over the embassy threshold.

Rocha, who was already on the shameless side of that threshold, managed to stir up a major uproar in the campaign. First, in February, he compared *cocaleros* to the Taliban in a failed attempt to install the "War on Terror" in Bolivia.

On June 26, four days before the election, he made a seismic declaration in Spanish: "I want to remind the Bolivian electorate that if you choose the candidate who wants Bolivia to go back to being a cocaine exporter, that

that will put the Unites States aid at risk," he said at an airport inauguration in El Chapare accompanied by President Quiroga. "A Bolivia led by the people who have benefitted from drug trafficking cannot expect the United States markets to remain open for traditional textile exports," he concluded. That statement had the backing of the State Department.

Evo responded at a rally: "I'm very pleased that the ambassador wants to act as campaign manager to Evo Morales." But he clarified that he didn't have the money to pay him for his services.

Hours later, Mesa presented his doubts to Sánchez Berzaín: "Why on earth would Rocha make these statements? It's a favor to Evo."

"Don't worry, brother, all of this is coldly calculated," said Berzaín.

The calculation, clearly cold, predicted that Manfred would fall in the polls from first to third place after Rocha's speech. The idea was to eliminate him from the second-round election seeing as how, the Goni team maintained, even Pluto, the droopy Disney dog, could beat Morales.

In fact, all of the political parties underestimated Evo's potential because they considered his influence limited to El Chapare, and not the beginning of a national trend. In addition, Morales' campaign had begun erratically.

Suspicious of his allies, Morales considered a possible agreement with Felipe Quispe, but in the end it didn't work out. Arguing that he was older, the Aymara leader demanded the presidential candidacy. "Evo Morales is a chameleon," he waged in the public accusations they later exchanged.

In addition, Evo had trouble coming up with an acronym to represent his candidacy during the election. The Court rejected both Political Instrument and Assembly for the Sovereignty of the People. Finally, he managed to come up with the party name Movement Towards Socialism (MAS, or "more" in English), registered to David Añez Pedraza, a retired leftist leader from the Bolivian Socialist Phalanx (FSB), whose socialism, in its origin, appeared to be more like national socialism than Marxist socialism.

The nomination of a vice presidential candidate turned into another quagmire for MAS. In February, Morales told the press that José Antonio Quiroga, director of the Bolivian publishing house Plural, would accompany him as his running mate. He saw him as a great candidate to seduce middle- and upper-middle-class voters who viewed him with a fiery mistrust on account of various types of prejudice. Nephew of the socialist leader Marcelo Quiroga Santa Cruz and former activist in leftist groups in his youth, José Antonio first heard the news through the media.

When Evo visited Quiroga in his office, Quiroga thanked him for the offer and wanted to know the contents of his platform, whether the MAS would become a registered party, and with whom they had political alliances. Morales responded that some intellectuals would elaborate the platform and that MAS was an instrument of the Trade Union Confederation of Bolivian Campesinos, but not a party in the traditional sense, and he was emphatic on the last point. "It is the decision of the MAS to go it alone. That's not up for discussion."

After thinking about it for a week, Quiroga concluded that his publishing house wasn't in the position to withstand an electoral campaign. Moreover, he disagreed with the MAS on some points, especially its refusal of alliances. Evo did not manage to twist his arm, but Quiroga did agree to join the campaign team.

When the MAS presented Morales' candidacy in the La Paz Coliseum, it asked Quiroga to attend. In the ceremony, José Antonio remained below the stage next to Filemón Escobar. During the speeches, Escobar went onstage to whisper into Evo's ear that Quiroga had agreed to be his running mate, but it was a lie. The leader took the microphone and invited the editor to come up on stage with him to speak. Quiroga hesitated but soon realized he couldn't ignore the applause of the 5,000 spectators. He went up and said, in a friendly tone, that the MAS could "play a role in the democratization of the country and democratize itself internally." Morales took the microphone from him and addressed his supporters:

"Since you want democracy, let's take a vote. Do you all want my *compañero* José Antonio Quiroga to be my running mate?"

Everyone answered yes. They put garlands on him and threw confetti, the leaders who were onstage hugged him, and Quiroga became consecrated as the vice presidential candidate. Evo and his brand-new (and very surprised) running mate walked from the Coliseum along the Prado—one of the busiest avenues of the city—where they heard cheers and shouts. On that walk, the editor repeated quietly that he had declined the offer. "You can't, little boss, the supporters have declared you," Evo responded.

The next day, Quiroga had to explain that what everyone had seen—his nomination—wasn't true. Distressed, Escobar came into Quiroga's office. "Evo is going to throw me out of the party, and they accused me of working for the CIA." Escobar confessed that he had lied to Morales, thinking that a middle-class guy like Quiroga wasn't going to say no to 5,000 *campesinos*. His calculation was wrong.

Quiroga called Morales to warn him that it would be a grave error to fire Filemón in the middle of the scandal and a bad way to continue with the campaign. In a matter of two days, he would have lost his vice presidential candidate and his primary advisor. Evo decided not to dismiss him. "It was one of the biggest political mistakes of my life," Escobar told me in May 2007. "I would have had to force Quiroga at gunpoint to be the candidate."

The Guevarist and human rights activist Antonio Peredo, the brother of Guido "Inti" (a Bolivian guerilla who fought with Che Guevara), was chosen to be the vice presidential candidate. The platform of the MAS, as Evo would admit years later, looked more like a list of petitions put forth by a union than a government program.

At first, Morales had little faith in the success of a national campaign; his sole objective was to return to Congress with a more numerous parliamentary brigade. This was especially true because the MAS stronghold was restricted to the valley of Cochabamba.

Evo began to travel around the country. He made most of those trips in an unpainted Nissan truck he bought with the $15,000 donated to him to contend for the 1995 Nobel Peace Prize. Morales took advantage of the structure offered by the *campesino* unions to organize his campaign.

He awoke a fervent following in the rural areas. In Los Yungas, for instance, he'd only planned 15 rallies in three days but ended up doing 39. From that point on, he became convinced that "*campesinos* would vote *campesino*" in Bolivian elections. In the eastern part of the country, by contrast, they were almost entirely unable to wage a campaign due to a lack of resources. Peredo visited the town of Riberalta and joined Morales in the city of Santa Cruz de la Sierra. "In Santa Cruz, they saw us as exotic and hardly greeted us," his then–running mate recalled. Fifteen days before the election, Morales was already enthusiastic: "With a little bit of money," he said to Peredo, "we win."

The MAS candidate designated someone he trusted to take charge of finances—mechanical engineer Iván Iporre. Because he made a living drawing diagrams and making calculations on chalkboards, Evo saw him as an economist. Although the party had allotted 1,100,000 pesos for official publicity, the decision was made to spend only 700,000. So, for the first time, they opened a bank account in the name of the MAS.

There were times when the party couldn't broadcast TV or radio spots because they were required to pay with funds not derived from state help.

Walter Chávez, the journalist in charge of the campaign in La Paz, only managed to gather $450 (provided by himself and Quiroga). That sort of epic poverty and scarcity stood in stark contrast to the staggering amounts their campaign rivals spent: $17 million.

Making the most of the benefits granted them by Ambassador Rocha's speech, Walter Chávez released an effective MAS campaign ad: "Fellow Bolivian, you decide who's in charge: Rocha or the voice of the people. We are the people. We are MAS [more]. Let's vote for ourselves on June 30."

Morales interpreted the events wisely. He said that whereas the other candidates would sell their mothers for a U.S. visa, he felt freer, more honorable, and more sovereign without one. When the opposition offered to debate with him, he responded that he'd prefer to debate with Rocha because he was the real "ringleader of the circus."

The MAS was the surprise hit of the election. Although preliminary official counts placed Goni in first place, Manfred in second, and Evo in third, Evo ultimately ended up second with almost 21 percent of the vote: 1.5 percent less than Goni and 721 more votes than the NFR. The determining results arrived from Potosí—they had been delayed by a snowstorm—a department in which there were congressional nominations that the MAS had left almost empty because their leaders didn't have trustworthy contenders and didn't foresee favorable results. Although at the national level the team expected to win between 7 and 15 congressional seats, they managed to win 35.

Morales felt more confident than ever before. He had bet journalist Mario Espinoza $500 that he'd come in second place. He heard the results in the home of Filemón Escobar while the recount continued on television. After his initial joy, he had a frightening realization: If he somehow managed to assume the presidency, it was possible he wouldn't make it to the end of the year.

According to Carlos Mesa (MNR's vice presidential candidate), the MNR was the reason that the MAS managed to get to second place. Five years after that election, although he didn't have any proof, he was suspicious: "I absolutely believe," he said in an interview for this book, "that they took Manfred out of second place and that the MNR worked to manipulate those 721 votes." The U.S. embassy's campaign in favor of their candidate also influenced the result. A survey indicated that they had caused Manfred and Jaime Paz Zamora of the MIR to lose 3.5 percent of their support. According to a later survey, 14 percent of voters said that they voted for Morales in repudiation against Ambassador Rocha's declarations.

At that time in Bolivia, if none of the candidates surpassed 50 percent of the popular vote, the president was elected with the vote of parliament members. A few days after June 30, an anonymous columnist summarized the electoral process, and the emerging picture was encouraging for Goni supporters: "You elect deputies, the embassy elects the president, and the deputies whom you elected elect the president whom the embassy elected."

With the final contest established between Sánchez de Lozada and Evo, Rocha set off to secure the votes for Goni that would have otherwise gone to Paz Zamora, who had come in fourth.

"But he can't even look at me, Manuel," Sánchez de Lozada said. "If you convince him, I am going on a pilgrimage to Copacabana [100 miles from La Paz]."

"I'll do it, Goni, I'll do it," Rocha promised.

Paz Zamora hated Goni because he believed that the MNR leader had circulated rumors in both Bolivian society and the United States that his party (the MIR) was linked to drug trafficking. The truth, however, was that the people who had most injured the reputation of the party were some of its own members, as well as several State Department officials. There were even several supposed "narco links" to drug dealer Oscar "The Bear" Echavarría among MIR leaders. Their arrests, especially that of Oscar Eid, Paz Zamora's right-hand man, caused a national scandal. Eid was in prison for four years, and his boss always believed that Sánchez de Lozada and Sánchez Berzaín had been the ones behind his detention.

The MIR, a political party originally created to fight against the Banzer regime that had assassinated MIR supporters, didn't hesitate to make official agreements with the ex-dictator in 1989 and 1997. These pacts allowed both Paz Zamora and Banzer to ascend to the presidency. "The best way to vindicate our dead *compañeros* is to ensure that their blood is not lost in vain, but instead that it becomes a victorious blood. And how can we vindicate them? By coming into government, triumphing and moving forward," Paz Zamora explained to me in the Hotel Alvear in Buenos Aires in December 1999.

Rocha knew how to manipulate the top members of the MIR and their leader. Any accusation of complicity in drug trafficking would exasperate them: "I'm sure you wouldn't want an ally of drug trafficking to end up in the Burned Palace," he told them.

Zamora was less bitter than Manfred, who wouldn't attend the July 4 diplomatic cocktail party because he held the embassy responsible for his defeat. While at the party, Zamora took advantage of journalists' presence in the entryway to denounce "Operation Evo Morales" and prolong the uncertainty of his parliamentary brigade's vote. He was attempting to negotiate a position of high power in the new government.

Evo was not invited to the cocktail party at the embassy, but he did send a few little coca leaves as a gift in honor of the U.S. Independence Day.

He decided not to make agreements with the established parties. "A healthy vote doesn't require negotiation," he said. What would happen if those parties gave him their votes? The MAS would run a transition government toward a Constituent Assembly, hold competitions for all public positions, and choose governors put forward by regional nominations. José Antonio Quiroga and Héctor Arce, Morales' lawyer, sat down and drafted that plan.

Nonetheless, Evo did put together a political team to meet with leaders of the MNR, MIR, and NFR. A sector of the MNR proposed making a deal. "With them, nothing," he answered. The NFR negotiator insisted that Morales and Manfred had been the victims of a fraud. He explained that they'd received a lot of pressure from the embassy to support Goni. The MIR didn't even flirt with the MAS. "For us," Oscar Eid recounted in an interview for this book, "Evo was in the world of prohibited things, and, moreover, we believed that the system could have fallen apart if he'd assumed the presidency."

Eid and Sánchez Berzaín were the architects who, for a time, kept the system from falling apart. They never reminded each other of their unpleasant years together as prisoner and jailer. In the mansions and hotels in the south of La Paz, the two entrenched parties carried out the postelection tradition of divvying up the ministries, embassies, and the ever-coveted National Customs, which was supposed to control contraband but was in fact a lucrative source of corruption. Eid and Sánchez met at Hotel Paris in Plaza Murillo. After long negotiations, they came to the magic number: 60 percent of the top positions for the MNR and 40 percent for the MIR.

The MAS leader took advantage of those days to develop close contacts with diplomats and representatives of international credit organizations. Separately, both the Chinese and Portuguese ambassadors suggested that he pursue the industrialization of the coca leaf.

Morales met with an IMF team led by Wayne Lewis. "We are always open to having a dialogue with you," Morales told them, "and so we accept your invitation to make our agenda known: Our dealings are based on the principle of reciprocity." Filemón elaborated on the idea of reciprocity, a characteristic of Andean sociability, and he offered to give them a lesson. Surprised, the IMF officials accepted.

Lewis explained that the IMF did support communist states and that their priority was the fight against poverty and corruption. Evo, during the least amicable moment, responded: "Poverty has grown because of certain IMF policies prompting the concentration of wealth."

His way of negotiating often combines understanding with tension.

Twenty-four hours before Congress would elect the new president, I met with Morales in a bar next to Torino, a $2-a-night hostel for backpackers where the campaign commander was working. The foreigners, most of them blondes disguised as poor Bolivians, hardly understood what was going on around them. Marchers from diverse parts of the country were mobilizing at that time in demand of a Constituent Assembly to reclaim the country and recover its natural resources.

I asked Evo whether he'd ever been to the U.S. embassy.

"Never," he replied.

I proposed that we go there to film part of an interview we were doing for a documentary by filmmaker Sean Langan of Britain's Channel 4.

"Let's go, we can see what the gringos are up to," he said to me enthusiastically.

On the way there, when we were talking about soccer, he said something that troubled me: He proposed that I be his ambassador in Argentina if he were elected president.

"But Evo," I countered, "I'm Argentine and the Constitution doesn't allow...."

"Little brother, the rules were made to be changed," Morales responded.

It was through gestures like this that he expressed his radicalism, his rupture with the past, and his vision for refounding the country.

In the doorway to the embassy, a security guard asked for our papers. He addressed Evo directly.

"Sir, you may not conduct your politics within the gates of the United States Embassy." Yet for more than 50 years, the embassy had been conducting its politics outside of those gates, and with particular enthusiasm during this most recent election.

Facing the Palace balconies on the night that the deputies inaugurated Sánchez de Lozada as chief of state, an embassy official with dual nationality told me how relieved they were by Evo's defeat. "We want the best

CEOs," he added, "like Vicente (Fox) or Goni. The traditional politicians had better start looking for work soon."

A few minutes later, the brand-new vice president greeted Morales: "I want to salute you, and I hope that we can do good work together."

"I don't see how that's possible with a traitor government like yours," Evo answered.

That afternoon, the MAS leader confided in me in the halls of Congress about a doubt he had—whether he should congratulate Sánchez de Lozada. The question was, as institutional head of the opposition, how many expected customs did he have to go through with? In the end, he didn't call him.

Morales met Hugo Chávez for the first time that night, an encounter captured in Langan's documentary. He had been eagerly awaiting that initial contact.

Chávez spoke to him about the Bible, and afterward he said, "Patience, Evo. Revolution takes time, you have to have patience."

At that exact moment, Bolivia's new government was already about to fall. With 30 minutes until the swearing in of the cabinet, Sánchez Berzaín received a fax with the names of the seven MIR ministers that Paz Zamora demanded be appointed. Goni didn't even know several of them, and he became enraged.

"I resign. This is a humiliation that I am not going to tolerate, goddammit. I'm not going to accept this fucking list."

Mesa tried to calm him down.

"You're going to go out on the balcony to say that you're resigning?" he asked.

"Tell that son of a bitch to call me himself or else I'm going to resign," Goni replied.

Sánchez Berzaín tried to put Paz Zamora in touch with the president. "If he wants to resign, let him resign," was the reply he ordered Eid to give to Berzaín.

At 11:00 P.M., five hours later than anticipated, Goni assumed control of the seven MIR ministers and the nine from his party. The battle over the seats in Roads, Customs, and Taxes dissolved because it remained in Mesa's hands, who was put in charge of "institutionalizing them," a euphemism that implied they would not be turned into niches of corruption.

Evo remained the opposition leader with a weighty parliamentary brigade: 8 senators out of 27 and 27 deputies out of 130. But there were a lot of them he didn't know. They were Aymaras, Quechuas, Guevarists, Marxist-Leninists, and various others. They organized workshops and seminars to train themselves and to establish connections between one another. Each one would hand over 10 percent of his or her salary to the party. One group, the one that Iván Iporre was in, met every Friday to chew on coca leaves and ask the *Pachamama* (mother earth), along with the hills, to enlighten and protect Evo.

The U.S. embassy had other plans for him. Documents declassified after the election reveal that it was the embassy's priority to counterbalance the strength of the MAS—"or its successor"—with political party reforms that would make the whole process more democratic and transparent and would prevent citizens from expressing themselves "through street protests." They referred to Evo as an "illegal coca agitator," situating him both in the margins of politics and outside of the law, thus denying him his status as chief of the opposition.

But Evo had already begun to undergo the transformation from *cocalero* leader to national leader. Distanced from the traditional left, the *foquismo* (*foco* means a guerilla center, which sparks a wider mass revolution) and the veneration of the institution of the political party, he embodied *campesino* unionism and those marginalized by the restricted democracy of the 1980s and 1990s. Although incorruptible, charismatic, and combative, he had a weak programmatic methodology. Refusals took precedence in his discourse: no to the government, no to imperialism, no to coca leaf eradication, and no to FTAA (Free Trade Area of the Americas). But he recognized it and established a new strategy after Sánchez de Lozada's assumption: "Go from protest to proposal."

During his campaign, Goni had had serious communication problems with what his gringo advisors called the *poblo* (bad pronunciation of the Spanish term for "the people"). He didn't perceive the profound "anti-Gonism" that proliferated in the country, which widely exceeded the support he had obtained (almost 22.5 percent of the total votes). Once in office, he began to isolate himself even more: He lived between the presidential house, the Palace of the government, and the official airplane. When he got in a car, they would put on his seatbelt for him and even his sunglasses sometimes. Despite the fact that the president has ten ceremonies to attend a year (the anniversary of Bolivia's nine departments as well as the country's independence on August 6), Goni only attended the celebrations of the foundation of the Republic and Santa Cruz day, because he feared friction with the *poblo*. By this point, he was completely dependent on two people: his right-hand man and minister of government, Sánchez Berzaín, who accompanied him to each one of his meetings; and María Paula Muñoz, his personal assistant. María decided such details of his day-to-day life as the lunch menu, the *siesta* hour, and which opera he would listen to, among many other things.

Between August 2002 and January 2003, Goni tried to start a dialogue and come to an agreement with Morales while also trying to make the United States more flexible in its fight against drugs. But Washington denied his most important request, that each family could cultivate a *cato* (1,600 square yards) of coca or, failing that, half of a *cato*.

This quest for mutual understanding with Evo was an attempt to mitigate potential blockades of streets and roads. Nonetheless, the ability of the government to begin such a dialogue had its limits. It couldn't accept the MAS demand to suspend eradication until completing an inventory of existing coca fields. The five meetings between Goni and Morales failed.

In January 2003, Evo warned that negotiations with the government would not be successful. His instinct told him that Sánchez de Lozada's desperation to agree proved his weakness.

The work in Congress began to frustrate him. His bench had presented 60 legislative measures, among them one to reduce the salaries of government employees and another regarding the recovery of natural resources. "They wouldn't give us an inch," declared Morales, because the systemic parties hindered each MAS initiative. He assumed responsibility for everyone with regard to the limitations of his parliamentary group: "I have to say, quite honestly, that my *compañeros* are good at ideological, political, and cultural discourse, but we lack technical expertise. Most of us come from the *ayllus*, the country communities." He became upset with a deputy who allowed himself to be tempted by money.

Impotent in Parliament, Morales opted once again for the fight in the streets. On January 13, he called for a protest with road blocks and a petition sheet for structural reforms. Figuring into the 11 stated reasons for the protest were the obstacles to passing laws presented by the MAS and the "handing over of gas" to Chile, referring to a plan to export gas to the United States through Chile.

Deaths from the January protests exceeded 12. From that point on, Goni wanted to destroy Morales but lacked the power and means to do it.

A few weeks later, the government had a major crisis—Black February. The IMF demanded that Sánchez de Lozada reduce the deficit from 8.5 percent to 5.5 percent. On February 9, Goni announced that taxes would increase: 12.5 percent for the average earner ($150). Among the multiple rebuffs, the one from the insurgent police demanding wage increases drew the most attention. On February 12, the Palace awoke to find itself without guards. A confrontation between the police and the army ensued that would end with 11 policemen and four soldiers dead. As a result of this incident, civilians protesting against the tax hike attacked several public buildings, including the Palace and the house of the vice president.

Sánchez de Lozada called an emergency meeting with the Cabinet that day at the unusually early hour of 9:00 A.M. (he generally didn't begin the day until 10:30 A.M. because he worked late into the night). He told them that, according to intelligence, Manfred had been the one to finance the riot. He concluded that he would only be able to cover the deficit with the economic help of the United States. Sitting in his bed in the Palace, he called the U.S. Under Secretary of Treasury John Taylor.

"We're going through a great crisis involving a police force mutiny," he explained in English, while listening to the stones breaking the Palace windows. "We need at least $150 million. And we need it this week."

The request exceeded Washington's annual assistance to Bolivia. Taylor responded that he could only offer between $12 and $15 million.

Goni became enraged. "It's a disgrace, goddammit, what the United States does to us. That wouldn't even be enough for me to buy cigars."

The crisis left 33 dead, 189 wounded, and an uncertain future. Bolivia couldn't resolve its economic crisis, Goni was left weakened as a chorus of voices called for his resignation, and Washington appeared to be putting certain limitations on its alliance.

But Rocha's enemy hadn't changed. On March 14, the new U.S. ambassador to Bolivia, David Greenlee, requested a meeting with the vice president. Without the arrogant style of his predecessor, he informed Mesa: "There is a plan to assassinate Evo Morales. Like any official who knows of an assassination plan linked to questions of the state or politics, I have the obligation to pass it along to that person. Since my government doesn't have a relationship with Evo Morales, I am informing you sir, and I ask that you please pass it along to him."

He handed him a document on yellow paper with capital letters without a heading or sender. "Information that is true and creditworthy has been obtained regarding the MAS party, that a coup d'etat is planned to overthrow the Bolivian government in April of this year. The leaders of the party, Evo Morales Ayma and Antonio Peredo Leigue, are the principal architects and ones responsible for the plan." According to the report, a splinter group from the MAS "would like" for Morales and Peredo "to be assassinated during the coup in April."

There wasn't actually any plan in the MAS for a coup or any interior conflict warranting a purge of that magnitude. Either the embassy was relying on bad information or it was part of a plan to create tension within the MAS. Or both.

The report ended: "We urge your collaboration to inform Morales about this attack in such a way that he understands and accepts the seriousness of this information so that he takes the necessary means to protect himself. To you, we urge that you confirm that this notice was delivered and, furthermore, that you report back to us afterwards as to Morales' reaction to the information herein."

After meeting with Mesa, Evo stated that there was a CIA plot to kill him.

"The United States embassy wants me out of circulation," Morales declared.

He held the Bolivian and U.S. governments responsible for an eventual attack against him. "Last year UMOPAR machine-gunned a human rights office in Iterezama knowing that I was there. Believe me, I understood the message," he said to the magazine *Nueva Economía* (New Economy).

Sánchez Berzaín was the one in charge of destroying Evo politically. In a meeting with government officials, he explained the plan: "We're trying to find out if he is linked to drug trafficking. Currently, we have three lines of investigation: (1) Cocaine, (2) Property, (3) Private Life."

After a few weeks, "The Fox" decided to suspend the investigation into Evo's private life because he didn't think anyone would care. The most solid line of attack, he told his people, was the second one: "We're going to see if this poor little guy, dying of hunger, might actually have 200 hectares."

He never found anything.

In that first meeting, he acknowledged that it would be impossible to buy Evo, but he was paying Felipe Quispe.

"I don't know how much you pay him," one of his interlocutors told him, "but it's not worth a damn. What the hell have you gotten out of him?"

"You don't understand, brother. With Quispe we've got to take the good with the bad. In the moment of truth, he'll fall into line."

A subsequent chain of events confirmed that Quispe would not fall into line. Either he was never paid anything and Sánchez was lying, or he did receive something but then did as he pleased.

Goni didn't learn the lesson of Black February. He told his team that he'd rather be a good president than a popular president. That was one of the reasons that they pushed him to go forward with the plan to export gas to the United States and Mexico at a low price. And to do it through Chile. This project reopened Bolivia's nationalist blood and fired up historic anti-Chilean and anti–North American sentiments that neither Goni nor Washington helped to alleviate. Morales and other social organizations rallied the cause of recovering the country's natural resources, which had been so effective during the War of Water. In brief, Sánchez de Lozada's last war on Bolivian soil had begun—the War of Gas.

"Goni, there's a risk of civil war," political analyst Cayetano Llobet warned him in a private meeting in June.

"I don't know what side you're on, Tano, but I am going to win that war," he answered.

In July, when Manfred Reyes Villa joined up with the government coalition (considered a failure by 78 percent of the population), an event that normally would have escaped national attention took place in the Pucarani district, in the Aymara Andean highlands. The people of Cota Cota murdered two livestock thieves. Shortly thereafter, the court ordered the arrest of the community leader, Edwin Huampu.

The call for his liberation was joined by another 80 calls from various organizations, such as the No to the sale of gas and the No to FTAA. On September 8, a protest composed of *campesinos*, chauffeurs, neighbors, students, and the unemployed carried those demands from El Alto to La Paz. "If Goni wants money, then he can sell his wife," was the predominant chant. Two days later, because Huampu remained a prisoner, Quispe and a thousand other people initiated a hunger strike and a roadblock throughout the Andean Highlands. The neighboring communities in El Alto had already called for an indefinite blockade. In a few hours, with the boost of the transportation workers strike, all communication between El Alto—where the international airport is—and La Paz was cut off.

"The War of Gas begins on the 19th," Morales declared, and he condemned the witchhunt for social leaders that had begun. In his case, they sought to link him to the Colombian FARC. Even Pope John Paul II seemed to hear him: He asked for the conflict to end in peace. On

September 19, the Committee for Defense and Gas Recovery, led by Oscar Olivera, and the MAS mobilized 50,000 people in La Paz and 20,000 in Cochabamba.

Sánchez de Lozada's spokesperson identified Evo as the ringleader of the insurrection and accused him of being a coup supporter. He was mistaken. Morales did not control the organizations of El Alto nor did he lead the protests, much less plan a coup d'etat. In a decision for which he would later be reproached, he traveled to Libya and Switzerland in the middle of what he called a "peaceful revolution in progress."

Meanwhile, the state forces murdered three people, including an eight-year-old girl during an altercation in El Alto. "Now, indeed, a civil war" was the new motto of the Aymara communities who didn't have the MAS or Evo as a reference, but rather Tupac Katari's insurrection. His "I will return and I will be millions," popularized by Eva Perón, would acquire meaning in El Alto, where almost three-quarters of its 800,000 inhabitants are Aymara. That identity, along with the strong link between the neighborhood committees and the unions, make the residents of the Andean Plateau a radical, organized community that has an enormous capacity for mobilization.

With La Paz isolated, the insurgents cut off the delivery of gas provisions into the city. The government commanded a war operation with tanks, helicopters, and hundreds of soldiers to clear up the El Alto—La Paz freeway: 25 civilians and one soldier died. These incidents caused an outcry against the president, and the middle class joined the conflict with hunger strikes in churches and plazas.

After the massacre, when bread and meat had become scarce among the citizens of La Paz, Mesa announced that he would distance himself from Goni and position himself for an eventual presidential succession. Despite the profound admiration that Mesa had felt for Sánchez de Lozada for years, he made this resolution as a result of the February crisis, those killed in the War of Gas, Goni's alliance with the MIR, a few cases of corruption, and Mesa's own ambitions.

One of the first calls Mesa received after his announcement was from Peter Deschazo, the assistant secretary of the State Department for Hemispheric Matters in Washington. As an ex-Bolivian embassy cultural attaché during the 1970s and an acquaintance of the vice president, his tone was unfriendly: "We would like to communicate to you, in the name of the government of the United States, that we will not accept, under any notion or circumstance, any government that is born out of the ousting of Sánchez de Lozada."

The State Department had charged Mesa with creating a conspiracy. The State Department's course of action after this was to keep Goni in the Palace at any cost. However, it proved too much of a challenge to abolish the law of gravity. The president was inexorably falling.

On October 16, more than 100,000 people flooded Plaza San Francisco to demand Sánchez de Lozada's resignation. The War of Gas already had 67 casualties and 400 injured. The plaza filled with miners from Huanuni (Department of Oruro), *cocaleros* from Los Yungas, young people, students, neighbors, the unemployed, and women from the markets of El Alto.

The latest command from El Alto involved going down to La Paz, traveling from the blockade into victory. They did this by foot, scattering stones and strengthening the pickets that acted as guards by night to prevent looting. Instead of shoes, many of them wore *abarcas*, sandals made from the remains of rubber tires.

The entire oppositional arc joined together, from Evo and the MAS all the way to Bolivian Worker's Center (COB), which regained a certain prominence.

That day, Mesa invited the U.S. ambassador to his house to assure him that he wasn't conspiring against Sánchez de Lozada and to request support in case he were to assume the presidency. The vice president sat alone in front of the living room fireplace, although his wife was listening from an adjacent room. The conversation is an eloquent testimony of how U.S. ambassadors in Bolivia operate in cases of extreme crisis.

"David, regardless of your good or bad intentions," Mesa said, addressing him in the familiar "*tú*" form, "you are going to have to recognize me if I become president. There is a new political situation that goes beyond the efforts of your government to keep Goni in office."

Greenlee responded, "I want to ask you to support him, Carlos, and don't take this as pressure. I want you to modify your opinion and make it public. You cannot separate yourself from him because your loyalty obliges you. The best that you can do for democracy is to strengthen a weakened president. Otherwise, you'll be the one who really brought about his demise."

While Mesa spoke with Greenlee, Sánchez de Lozada continued to stand by his power. He believed that the measures he'd proposed hours earlier—a consultative referendum on gas policies, a revision of Hydrocarbon Law, and incorporation of the Constituent Assembly to the constitutional regime—would soon start to take shape and buy him some time. Plan B could be summarized with a phrase attributed to Sánchez Berzaín: "Maybe we won't make it with 999 deaths, but with 1,000, maybe we will." The then–minister of defense asked the president how far he was willing to go.

"As far as Salvador Allende," was his answer. Allende, the Chilean president who remained in the Palace to confront the military coup led by Augusto Pinochet on September 11, 1973, committed suicide as a last recourse.

Although Goni and Allende didn't resemble each other at all, Sánchez Berzaín found courage now that he knew Goni would fight to the end. So he raised the death toll: "With 2,000 deaths we stay in the Palace but with a very high political cost." Sánchez de Lozada's family pressured him not to imitate Allende or anyone else for that matter: With a calculated fortune of $200 million, he had other considerations to keep in mind.

"Goni, you bastard, you'll pay for this disaster," or "Goni to the gallows, and the people in power," the protestors in La Paz shouted. While thousands of marchers arrived on foot from different parts of the country, the Medical Association of La Paz declared a general alert, and hundreds of tourists were evacuated.

In southern La Paz, Mesa's chat with Greenlee had grown bitter.

"It seems rather strange to me," the vice president told him, "that you confuse my loyalty [to Sánchez de Lozada] with subservience. Weighing the development of his government against putting a stop to these deaths, there is reason, ethics that force me to...."

"Don't come at me with that crap," Greenlee interrupted. "Don't disguise your true intentions of becoming president, which is what you're after."

"David, you can't understand because you're from a country of double standards like the United States."

"I won't tolerate you insulting me or my country," he replied and tried to leave, but his host prevented him.

"And what have you done? This has been one insult after another. You don't insult me and I won't insult you."

Somewhat calmer, the ambassador told him that he felt a great identification with Bolivia, that his wife had been born here, and that what was happening was painful for him, too. "The elite has governed very poorly. I've never known a country as racist as this one. You all, the elite, made a democracy of exclusion. You aren't self-critical, you're incapable of establishing institutionalism, and you live in corruption."

Later, given both of their uncertainty about what would happen at the end of the conversation, Greenlee tried to reaffirm his main point: The United States would not recognize a president who came into power out of the "destabilization" of the country.

"Goni is not resigning. They are throwing him out in street movements. The United States can't redefine democracy based on who has the ability to bring a group of people together to oust presidents," the ambassador told Mesa.

Sánchez de Lozada resigned on October 17. One of his advisors relayed the decision to Mesa in the mid-afternoon and informed him that they would visit him at his house to establish a few conditions, but they didn't even have time for that. After recording a message and editing the letter that he then read in Congress, Goni fled. The road he traveled in Boliva had begun at the Military School of La Paz, continued in El Alto, and ended in Santa Cruz, where the peace stood in stark contrast to the western insurgency. From there, he flew to Miami, and days later, in Washington, he announced: "It's very possible that they will take power in a nondemocratic way in Bolivia and that the country will be transformed into a cocaine-exporting version of Afghanistan."

On October 17, before Goni's resignation was made public, Deschazo called Mesa, and told him: "The State Department has done a very thorough study of the crisis, and should it come to pass that you have to take charge of the presidency, you will receive the full support of the United States."

Representatives of Lula and Néstor Kirchner had arrived in La Paz the night before in search of a peaceful end to the crisis. Meeting in Calafate, Argentina, on October 17, the presidents would take credit for the resolution, but nothing could have been further from the truth. In fact, the Argentine ambassador in Bolivia had been at the point of running off to his native Jujuy in an "escape plan," as the sources of the foreign ministry in Buenos Aires admitted to journalist Walter Curia.

Goni's flight was the principal reason for the truce. The marchers returned to their territories, victorious. Although they still had to bury the dead of October, they guaranteed to keep the peace.

Definitively, the War of Gas knocked out Sánchez de Lozada, stopped his gas exportation, and set up the October Agenda, which called for gas nationalization and a constituent assembly to refound the country.

Although Evo came out triumphant, he did not direct the uprising. He was not the general of the War of Gas but rather one of the many officials in a vast network of organizations and movements. As in the War of Water, the masses had taken over. This time, it was predominantly run by the Aymara insurgents of the high plateau, their neighbors in El Alto, and hundreds of supporting clusters.

Morales traveled to Havana in the first week of November, where he spent 24 hours with Fidel Castro. "Evo, the indigenous people are good at overthrowing governments, but now they have to learn to govern themselves," the commander told him. After this meeting, Morales took it upon himself to formulate a government agenda.

A month later, with the War of Gas still fresh, I visited him in what he called his room of La Paz. The apartment is located where Manko Kapak becomes a meandering and unpredictable street. Furnished with one- and two-seat violet armchairs, two cables hung from the ceiling, one with a light bulb socket and bulb, the other bare.

"I detested politics before, but now I've learned that it's fundamental to know how to be involved with them," he said, remembering what his fears had been in 1995.

He spoke of his children's panic about the attacks against him. Eva and Álvaro would worry every time two days went by and they didn't see him on the television. They didn't know that on October 15 the security team had arrested someone who came up to the MAS leader holding a revolver.

He changed the subject. He said he'd heard Julio Iglesias by chance and that he was charmed by his romantic quality, but he continued to prefer Savia Andina. I foolishly asked him whether he'd seen *Bolivia*, the film by Adrián Caetano that premiered in Argentina in 2001. He answered that he'd only been to the movies once in his life, to see a film about the soccer player Pelé. "I was impressed by the size of the screen."

At 10:00 P.M., Álvaro García Linera and Filemón Escobar arrived. Evo's eyes were bloodshot from exhaustion. "We have difficult months ahead but with great changes," he stated.

Bolivia was irremediably split in two. There was the west, the indigenous and rebellious Bolivia of the War of Gas, which, through the force of their marches, demanded decolonization of the country, nationalization of natural resources, and the end of Supreme Decree 21.060. Then there was the east, with Santa Cruz at the helm, calling for more regional autonomy to maximize the benefit of their land, rich in natural resources, and state authority to confront street and road blockades.

I asked Evo whether he would change the name of the country if he ever made it to the Burned Palace.

"I don't want to say...there is oversensitivity," he told me.

"Popular Republic?"

"No, but Native Republic of Bolivia is a possibility, don't you think?"

The rules, as well as the names of countries, he figured, were meant to be changed.

Chapter Five

THE PALACE
(APRIL–MAY 2007)

Morales governs from the head of a wooden, rectangular table, with his back to Plaza Murillo. For security reasons, and also out of habit from his time as a union leader, there are few moments when he's left alone in his office, which has an impersonal air. The floor is hardwood; the curtains made of velvet; the carpet, Persian; the tables, most of them, low to the ground and small; some of the window panes display the Bolivian coat of arms. Light comes from chandeliers with eight spiderlike arms, but there are also a few spotlights fixed into the ceiling, pointing out the balance, or the conflict, between new and old. Serving as an additional reminder is the television set sitting in a nineteenth-century hutch.

On that April afternoon in 2007, Morales had just woken from his *siesta*, mandatory since his March illness. The Cuban doctors diagnosed him with a sinus infection, in addition to performing surgery on his eyes, and demanded that he look after himself and rest every afternoon. He had neglected his body.

Since then, Morales lies down for an hour or an hour and a half in the room adjacent to his office. Nobody knows exactly how much he sleeps because he makes calls on his cell phone from the bed. It's generally a moment of relative solitude.

"Where've you disappeared to, big boss?" Evo greeted me.

After we exchanged "How are you?" he monologued for a good while almost without interruption. As in his public speeches, the subjects do connect to one another, although sometimes those connections are imperceptible to his listeners. He looked more executive and more concerned with management than the Morales of 2006.

They forgave half of the debt. And I thought that after doing so it wouldn't be possible to ask for any more credit. I was against the idea of credit before because I thought that one should have to use the money he had and that was that....Japan, for instance, forgave the debt, but we continue to work together. I have problems with the institutions that have to monitor money. The people should take care of it....In 13 years, $250 billion have been wasted in reserve expenditures. The ministry employees had $3,000 salaries and bonuses of another $3,000. I only wanted to earn 5,000 *pesos* ($660) per month, which is what I need for my children's pension, but they told me that if I asked for that, all of the ministry employees would have to be making less than me....As a union leader, I just needed enough to get around and to be able to eat: It's no different over here, and since they pay for my mobility and food, I don't need any more....Some colleagues don't let themselves get involved in the bureaucracy, others spend all their time looking at the clock because all they want is to go home....I wanted to increase 50 percent of [teacher's] salaries, but the economic team told me that the treasury didn't support it. Last year we increased 7 percent, and this year we increased another 6 percent [inflation was from 4 percent]....I've just managed to understand all this about the fiscal deficit and surplus: Before becoming president, I didn't know....Since 1970, the State has always had a fiscal deficit. And we didn't go to the United States to ask for money in order to pay our Christmas bonuses, we're paid in advance....Nor have we asked the IMF or the World Bank....For every $10 that comes into the State, $2 comes from gas....The reserves were $1.7 billion, and now they're at $3.5 billion. The Bolivian *peso* has risen in value against the dollar....In the polls, I have 40 percent compared with my next opponent's 8 percent....We began with a debt of $5 billion: Each Bolivian owed some $500 and now less than $200....And in only a year and a half of government, we can't just change the model of 500 years or even of 20 years....Before, I knew about *coca* and now I know about hydrocarbons. After its nationalization in February, the deposits in the Vinto mine went up in 30 days. Since we have a little more capital, certain sectors keep asking for more and more.... I want for the right to vote to begin at the age of 16. In the country, a kid works as soon as he can walk. At six or seven years old, he's already scaring the birds away so they don't eat the quinoa. I did that.... At 16, one should be able to vote and also to be elected.... The ministers would have to spend hours listening to the *cocaleros*.... There is a *campesino* problem, which is the gap between the countryside and the city. As long as that problem goes unresolved, the problem of Bolivia will not be resolved.... Often in the city one gets lost in an organization on account of small things, and that just doesn't happen in the country.... Look, I never even thought I'd be mayor, and now I'm the president.

That afternoon, he spoke as mayor and as president. The first year of his administration had ended with a paradox: very good economic numbers (poverty and unemployment went down, for the first time in 30 years there was no fiscal deficit—there was even a surplus—and the external debt was reduced by half) and an increase in political difficulties due to conflicts between different regions and social sectors.

The Evo of April 2007 had already incorporated the concerns of governing into his radical rhetoric. The Palace, in which he had always feared being closed up and subject to alien protocol, had begun to shape him.

He also worried about the bad performances of some of his ministers. A few of them had cried during an evaluation: "You know how our female *compañeras* are more sensitive." He demanded, among other things, his same level of commitment. If it were up to him, he would select ministers without family and divested of any interest outside of politics. That had been his crucial choice—to live his public life with few excursions into his private one.

Morales continued to obsess over every detail. That afternoon he called the mayor of La Paz so that he'd get a few street lights in the Plaza Murillo fixed, and he informed the mayor of Cochabamba that they would be bringing in cement to build a street in his city.

After this initial monologue, and through the end of a month, I would see how Evo governed the country from the Palace and witness his everyday routine there; I would attend Cabinet meetings, his tête-à-tête with certain ministers, his encounters with mayors, parliament members, businessmen, officials from international organizations; his long sessions with his most intimate circle. But I would also accompany him in less public routines,

such as watching television or sharing locker rooms with old Bolivian soccer legends. We would talk about the issues of his presidency as well as less
immediate ones, such as the kitchen in times of bachelorhood.

"I don't expect to be in the secret meetings of the Palace," I told Morales,
innocently.

"There aren't secret meetings here, boss," he teased me.

He clarified that when staying in the Palace, he had to leave fairly frequently. The Palace is stifling—the air doesn't flow, it's impossible to tell
whether it's night or day in many of the rooms, and most of the furnishings
and decorations are oppressive. He maintains that while the government is
located in the Palace, the real power resides elsewhere.

Morales went down to the Central Hall and sat between the presidents
of the Children's Chamber of Deputies and the Chamber of Senators. The
president of the Lower Chamber, Héctor Mamani, spoke first. He was
16 years old and looked like an extremely thin version of Evo, with a more
pronounced nose resembling a wolf's snout. He had a particular way of
referring to himself. "My person would like to say something: We want to
participate in creating a project for change," he said. About a hundred little
junior deputies and senators had hot chocolate and took pictures, and some
of them laughed at a guard's face.

In his turn, the president told them his agenda for the day. From 5:00 to
6:00 A.M. he would meet with advisors to talk about the Venezuelan energy
summit. Afterward, he would devote himself to the Corocoro mine situation. "How are we going to be able to get a hold of the $100 million needed
for its reactivation? I've been thinking about this since I got up, kids, and I
want you all to hear the information first hand," Morales stated.

Later, he offered them a definition of the presidency: "It's like being
the father of a family. You work and work so that the family can eat and
educate itself."

Many continued joking among each other, and some were making a
racket.

"Kids, I wasn't able to study economy or law, but I don't regret it," Morales
said. "I learn here. When I was little, my parents taught me to be respectful
and humble. My father told me, 'Evito, if you want to be respected, respect
the elderly and the young.' "

The children were now divvying up boxes of sweets.

After that event, he began a trip that, with brief layovers in Caracollo
and the city of Cochabamba, landed in the department of Tarija. His

photographer, Noah Friedman-Rudovsky, accompanied him, along with Sacha Llorenti, vice minister of coordination with social movements and (in practice) also his private secretary.

In the helicopter, they put earmuffs on Evo and gave him sunglasses because of his eye operation. In Caracollo—a town along the highway serving as the main artery between La Paz and Cochabamba—he handed out computers. "He's a human being, not a god," a teenager shouted upon seeing the weeping and madness that Morales had caused. After the function, Evo gave a toast with the dark beer of the region. He offered some to the *Pachamama*, the Mother Earth.

Tension with the press was already a part of the presidential agenda. In Cochabamba, during a national meeting of the radio stations of indigenous groups, he assured them that 90 percent of journalists sympathized with the government, but that it was the owners of the media channels who were anti-MAS. "My parents taught me to pray with my eyes closed, and Unitel claimed that I fell asleep in mass. And they took photos of me scratching my nose!" he complained. "Tell the people our tragic history and you will make them cry," he suggested to the reporters present. In his eagerness to intervene in every detail, he suggested the programming for a chain of community radio stations.

"From 6 to 9 the national channel, from 9 to 12 regional programming, news at 12, and from 6 to 9 national news again. If all goes well, we'll set up a television station," Evo promised.

Fifteen minutes later, he entered the headquarters of the Committee of the Six Federations of the Tropics of Cochabamba. In his permanent office there, he paused at a poster with the candidates of the 2002 election. While he listed the future positions of the women in the photo as parliament and ministers, I said that he looked much younger.

"What are you trying to say to me, brother?" he asked.

It bothers him to see that he's gotten fatter in the photos of himself as president, and the old photos only prove just how much his belly has grown. He got mad at a congressman for his failure to coordinate the cancellation of a meeting.

"This isn't right, brother," he protested, plastering his arms straight by his side.

He went up to the fourth floor, where 15 neighborhood leaders, promoters of the construction of a stadium in Cochabamba, were waiting for him.

He explained to them that there was only $1 million for the project. "If I learned anything here," he said looking each of them in the eyes, "it's to know when a project costs less than what it says. I have become an expert—they can't fool me anymore."

His tone differed from the one he uses at public functions. It was drier, more categorical, and more to the point. He instructed the leaders to eliminate the part of the proposal that involved building on private land.

"But we'll convince the neighboring land owners," a leader argued.

"I want to be responsible, *compañera*. Run my proposal by your supporters, and we'll make a decision by the weekend," Evo said.

Two security vehicles were waiting at the door. The first, the one that Morales got into, took off, its tires screeching, and the second was delayed ten minutes because a guard had forgotten the lamb's leg that had been given to Morales as a gift during the lunch in Caracollo.

At 5:00 A.M. the next day, it was pouring rain in Cochbamba, so the colonel in charge of the presidential plane called a commander in Tarija to check on the weather because nobody was answering at the airport. The commander got out of his bed, looked at the sky, and reported: "Clear." With only this certainty, the plane departed.

Tarija is located in the hottest part of the valley. It lives in a dream created by a double illusion, that its gas will make it both the Bolivian Kuwait and immensely rich. Eighty-five percent of the gas and 84 percent of the condensed gas of the country come from this department. The incomes produced by hydrocarbons went from 6 million in 1997 to 237 million in 2007.

The delegation, joined by ministers and vice ministers, was put up in Los Ceibos, a four-star hotel on a wide avenue divided by a boulevard. There, Evo was to meet with mayors who were to receive finances from a special fund from the Venezuelan government that would be distributed among the nine departments in Bolivia. In the mezzanine decorated with red columns and ceramics forming a chess set, Morales sat with the mayors, all of them opponents, listening to the experts who would study the projects; farther off was a table with hot and cold drinks.

Morales explained the procedure: "We look at the project, its cost, and how long it would take to complete. We'll say which ones we have approved and will hand over the checks by this afternoon."

The first mayor presented a plan to export onions to Mercosur, making it clear that, because it had already received some financing, it only needed $16,000 more. The second one requested $35,000, $24,000, and $25,000 for different buildings on a school campus. The third mayor requested $188,000 for a potato crop renewal plan. The fourth, from Río Pilcomayo, said, without blushing, that he needed $119 million for a grape cultivation and exportation project.

The president informed them that they had to execute their projects in one year's time. "We will repair that road," he indicated to one of the mayors. To another, he said he would proceed with only four of his six requests. To a third, he demanded that he lower the price. Only one tried to talk back to him, claiming that he lacked resources to organize a tender.

Morales, in his role as executor, stayed away from political subjects.

Later, he traveled by ground to a housing development presentation in San Pedro de Buena Vista, which was almost canceled due to lack of attendance. The development was just a group of brick houses without plaster facing green hillsides covered with cornfields.

"I have been a tenant," he said in his speech. "When I came to Oruro, I rented a room in a house. I couldn't yell or have guests over. I don't mean it that way [he laughed and those present laughed with him]. One time I came back to Cochabamba at 11:00 P.M. and slept in the market. Some people were still outside drinking, and I asked if I could lie down off to the side until the morning. I know what it's like not to have money or a home."

This is a constant in Evo's public discourse. The story of his life is the story of the pain and scarcity in the country, and his governmental decisions are his way to begin to remedy them. And this is why a son of Bolivia can aspire to be seen as its father.

Another stop on the journey, the Tarija neighborhood Cuarto Centenario, showed more signs of that same scarcity. He inaugurated a school painted sky blue with fluorescent lights, chalkboards, display cases in the classrooms, and a gated perimeter. Surrounding it stood precarious dwellings without running water.

From there, the president flew to Padcaya, a town with a population of 20,000, to inaugurate a rehabilitation center for the disabled and to distribute computers. The microphones didn't work, but the megaphones did. A blind violinist played a short number. Morales told another personal story to contextualize the ceremony and give meaning to the government's action: "In my first trip to Europe, I had to talk on the phone, which was very expensive because I didn't know how to use the Internet. Now I understand how important computers are for communication."

On the next helicopter flight, he noticed green specks on his shirt—from a garland of leaves—and concluded that he should bring one shirt per event. When the helicopter, a Venezuelan Superpuma, landed in some cornfields, his face was covered in dirt. A *campesino* reassured him, "Don't fear, the earth here is sacred." Morales had arrived in Emboruzú.

To expand his consensus and popularity, Evo believes he should visit the places ignored by cartographers. There was no press at the event, only 200 townspeople. Illuminated by the orange dusk and a few light bulbs strung between the trailers of two trucks, they awaited the inauguration of a citrus fruit processing plant to be managed by a cooperative.

The minister of production and micro-business, Celinda Sosa, explained that the machines they looked at in Tehran wouldn't work. Morales warned them that if they failed in the administration of the cooperative, it would go back to being a private business. "We have to assemble an economic branch with associations and cooperative members. Unions aren't always enough."

Returning to the hotel, he handed over the checks for the nine projects totaling $1,388,996. He made it clear to the mayors that there weren't any sort of political conditions tied to the money. The mayor of San Lorenzo, who received the most ($427,000), got drunk on corn alcohol. In contrast, the one who asked for $119 million would have to make do with $89,363. Morales requested applause for Venezuela. And they applauded.

Days later, a Tarija mayor would send a photocopy of one of these checks to the U.S. ambassador, who would show it to Bolivian officials with obvious qualms.

A similar uneasiness occurred in the opposition when it was reported that the money from Caracas was deposited into the nation's General Treasury without record, violating the regulations in place. The president denied that accusation and left the oversight of the projects in the hands of an auditing unit. When its manager, Pablo Guzmán, outlined the risks and scandals that could emerge, Evo responded: "If they send me to jail, I'll go. I'd rather make a change, or at least to try to, than do nothing. If I end up in jail, someday, the people will get me out."

After the ceremony of the distribution of the checks, the president called me to his room for an "international evaluation" of the tour. His spokesman, Alex Contreras, and vice minister, Llorenti, were with him. A map with potential cross-country routes hung on one of the living room walls. "I've had very little time to study it," Evo lamented. Days earlier, he'd made a five-hour flyover from Guayamerín to Cobija to inspect the benefits of a cross-country route.

Sitting in a wicker armchair, he looked at his cell phones and told them to shut up. One of them featured Ernesto Guevara on the screen. "That's my line," he said, showing the photo to the General Secretary of the Andean Community of Nations (CAN), Freddy Ehlers. His two telephones ring all day, and often Evo himself answers.

Sometimes the calls are from women wanting to devote their lives to him. Months earlier, one of them confessed that she was afraid they would kill him. Others' fear for his well-being has been a constant in his life, which the rank of president has not diminished. He tries to have his closest associates take measures to protect him as a means of reducing the number of official guards.

Once relaxed, he described the traits that he looked for in a mate—athletic, politically left, young, a good person, fun. Someone to take care of him and caress his hair. "I like to cook with her, which isn't the macho style," Morales added. His relationship with food, though, was more a measure of the extent of his political activism than how he related to women. As a young leader, a cylinder of cooking gas would last him four months. When that stretched out to a year, he realized how much his life had changed.

At that moment, he did in fact receive a call from a woman—the president of Chile—and he went to his room.

"I'm meeting with Bachelet on Tuesday," Morales announced when he came back.

The conversation turned to politics. I asked Evo why he continued to concentrate so much power in himself and why he personally made so many decisions every day.

"Well, I have to follow the issues. Think about Fidel and Chávez—they know every detail. And also, so many things occur to me," he explained.

"You tell the *cocaleros* not to increase the production of coca because that depreciates its value. Doesn't the same thing happen to the word of the president? With so much discourse, so many press conferences and statements, won't your words depreciate?" I asked.

"I want to be in contact with those people, to get through to them. They have not had a relationship like this with any president," Morales responded.

I criticized how he sometimes generalizes his attacks on the press. "Yes, we have to maintain a dialogue with them," he conceded.

Mario Cossío, the governor of Tarija and an opponent of his government, was waiting for Evo one floor above. He claimed that there was a plan afoot to destabilize him. The president denied it and urged him to come to an agreement with the social organizations because that would guarantee him political stability. Before saying goodbye, Evo asked for the key to the stadium to be able to play soccer and deliver tractors the next day. The governor said that he could have it, but he didn't follow through on his promise.

"I'm not going to call him. I don't kneel to bastards," Morales asserted. He set off and moved the event and tractor delivery to the city market. The Venirán tractors, manufactured by Venezuela and Iran, shone in the sun off to the side of the event, along with fruit trucks. There was a police sniper on top of a water tank. Security had removed a protestor carrying a placard that proclaimed, "No to the corruption in the MAS."

Evo's dispute with Cossío didn't make him lose his conciliatory tone. At 7:30 P.M., he met with the Civic Committee of Tarija, another opposing group, but one with which Morales chose to maintain a tolerable coexistence.

The tour ended with a racquetball game and a barbecue. At 9:00 P.M., the president started bouncing a ball against a worn-out cement court painted light blue with white lines. Dressed in a black polo shirt with the inscription "Cancún" and the shorts of the Bolivian soccer team, he played two against two. Afterward, he invited the entire delegation, including security, to eat steak, and he made a couple of toasts.

Before midnight, he traveled to the island of Margarita, Venezuela, for the first South American Energy Summit. While there he had a confrontation with Lula and a minor altercation with Chávez.

In the presidential suite of the Hilton Hotel, Evo revealed to the Brazilian president Bolivia's intention of buying the Petrobrás refineries currently being run out of Brazil as part of his carbon policy, increasing Bolivian state presence throughout the entire chain of production.

In the harshest meeting they'd had up to that point, Lula responded that if that happened, Brazil would stop investing in Bolivia. "We prefer to sell everything," Petrobrás president José Gabrielli specified. Future prospects were not encouraging: Brazil asked for $200 million for the refineries, and Bolivia offered $60 million.

In the end, Lula tried to reconcile the two.

"Let's not put our relationship at risk for such a small amount," Lula said.

He asked that Morales understand his situation in Brazil: "I don't have the majority in the parliament, and the media groups are hostile." They agreed to continue negotiating.

Evo was troubled by the conflict over biofuel in the summit. Brazil, Colombia, and Chile pronounced themselves in favor of its use, whereas Venezuela and Bolivia refused it. Chávez met with Lula, and they agreed that there would be a final document favoring Brazil's position: "Without that document, the summit will be considered a failure," the Venezuelan explained to Morales. Somewhat angry, Evo responded that he didn't agree with this reasoning because he prioritized the care of Mother Earth over the summit's outcome.

In the written declaration finalizing the summit, the participants expressed their "recognition of the potential of biofuel to diversify the South American energy matrix." Next to his signature on the declaration the Bolivian president wrote by hand, "with a difference of opinion in regard to the biofuel matter."

Still upset, he landed in La Paz. His mood worsened when he learned of a conflict that had erupted in Tarija hours after his departure. The provinces of Gran Chaco and O'Connor were disputing the Chimeo site, where the Spanish company Repsol runs the Margarita mega-field (13 trillion of the total 48 trillion cubic feet of petroleum estimated in Bolivia), provoking confrontations between the local people and security forces. Morales thought the conflict was under control even though the mayors of the two principal towns in Gran Chaco—Villamontes and Yacuiba—were already on hunger strikes in demand of a solution when the Venezuelan checks were delivered to the other mayors. In fact, these local governments of Tarija and the national government had spent months blaming each other over who should have brought the conflict to a resolution.

When he arrived from Isla Margarita, he urgently called his inner circle together in the San Jorge residence. After a few minutes, he heard about the death of Derman Ruiz on the radio: A bullet had shattered his left leg, and he died from blood loss. According to the official version, Ruiz and a group of protestors had tried to shut off the valves at the Transredes plant, which supplies gas to Argentina and Tarija. There was a long and uncomfortable silence in the room. Evo lowered his head. After he was over the initial shock, he said that there was an internal conspiracy. He first came down on Fabián Yaksic, the vice minister of decentralization. "I told him to be there and he wasn't," Morales exclaimed.

The official line consisted of holding the governor of Tarija responsible for the conflict. It was based both on the political interpretation and a report by Tarija leaders, which alleged that one of the vice mayors had paid demonstrators money to join together. Morales requested that the government of Potosí arbitrate the dispute between the two provinces, and it announced that García Linera would lead a dialogue initiative.

The president was sure that the crisis was bigger than a single regional conflict: It put nationalization into question, even the control of national territory.

Faced with the risk that the issue would brim over and even lead to the seizure of oil plants, Evo wanted to know the options for a military intervention. "It's going to be very difficult," Minister of Defense Walker San Miguel warned him, fearful that there would be more deaths. On Wednesday at 6:30 A.M., after two hours of sleep, the Cabinet meeting began. "We didn't come to government to have blood on our hands," Morales told his ministers, "and another Bolivian is dead." He requested a political assessment from each of them. Many called for a stricter government. The president complained about the lack of solutions. Demonstrators took control of the Transredes plant. They threatened to set off explosions and managed to close off the gas delivery valves to Argentina. In Yacuiba, the looting and confrontations went on. At 5:30 P.M., the president received, via fax, an intelligence report confirming that 60 members of the security forces had been taken hostage and that a "mob" had raided the Transredes gas pumping plant. Because those working in the house of government that night forgot to turn on the lights, the Palace remained in shadows.

Called on by Morales to give an explanation of Ruiz's death, Chief of Army Freddy Berzatti assured him that his force had not shot the fatal bullets despite reports to the contrary. He also said that every incident involving the police had ended badly. Because Evo trusts the armed forces more than the police and his intelligence reports, he decided that the military should try and restore peace in Yacuiba.

In the Cabinet meeting that afternoon, the minister of the presidency, Juan Ramón Quintana, proposed that the operation be executed that night. They needed tear gas, but the government didn't have any. Urgently, he requested that the Argentine government provide a few cartridges through a border regiment. Evo asked about the proportion of troops to occupants, and he became more nervous when he found out that they had Molotov cocktails. "Could they destroy anything?" he asked. It worried him that the occupation of oil wells could become the norm.

With the hours slipping by, Evo became convinced that Cossío was relying on the support of transnational businesses. The oil companies began to apply pressure. With each fax directed to the presidency, Petrobrás and Repsol asked what was being done about the shortage. Because the crisis had reduced the amount they were able to export, Bolivia had already lost $980,000.

This conflict was representative of those often faced by the Bolivian government. It combined a confrontation with the governor of an adverse region, an internal dispute over natural resources, external pressures for the guarantee of a gas supply, and the ineffectiveness of the state to diffuse social tensions and disputes.

On Friday, the army regained control of the Transredes and Gran Chaco plants and established a round of conversations with the municipalities.

On Sunday, the president worked on another issue.

In the Plaza Murillo at 7:30 A.M., he listened to the Oruro Imperial Band, the one in which he had played as an adolescent. A child came up to him to ask him a question:

"Hello, are you Juancito Pinto?" the child asked Evo.

Juancito Pinto was the name of the state voucher program for schoolchildren.

The president headed south to a private residence with gardens in Huajchilla to conduct reviews of the government's progress with mayors from his political party, just as he had done with the senators and deputies. He began his speech with a reprimand.

"Not even half of us are here, and it's already nine.... Turn off your cell phones."

A few baseball caps and straw hats stood out among the group. When a cell phone rang, he shot a death stare to the person who attended to it.

In his monologue, he demanded further commitment from them, that they not focus so much on local issues, that they politicize themselves more, and that they defend two of the pillars of the process, the nationalization decree and the Constituent Assembly.

"You all continue to be leaders, and you have to work as leaders all week long. If you aren't committed, you should just leave," Evo said.

When he went out to the garden during the recess, he requested that lunch be served at 1:00 P.M., and he asked to hear the news on the radio. He was bothered by an opponent's accusation that, in a private meeting, his sister, Esther Morales, had said there was already a written constitution. Sensitive to the mentioning of his family, Evo decided that his sister shouldn't have a public presence.

He went back to the room and made note: La Paz, 34 of 80 mayors; Cochabamba, 60 of 90; Oruro, 9 of 15; Santa Cruz and Beni, none. He openly expressed his anger.

"There has to be discipline, if not, we're going to start suspending pay. We'll reduce the salaries of anyone who falls asleep [laughter]."

The mayors spoke afterward, even the sleepyheads. If they began their speech by saying "Mr. President," Evo corrected them: "Get to the point." One said that the external debt was no longer discussed. Another requested an official seminar with information and analysis. Another acknowledged that they lacked training, unity, political information, and self-evaluation. Another complained that the media had been bought. Another requested that they publicize the ten points of the government program. Another lamented that he never received the information that the vice president had just given them about the nationalization decree. Another requested the nationalization of the telecommunication industry. In general, the mayors expressed excessive respect for the president, almost fear. There wasn't time for debate.

Evo concluded the ten-hour meeting, which had only had one recess and lunch of *milanesa* (a South American fried meat dish) with french fries:

> Sometimes I have to call ministers to the palace just so they'll send letters that they didn't send.... Another weakness of ours—information. I was thinking just now about how to get ads, jingles. We can't help some of the radio stations that sympathize with us because they're illegal and can't register. We can't buy a TV channel—ATB is for sale, but it comes out to $20 million.... If only there were a left-wing newspaper, some means to disseminate information weekly.... It has to be information by word of mouth.

Every morning, the president receives a report with a map of the social conflicts that greet Bolivia that day. This report is called the Early Alert Conflict System, and it is prepared by the vice minister of coordination with social movements. It describes the organization involved, the subject, whether it's a crisis, pre-crisis, anticipated, or latent, whether the trend is growing, diminishing, or steady, the demands, the means of pressure, the response, the current status, and the government sector responsible for handling it.

The April 24 report recorded 11 conflicts, almost all growing, but none with the red mark of crisis. A mixed front had resulted in strikes, protests, and marches: *ropaviajeros* (sellers of old clothes) demanded a three-year prorogation for the free importing of clothing; the disabled, an annual voucher of 5,000 bolivianos ($660); teachers and health workers, wage increases; and the list went on.

On the external front, negotiations with Brazil were not advancing, and the purchase of ENTEL shares by Telecom-Italia created complications. On April 2, a supreme decree formed a commission to work on ensuring that ENTEL went to the Bolivian state, which required 47 percent of the shares of the capitalized company.

Because the nationalization decree was enacted on May 1, 2006, the Latin American Labor Day, many expected a similar surprise on that day in 2007. The U.S. ambassador, Philip Goldberg, was among the anxiously expectant bunch. Goldberg's secretary called Paola Zapata, Evo Morales' personal assistant, to request an urgent lunch with the president. Zapata responded that they could do it in writing.

"But we always use the telephone," Goldberg's secretary insisted.

"We'll be expecting your request," Zapata responded.

This new requirement reflected just how much the relationship between the U.S. ambassadors and Bolivian presidents had changed.

On April 30, a fax directed to Morales came from Telecom-Italia. In English, the company asked for a meeting in Río de Janeiro, San Pablo, or Miami with executive officials to resolve the conflict. It also denounced the government for "launching a press campaign with the deliberate interest of fostering rancor in Bolivians against Telecom" during April 2007.

"We won't go to Miami or San Pablo or Rio de Janeiro," Evo decided when they handed him the translated version of the fax.

He was campaigning against the International Centre for Settlement of Investment Disputes (ICSID), an organization dependent on the World Bank and dedicated to arbitrating conflicts between companies and governments. "The only time it ever ruled in favor of a country was in a case involving the United States. That's why it's the ICSID that should be eradicated and not the coca leaf." His strategy for resolving the conflict with

Telecom and Petrobrás consisted of contesting the ICSID and having the legal battle in Bolivia regardless of the fact that the original contracts—signed during the old regime—contained a series of extraordinary benefits for the companies.

Three days before May 1, Petrobrás and Telecom came to an agreement with one another. They announced that, if the unilateral decisions persisted, they would turn to "international courts" in the case of Petrobrás and "an arbitration" in the case of Telecom. Both paths would lead to ICSID.

May 1 arrived with several conflicts and one additional problem. The government had allowed a rumor to spread that there would be great announcements comparable to those of 2006.

That day's Cabinet meeting began with the ministers' reports on the measures that they would later announce: the creation of 230,000 jobs (160,000 temporary and 70,000 permanent), the restoration of COMIBOL (Miner's Corporation of Bolivia) services with the goal of recovering a state presence in mining, an increase in the national minimum wage from 1,500 to 1,525 bolivianos per month ($65.60), the prohibition of new mining concessions, and the declaration of Bolivian territory as a fiscal reserve.

The Petrobrás conflict over the purchase of the refineries—perhaps the most complex—went on without resolution. It had been rumored the night before that the state would recover the plants. In a panic, the Brazilian ambassador of La Paz, Federico Cézar de Araujo, indiscreetly asked the head of the Bolivian armed forces whether there had been any movement of the troops. Upon receiving "I don't know" as a response, he inferred that there had been. He feared that on May 1 Morales would show up at the refineries riding in a helicopter.

The president tried to advance a radical decree in which Petrobrás would no longer act as owner of the refineries and would therefore become a lender of services, thus changing its legal status. In that day's Cabinet meeting—one of the most tense up to that point—they argued about that idea. "I would issue it just like this," Evo said, stressing that Brazil was not cooperating with his government or contributing to the bilateral relationship. But he gave in to the reconciliatory position of his minister of oil and gas, Carlos Villegas.

Although two intelligence reports warned him that he might be attacked or a whistle blown by teachers and health workers, Evo decided to march with the Bolivian Worker's Center (COB) after the Cabinet meeting anyway. During the previous week, the union leaders had asked him for raises, a building for their headquarters, and a community radio station. Morales, in a gruff leader-to-leader talk, scolded them for being involved too little in supporting and participating in his administration, and he told them to catch up, given that the miners held a power and influence in the COB that didn't correspond with power distribution among popular sectors in present-day Bolivia.

"Force, force, force, *compañero*, yes, the fight is hard but we will overcome," Evo sang in the march that he joined from the cemetery. Closely guarded by Llorenti and the vice minister of governmental coordination, Héctor Arce, amid cheers and salutes, the president saw how the country's informal economy continued to grow in the street markets, which, according to some estimations, came to 70 percent.

The event in the Plaza Murillo was so haphazardly organized that the sound engineer hadn't begun his work until midnight the night before the event and finished just in time for the beginning of the speeches. When the president went out on the balcony, he saw his face reproduced and enlarged on the Jumbotron, soldiers and *campesinos*, offerings to the *Pachamama*, a man dressed as a condor, YPFB workers in their helmets, and the smoke of a ritual. Some bands played in the background, and the crowd shouted sporadically, "*Jallalla*" (Aymara for "hooray").

Leaning his hands on the red of the flag, he gave a manager's speech, which centered on the numeric data. In addition to his use of symbolic langauge, he began to defend his status as a doer, someone who fulfills his promises. His speech, however, contained one slip, his reference to himself as God: "Mayor Caranavi told me that nationalization is a blessing from God, from God Evo. I was startled; I am just Evo, nothing more, but sometimes I am considered a devil along with Fidel and Chávez."

After the ceremony, he set off to the Hernando Siles Stadium to play a soccer game as a fundraiser for the medical treatment of the soccer player Óscar Sánchez. As he warmed up, he passed his childhood smile around with the other players, the old greats of the 1994 Bolivian national team, such as Diablo Echeverri or a dexterous Milton Melgar, his vice minister of sports. Evo had watched that World Cup, the third one Bolivia had played after 1930 and 1950, in the tropical heat of Iterezama, in El Chapare. Now those same players selected him as captain for their game against The Strongest (the opposing team, whose original name is in English).

During the match, he collided with ex-professionals who still had the physiques of pros. His team won, 2 to 1, and his best contribution was an assist that almost resulted in a goal. Afterward, he claimed not to have heard the whistles that came down from the grandstands every time he touched the ball.

Sitting in one of the little wooden boxes for the players in the locker room, he saw how the ex–World Cup players teased Melgar. "Vice minister, sir, you forgot to order hot water," one of them mocked. Although they couldn't bathe there, they still took pictures with five contestants in the Miss La Paz pageant. The penetrating sweat from the game permeated the locker room. Carlos Borja did his best to get the contestants' cell phone numbers. Sandy, one of the local players known for his rough game, asked the president whether he'd been eating a lot of *chicharrón* (seasoned pork rinds) because he noticed he had a big belly.

At 6:00 P.M., Morales arrived with Llorenti to the San Jorge residence. He wore blue pants and a sweatshirt with the inscription "Presidency of the Nation," and he sat in the first-floor living room. He tuned into the last few minutes of overtime in the Championship League Semifinal between Liverpool and Chelsea.

The house waiter offered him refreshments and coffee, and Evo asked for fruit. "Complete nourishment," he exclaimed after eating three kiwis. His phone rang, but because Llorenti answered, the caller hung up. Immediately after, it happened again, so Evo decided to take the call. The vice minister said next time he should answer the phone "Hello boss" to sound more like Morales.

There was something disconcerting about it all. The person who had showered at 4:30 A.M., attended extremely tense meetings to define decisive decrees, marched with the COB, addressed crowds, and played a soccer game in the most important stadium of the country didn't suffer the effects of hypereuphoria or hyperexhaustion. He was eating fruit, watching television, and making jokes as if it had been just any other day.

At 7:00 P.M. that night, the minister of treasury, Luis Arce, came in to discuss the demands of the teachers—rural and urban—and the health industry workers who were all asking for 7 percent salary increases. The government, in both cases, was willing to go to 6 percent.

Arce, dressed in a plum-colored shirt and a corduroy jacket, explained to Evo that there were other issues to resolve beyond the difference of the 1 percent increase. Evo looked back and forth between the television and the minister and held onto a lamp cord with his hand. Very formally, Arce admitted that a group of rural teachers—about 1,500—were working 120 hours a month and only being paid for 104.

"What's your suggestion, boss?" Evo asked.

"It's possible to raise it a little, from 104 to 108 hours as fixed pay [this isn't just a little group in the minority], and it would be beneficial to discuss a wider and more major law next year," Arce responded.

Morales agreed. He asked what the total payment was.

"Two hundred million bolivianos [$25 million]," the minister answered.

"Offer them 106 hours," Morales ordered.

With the urban teachers, it seemed more complicated. They were demanding a voucher that involved 50 million bolivianos a year. Evo figured out a strategy: fix things with the rural teachers first so that they would consider themselves obliged to cede their position. Because there remained some doubt as to the amounts, he used Llorenti's cell phone calculator.

The minister of education, Víctor Cáceres, came in. He asked the president, in an obsequious manner, whether he had accounted for the third goal of the day in the stadium because he had already made two, the march and the speech. Morales didn't laugh.

"Let's eat, bosses," Evo said after saying goodbye to the ministers. Evo commented that the house waiter had told him that Yolanda Prada, Banzer's wife, used to show off bundles and bundles of money, that an ex-president went to bed with an underage girl and afterward named her mother as an ambassador, and that ambulances once transported money back and forth.

When the waiter entered, he didn't look like the keeper of so many secrets. Tall and dark haired, he limited himself to serving little pieces of beef and chicken, puree, rice with cheese, yucca, *chuño*, potato, chili peppers, and *mocochinchi* (dried peach) juice. Morales requested soup and asked whether it was the same one—quinoa—that he'd eaten for lunch the day before.

He spoke about one of the biggest subjects of the day—the decree of the Petrobrás refineries. "I didn't sign it because I had technical doubts," Evo said. His trust in Lula had been dissolving since May 1, 2006. Evo said that he continued to care for him, but that he had doubts as to whether it was reciprocal.

Unlike Brazil, his relationship with Argentina and Kirchner had progressed beyond his expectations. He fantasized about an event for Bolivians in Argentina in the Bombonera soccer stadium. He asked how much it would cost to rent the stadium and whether Kirchner would play. "I told him that though he's letting the opposition go ahead and talk about

Cristina running, in the end he'll be the final candidate." He bet $100 that the Argentine president would seek reelection.

The subsequent half hour of his attention was captured by a game of beach soccer between Peru and France in Río de Janeiro.

On May 2, a year and a day after the nationalization decree, the oil contracts were registered in the Burned Palace. Morales spoke to the businessmen in the room of mirrors:

> Legal security is important, but it's also reciprocal: You ladies and gentlemen must respect the Bolivian laws.... Before the contracts that previous governments signed were secrets, but now they're constitutional and transparent.... If we had the resources, we wouldn't look for partners.... I thank Mother Earth, the *Pachamama*, and ask her that the oil continues to appear.

He should have asked the *Pachamama* for a quick resolution for the mess that relations with Brazil had become. On Sunday, May 6, the decree that Minister Villegas had worked on in secret was enacted: It granted the Bolivian State Petroleum Company (YPFB) a monopoly on the exportation of residual fuel oil, which, as an ulterior motive, sought to lower the value of the Petrobobrás refineries.

The decree had terrible repercussions for Brazil. Silas Rondeau, Villegas' counterpart, condemned Morales for not being loyal and said that he should have told him about the decree. The Brazilian government publicly summoned Bolivia to conclude the negotiations over the purchase of the refineries. In 1999, Petrobrás had paid $104 million for them, and in 2007, it first requested $200 million, then $180, then $153, then $135, and finally stuck with $112 million as their final offer. "If we don't get a fair price," Lula declared on May 8, "we'll appeal to the international courts." Just one day later, he cooled down somewhat. He attributed "oral radicalism" to Morales and announced that his colleague "cannot ruin the historical relationship between Brazil and Bolivia."

From Cochabamba, he received this response from Morales: "I don't know where all of this harsh discourse is coming from. We always try to resolve these conflicts through a dialogue."

Evo met with Villegas and Álvaro and offered $112 million. They estimated that it would cost $630 million to construct a refinery, and it would take four years to build it. The difference between $630 million and $112 million left no room for hesitatation.

"Let's make peace," the president ordered.

On Thursday, May 10, the purchase of the Petrobrás refineries for $112 million was announced.

A president can meet with Miss Bolivia and fly to one of the poorest regions of the country directly afterward in a single day. That's what Morales did on that May morning.

Jessica Jordán, a Beni woman with the air of a young Julia Roberts, would represent her country in the Miss World Pageant. She had won the highest national beauty contest in June 2006. Among the eight governors who attended—a demonstration of the social importance of the event— Mario Cossío of Tarija stood out the most. The volatility of Bolivian politics is curious: A year earlier, as president of the chamber of deputies, he was close to becoming chief of state.

"Do you think that autonomy is important?" he asked Jordán, committed to his new responsibility as a member of the panel of judges.

"Yes, but for all Bolivians, not just those in Santa Cruz," Jessica answered.

In the Burned Palace, however, Jordán was receptive to the official discourse. The president called her "*compañera miss*" and asked her to speak of nationalizations and the process of change during the Miss World Pageant. (In January 2010, Jordán was nominated by Morales to run for governor of Beni, an eastern department unsympathetic to the government.)

During the trip to Sacaca, a town with a population of 18,000 in the arid north of Potosí, Evo pointed to a tall and far-off peak surrounded by mountains and remembered something from his childhood.

"I brought my llamas out there. I was 13 or 14 years old," he said, pausing thoughtfully.

He used his index finger to outline his route: a zigzag through a rocky region without farmhouses or streams. "I bundled up tight so I wasn't cold, but sometimes I was hungry," he explained as he retraced in 30 minutes an expanse that, as a shepherd, had taken him ten days.

In Sacaca, the sun dries out and cracks the earth until it is almost useless. In his speech, the mayor of the town explained that they'd already received an ambulance and were negotiating a donation of two tractors. The townspeople who had gathered asked for more: a community radio station, paving the road from Sacaca to Oruro, and improvements to the hospital, among other things.

Morales has to live with these demands. Covered in garlands, he recited statistics from memory: Sacaca went from a budget of $100,000 to $1.1 million as a result of the nationalization decree. That increase should have translated into the general well-being of the community.

He asked the townspeople not to overlook the possibility of organizing themselves, and he complained about the protests of teachers and health workers. "We *campesinos* don't know about salaries or Christmas bonuses!" he shouted. He announced that he was going to inaugurate the Coliseum. "We're going to play soccer. If I lose, another Coliseum. If I win, a beauty queen." A duet sang that the woman has to be a guerilla and that she must give birth to working-class children.

Back in La Paz, Evo noticed that his shoes were dirty. Because the Palace shoe-shine wasn't there, his security guard looked for a substitute in Plaza Murillo. The youngster he found wore a red scarf on his head, a Michael Jordan jersey, and the dumbfounded look of someone entering a place that he'd only seen from the outside.

The shoe-shine had to wait a few minutes on the third floor, where the hallways form an open area. He contemplated the portentous black and red carpet, the stained-glass arches, the chandeliers in the stairwells, a green and white marble archway, gilded details, the carnations that are changed every other day, a full-length mirror, and the Thorvald watercolor that likely portrays Titicaca Lake. While waiting for his work, other people did theirs: The secretary of the president was rewriting a letter underneath a photo of Ernesto Guevara, the security guards were talking on their walkie-talkies in code, and the chancellor went into the elevator with his bag reminiscent of a freebie from a dental conference.

At 9:00 P.M., the president walked the two blocks separating the Palace from the vice presidency. "Evo, we love you so much," a woman shouted at him, raising her hand and displaying her palm.

The MAS deputy bench was waiting for him in the central hall. The president took note. There were obvious absences, such as seven Oruro representatives.

He scolded them:

Apart from the oil contracts, not much else has been done.... From here to Yacuiba [in reference to the Tarija conflict], the actions of the oil companies are political and deserve a political response.... Yesterday I got together with our *compañeros* in northern Potosí. The problem is that the ministers don't pay them enough attention....I met with the members of the cooperatives, and they informed me that they'd made an agreement with the ministry, but the ministry never told me....And now I'm going to ask *compañero* Martín not to write this down.

He laughed, looking at me. It was in reference to a topic that he'd already spoken about publicly—that the mayors, some of them potential contenders for the presidency, were coming after him and that was why they raised conflicts.

"The social movements," he continued, "are in need of new flags."

He asked for a coffee before continuing:

People whistled at the health workers and the *ropaviajeros*....The most recent conflicts are political....Our weakness is the little information we have....The people believe us. Even if we lied to them, they'd believe us, but we shouldn't lie to them, and we're not ever going to lie to them....If you have something convincing against the enemy, that's real and not just gossip, then let 'em have it.

It sounded like a training introduction.

Deputies, we have to approve laws....Work weekends, find something impactful, something novel....I am going to complain publicly if you don't pass anything, if you don't find anything....I know that many of you would earn more money in your private activities, but you're here to bet for the well-being of the country.

He asked for another coffee, and this time they added four spoonfuls of sugar that he neglected to stir in. García Linera spoke. "Congress is lacking an astuteness....There are communication problems....If you all don't fight your battles, the president has to fight them for you."

As the vice president spoke, eight deputies fell asleep. The eyes of almost everyone present were red, and those of the president were red and squinting. It was 10:45 P.M. In addition to coffee in plastic cups, they distributed bologna and cheese sandwiches.

In front of Morales, the deputies had submissive attitudes. One called for self-criticism. One colleague complained about how hard it was to get media attention. Another responded that to reach the people, you have to go door to door. At that point, Evo sneezed, and when an assistant came by with a tissue, he took advantage of the interruption to conclude the meeting.

"You don't have to wait for the Constituent Assembly to make changes, the ability to make changes is also in your hands. . . . I understand that many of you leave your families for other families [laughter]." Morales was joking about the alleged double lives of several of the deputies and senators.

At midnight, he went to a dinner at the Venezuelan embassy. The next day at 7:00 A.M., he began a Cabinet meeting that I attended.

"Good morning bosses, what's on our agenda today?"

The ministers gathered around the oval table in the Cabinet room. The fluorescent lighting created an almost hostile whiteness amid the columns, watercolors of the national heroes, and unlit chandeliers. The president was in front of a giant screen onto which an advisor's laptop was projected. Within his reach were a few tissues and a little bell to call his listeners to attention, which he would never ring.

While the minister of defense expounded about vehicle purchases, Evo took notes in a notebook, his knees positioned slightly apart. For his first contribution, he launched an attack against Minister of Education Víctor Cáceres.

> I'm very upset with you. You made an agreement with the teachers that affects the General Treasury of the Nation without telling me. Álvaro and I have both asked you about it, and you told us that you didn't do it. That is disloyalty, *compañero*—you've acted as the head of the teachers. I'm not going to follow through on the promise you made them, even if the teachers strike for the whole year.

The minister, who had straight hair combed to the side, eyeglasses with grey frames, a jacket, and a brown sweater, looked steadily at the president without showing anger or resignation. He seemed to turn off his face. He didn't even attempt a defense.

Evo left the meeting to answer one of the calls his assistant had taken. "How do they look, big boss?" he said into his cell phone. Three minutes later, he came back to the room and distributed pins with a design combining the Bolivian flag, the Andean Wiphala flag, a coca leaf, and the MAS flag and acronym.

"It's mandatory to wear them," he instructed the ministers.

When Evo sat down, he took up his anger with Cáceres again. He explained to the rest that when a measure involved treasury money, they had to speak with the minister of the treasury. "We have to continue having surplus," he told them, warning:

"If they censure you, you remain in the Cabinet. Because that shows that you're doing a good job."

Censure is a mechanism through which the opposition can call for the probation of a minister, and the president must either correct or remove the minister in question.

Dressed in black with Mao collars and white shirts, the servants came into the room carrying trays of bread, strawberry juice, pastries, fried eggs, and bacon.

The president continued with a speech that was more political than technical.

I'm worried that ministers don't place enough importance on communicating with the people. If someone attacks the ministry, you've got to come out. When people hear in a taxi that they're dragging us in the dirt and no one responds, the right wing gains momentum. Last night I requested that the members of parliament conduct one interview per day. I'm going to request five from all of you [laughter]. The Chief of Press should be like the chauffeur, going everywhere in the ministry. I am going to do a monthly follow-up.

He paused, played with his fried eggs, and asked the vice president, "Which law are we working on?"

"The one about financing political parties," García Linera replied. He explained that the law granted around $30 million to registered political parties.

"How much is repaid to us?" Evo asked.

"Sixteen," García Linera replied.

"Political parties often use that money against the government. I propose we reduce that amount by 50 percent," said Héctor Arce, vice minister of governmental coordination.

"We, the MAS, need the money for the electoral year too. We have to be realistic," Minister of Public Works Jerjes Mercado requested.

"A change in the law," Quintana, minister of the presidency, said excitedly, "would show that the MAS party is frugal, and that is seen by society as a very good thing."

"We have ethics," concluded Morales, "but we don't have money. We've always paid it back, and when we've overspent, it has given me terrible headaches. I think that the cut has to be 100 percent. I'll consult the social movements and the national leadership of the MAS."

The vice president didn't seem to support a cut of that size.

Evo said that the armed forces would receive $50,000 for sheets, repairs of the barrack bathrooms, and to solve other problems.

He moved his hands to lean on the table, transitioning to the agricultural revolution and directing his words at two of the ministers present:

Compañera Celinda [Sosa, of Production and Micro Enterprise], I'm concerned that there aren't enough sugar cane milk processing machines. Brazil is moving toward biofuel and the value of cane is going to rise.... *Compañera* Susana [Rivero, of Rural Development], we've got to create a very large State Cooperative Mill.... I'm upset with the vice minister of gender and generational matters (Maruja Machaca).... We have to get rid of her, even if she is a *compañera*. Let the Federation [of Women] propose candidates to us.

The third woman present, the minister of justice and *cocalero* leader, Celima Torrico, wearing Colón shoes, a traditional maroon skirt, a white blouse, and her hair tied back, spoke very little. But she spoke more than the minister of water, Abel Mamani, who didn't even open his mouth.

The minister of treasury requested an information technology revolution. "We don't have data, statistics. If an investor comes to Bolivia wanting to open a pharmacy, he won't know how many there are."

"The measures we have taken are good," Evo concluded, "but we have to follow up. You are a minister [of education], but you've been acting as a union leader.... Thanks for the meeting, *compañeros*."

Some of them applauded.

A few minutes later, the president began a press conference with foreign correspondents to wage the battle against the constitutional tribunal outside of the country. "It's illegal. Instead of justice in Bolivia, we have injustice. The court is seen as the most corrupt of the powers of State."

He went down to the central hall, filled with workers in yellow overalls with the inscription Tupiza Micro Enterprise, Bolivian Administration of Roads, Potosí. The hostess and the one responsible for the roads, Patricia Ballivián, was conversing with the president of the Inter-American Development Bank (IDB), Alberto Moreno. She had a modern look with her black sweater, corduroy pants, and bodily posture, but with white pearl earrings lending a conservative note.

A poet burst into the room reciting lyrics to the roads, and he moved around as if possessed by his own words. Afterward, offerings for Morales were presented. García Linera and Moreno arrived with wool and cloth hats, ponchos, and a few other items. The IDB president wasn't much taller than four feet and nine inches, and the hat they gave him went past his ears, making him look even smaller.

"When we met with the president for the first time," Moreno said from the lectern, "he took out a map and talked about the march up North. 'Development is in the roads,' he told me. His dream is to connect the jungle with the sierra and to unite Bolivia, South to North."

Evo reciprocated the praise in the first part of his speech:

Today we commence the longed-awaited plan, march toward the north. East and west, west and east will be united with this $120 million credit.... The IDB forgave us a billion dollars, but they go on lending, and they don't have any conditions except that we spend the money. The conditions of the past are no longer.

In the second half of his speech, he scrutinized the construction estimates and the pre-feasibility and feasibility studies, nearly sacred to the IDB.

"Forgive my candor, Señor Moreno," Evo closed.

Sunk deep in his armchair, Moreno gave him the best smile he had for situations like this.

On May 21, I spent the last afternoon I had with Morales in his office. Alone, recently arisen from his *siesta*, his hair wet at the tips, his eyes narrowed, and his coppery skin imprinted by his pillow, he was sitting at the head of the table with his back to Plaza Murillo. By the tenuous late afternoon sunlight, he wrote down that week's activities, slowly and in print letters. His planner is a black notebook customized with presidential letterhead, in which the red lines begin at 4:00 A.M. and end at 1:00 A.M. They don't make commercial planners for his routine.

"You must be the only president who annotates his own meetings," I said.

"It's just that I'm fed up with some of the secretaries: They mess up their work sometimes," Morales replied.

Evo's memory allowed him to fill in all of the activities hour by hour: He jotted down his soccer games, inaugurations, speeches, and travels. When he forgot the name of a school, he called on Chancellor Choquehuanca to recall it.

As Morales continued to be absorbed in his agenda, he wrote coliseum with an "s," but then hesitated and asked me whether it was spelled with a "c" or an "s." He proceeded to run other spelling doubts by me. He didn't get embarrassed. It's just another rupture with the times. Before, the president of Bolivia, in addition to being white or *mestizo* (of European descent), had to demonstrate certain knowledge learned at university, school, the armed forces, or other predetermined social circles. Morales came without that knowledge, without the general culture of the middle and upper class, and has demonstrated the flaw of this imperative of the educated chief of state.

Evo's midday bad mood had already lifted. He'd gotten angry when he found out that they didn't give lunch to the *campesinos* from the northern Potosí *ayllus*, who had come to the Palace to resolve a conflict. "We *campesinos* eat a lot," he explained. In those details, he makes use of a certain dose of his stature. He feels that he should take care of *campesinos* visiting the Palace so that they know the president cares about them.

That morning he was very hard on the police chiefs: "Are you guys going to take care of me or am I going to take care of you?" The week before, one of the police guards had leaked to the press where Evo sometimes sleeps. Thus, he decided to replace the police guarding the third floor of the Palace with civil guards. The police chiefs responded with apologies and compliance but requested, as does every institution that deals with the executive, equipment and training. In other words, they wanted money.

His communication advisor, Víctor Orduna, joined the table with a press release published in the daily paper *La Razón* about the supposed influence of Hugo Chávez over Morales. The president asked whether it was worth the trouble to respond. Orduna assured him that the release didn't offer any new information and that it contained errors. One of the mistakes made him laugh. According to the article, the Venezuelans would conspire in the Ritz Hotel in La Paz. He dialed the number of the Venezuelan ambassador, Julio Montes.

"Yes, with Julio. It's Evo calling."

Morales joked with the ambassador about that release. "Julio wouldn't go to the Ritz even to use it as a one-hour motel," he'd later say. García Linera told him that CNN was trying to interview the vice president on the *La Razón* story. "It's not worth it," Morales concluded.

Llorenti told him about how they'd tossed a coin to elect the first presidential delegate from Potosí. Morales asked who it was, hugging the wooden table. That gesture revealed his nervousness, as did few others. He slammed his fists on the table, lifted his pant legs to scratch himself, and asked the palace waiter for something to eat because, he said, he'd barely had any lunch.

The most serious member of his intimate circle, Minister of Government Alfredo Rada, arrived. Morales explained that they made jokes in the Palace to reduce tension. "Even *compañero* Alfredo laughs with us now." The minister affirmed with a nod and, becoming serious again, gave an overview of the transportation strike.

"There is no reason to stray from our proposal, but there doesn't have to be a roadblock tomorrow, and they should come here to negotiate," the president demanded.

Rada had more bad news: Cooperative workers were threatening more blockades, and fresh conflicts with unions and social organizations were beginning to emerge.

García Linera, sitting in front of the president with his open laptop, was suffering from the pain of a recently operated hernia. The president of the Chamber of Deputies, Edmundo Novillo, joined them. He recounted how negotiations over the law of education had gone and that he was waiting on the plan for the submayors' law. "Get it done, big boss," Evo told him while reading the daily newspapers of Oruro and Potosí. Last, Novillo reported that the opposition was trying to negotiate positions to maintain a subcommittee in parliament.

While Novillo was speaking, Morales burst out laughing. He showed the room the cover of a local newspaper featuring Evo with another man standing in front of a mock-up of a building. He explained how the other man had shut right up when Evo ascertained that the construction would cost 50 percent less than what he proposed. "There are many crooks," he concluded as he grabbed the freshly baked *cuñapé* (cheese bun) that they brought with his afternoon coffee.

Llorenti pointed out that the government criticisms of the judicial system had been well received in radio surveys. Sixty-two percent said that the church should dedicate itself to prayer and politics (the minister of the presidency had said that the church had to pick one or the other). They reviewed the statements of the Pope, who declared in his Latin American tour that evangelization in the New World did not represent the imposition of a foreign culture, and he addressed, without giving names, the continent's authoritarian governments. García Linera tried to contain the president's ire so he wouldn't issue a response. Evo recalled how a Cochabamba bishop once tried to buy him off many years back.

They brought him an official agenda, over which he laid down his cell phones. The vice president told him that the MAS could rely on a majority in the security committee in the Constituent Assembly—but that two of its deputies defended the interests of the police more than those of the governmental party. Morales asked García Linera to meet with the deputies. The group discussed a flurry of subjects. The president said that he was worried about agriculture and the People's Trade Agreements. He called for ideas for a speech in a seminar on the defense of humankind. "Beyond Iraq and ecology, what else can I say?" he asked.

He suggested that I come with him on the tour through the city of Sucre—similar to the one through Tarija—and that I stop going back to Argentina.

"You know I can blockade the airport, right?" Evo asked.

When I responded that I would try to go to Sucre with him, he gave me his hand, and I understood that he was asking me to leave his office.

"I'm not throwing you out. When I want someone out of the Palace, I say to him, 'Get out,' and he goes."

In Oruro, when he was ten years old, they took the first photo of him. *Personal archive of Evo Morales*

The only known picture of Morales in a tie, during the last year of high school in Oruro, 1977. *Personal archive of Evo Morales*

Military Service in La Paz, 1978. *Personal archive of Evo Morales*

In a *campesino* march, 1994. *Personal archive of Evo Morales*

In 2007, during his second August 6 (Bolivian Independence Day) as President. *Photo: Noah Friedman-Rudovsky*

Delivering a speech from the Burned Palace to a crowd gathered at Plaza Murillo in the city of La Paz. *Photo: Noah Friedman-Rudovsky*

A truck painted with Morales' face used in the 2005 electoral campaign. *Photo: Noah Friedman-Rudovsky*

With a garland of coca leaves in a rally at El Chapare, Cochabamba. *Photo: Noah Friedman-Rudovsky*

Wearing his famous sweater in a meeting with *campesino* representatives. *Photo: Noah Friedman-Rudovsky*

Attending a ritual in Tiwanaku (La Paz department) with indigenous leaders from all over the continent in October 2006. *Photo: Noah Friedman-Rudovsky*

In Cota Cota, near Lake Titicaca, during one of the games in which the presidential team lost. *Photo: Noah Friedman-Rudovsky*

A rally in Yamparaez (Chuquisaca department) during March of 2007. *Photo: Noah Friedman-Rudovsky*

With Hugo Chávez, on one of his visits to Bolivia. *Photo: Noah Friedman-Rudovsky*

On a visit to Havana, with his two main allies outside of Bolivia: Fidel Castro and Hugo Chávez (April of 2006). *Bolivian Information Agency*

Presenting a coca leaf during his first speech in the United Nations headquarters (New York, September of 2006) *Photo: Noah Friedman-Rudovsky*

At an International Summit with new colleagues such as Angela Merkel, Michelle Bachelet, Jacques Chirac, and the former Secretary General of the United Nations, Kofi Annan. *Photo: Noah Friedman-Rudovsky*

Chapter Six

NOW IS WHEN
(2003–2006)

For its elite, the Bolivian east represents modernity, free enterprise, success, and the gateway for the country into the rest of the world. They see themselves as friendly, hospitable, and devout entrepreneurs. The west, according to them, represents stagnation, Indians, leftism, and isolation. The east is an archipelago of departments led by Santa Cruz, the richest of the country. Extending from the vast *Chaqueña* plain to the Amazon and the Andean foothills, Santa Cruz cultivates soybeans, extracts gas and petroleum, and enjoys warm temperatures. The west, whose symbolic center is La Paz, stretches over a high, cold plain. The minerals that were once its wealth, silver and tin, have recovered markets and something of their previous value in recent years.

In October 2003, during the fall of Goni Sánchez de Lozada, Bolivians and the world witnessed the clash—not just ideological—between the east and the west. In Santa Cruz, the majority followed the uprising in La Paz and El Alto as a spectacle that burst forth from their televisions. In the city of Santa Cruz de la Sierra, there was a minor confrontation between two groups. *Campesino*, indigenous, and student sectors marched in demand of the president's resignation. They faced activists from the Pro–Santa Cruz Committee and other similar organizations calling for institutional continuity—that is to say, the continuation of Goni in the government—and supporting the exportation of gas to the United States via Chile. The battle was waged in 24 de Septiembre Plaza—the main city square—which the allied groups of the Pro–Santa Cruz Committee eventually occupied. They celebrated by singing the anthem of the department.

The Pro–Santa Cruz Committee, self-titled the "moral government of people of Santa Cruz," is the major representative of the Santa Cruz elite and Santa Cruz-ism in the conflict with the west. By 2003, they could rely on extensive social support and a great ability to mobilize the middle class.

During the October uprising, the committee underwent a radical change. After the forced resignation of Sánchez de Lozada, it called for a fundamental transformation of the political system "to avoid the excision of Santa Cruz from Bolivia." From their point of view, the country was mutating. The social movements of the west had brought down a president and managed to set up the so-called October agenda, demanding the nationalization of natural resources and the convening of a constituent assembly that would refound the country. The eastern elite launched a series of maxims: autonomy, election of prefects (governors), and the end of roadblocks. "Now it's possible to easternize the westerners," declared Rubén Costas, the then-president of the committee.

From the perspective of the Santa Cruz elite, the history of Santa Cruz's relationship with the west had been one of denigration, scorn, and imposition.

During the nineteenth entury, Santa Cruz felt discriminated against and neglected; twice the department rose up in arms demanding a new relationship with the Central State. In 1876, the rebellion was led by federalist Andrés Ibáñez, whose egalitarian discourse rallied the opposition of the elite in his land. In 1891, the Revolution of the Domingos (Sundays) took place, named thus because it began on a Sunday and because of the names of the military leaders who headed it: Domingo Ardaya and José Domingo Ávila. Both putsches failed, but they initiated a series of demands from Santa Cruz to the Central State.

Later on, during the first half of the twentieth century, the Santa Cruz elite requested integration through peaceful means. In the first three decades, they prioritized the construction of a railroad, to connect east and west. The 1952 National Revolution, led by the Nationalist Revolutionary Movement (MNR), became the main unifying force between the west and Santa Cruz. The MNR launched the "March Toward the East" plan. With the goal of economic diversification—to make the country less dependent on mining—they populated large expanses of territory in Santa Cruz and the neighboring departments. The Santa Cruz elite, represented by the Pro–Santa Cruz Committee (founded in 1950) and by the Bolivian Socialist Phalanx (FSB), defeated the MNR and governed the city between 1957 and 1959, when the Central Power used the armed forces to recover control of Santa Cruz. The committee suspended its activities until 1965.

During the 1960s, Santa Cruz sought to modernize itself, demanding services such as water and sewage. Because these services never came, the city built them using its own resources. The elite have stressed these achievements to establish the idea that today's Santa Cruz de la Sierra is a city created without the support of the Central State. Water, electricity, and other services are in the hands of cooperatives run by two of the city's secret societies, Gentlemen of the East and Toborochis.

In August 1971, the Santa Cruz elite collaborated in the coup that brought Hugo Banzer Suárez to power, one of the three Santa Cruz presidents in Bolivian history. Banzer's dictatorship from 1971 to 1978 propelled the first great Santa Cruz economic boom. He granted many benefits to the most powerful inhabitants of the region, including state credits and a devaluation that benefited agro-exporters. He also gave over state lands to a group of Banzer supporters and wealthy families. Drug trafficking played a role in this expansion, and it wasn't minor, according to what academic and journalistic investigations have revealed.

The second moment of significant economic boom took place after the implementation of neoliberal measures in 1985. Foreign investments in petroleum and hydrocarbons, such as those made by YPF-Repsol and Petrobrás, along with profits from the agricultural industry, transformed Santa Cruz into Bolivia's economic engine and the primary destination for internal migrants. The population of the department's capital grew from 50,000 inhabitants to 1.2 million over 30 years. According to sociologist Fernando Calderón, the end of the twentieth century found Santa Cruz "more Bolivian than ever." But in the first years of the twenty-first century, it would find itself in more conflict with the west than ever. Evo Morales, an incarnation of the western highlands, became a favorite target for attacks leveraged from the east. He wasn't the only one.

On October 17, 2003, after replacing Sánchez de Lozada in the presidency, Carlos Mesa assumed the role of tightrope walker. He tried to establish a balance among the east, west, other political players, and the Congress, in which the traditional political parties were still in the majority.

He also struggled with the pressures of foreign businesses and governments, which, faced with uncertainty, demanded guarantees. Mesa lacked his own party and experience as a politician and as an administrator.

The president received me in his office on the first Thursday in December 2003. The Palace, silent and deserted, reflected the lack of confidence in his staying in power.

"From an objective point of view, the worst that can happen to a person these days is to become the president of Bolivia," he began with a smile, and it wasn't easy to refute.

To explain how he would continue to govern, he stood up from his armchair, revealing his six-foot stature, and looked for a poll that gave him 82 percent approval.

He believed in those statistics but more still in his oratory capacity. Mesa's presidency was a long succession of speeches delivered from memory. He wanted to prolong his relationship with the public through the good image he'd earned in his career as a journalist, television anchor, and historian.

Other presidents snubbed him. He had confirmed a meeting with Néstor Kirchner on November 15 in the Ibero-American Summit in Santa Cruz, but the Argentine missed the appointment. He did, however, meet with Morales, who had become a parallel chief and leader of the anti-summit that was mounted in the city.

Kirchner, like the U.S. government and Hugo Chávez, expected his government to be short-lived. But Washington was more concerned about Morales' future influence. Days after his meeting with Kirchner, a U.S. official brought a document to the Argentine chancellor, in which the *cocalero* leader was defined as a "Narcotics-Terrorist."

Evo's relationship with the Mesa administration had a foundational moment. It occurred when Morales opposed the creation of a revolutionary junta, after Sánchez de Lozada's fall, with a package of radical measures, including the expropriation of oil companies that some organizations were pushing. Costly as it was for Evo to expose himself to left-wing criticism, he still contributed to the presidential succession of Mesa.

At the outset, Morales wanted to establish a coexistence with Mesa. To his political team, he held that they should support the new president in order to attain certain demands of their own, such as the Constituent Assembly and a new hydrocarbons law. He announced that they would refuse positions in the executive branch despite Mesa's insistence to the contrary. In the meantime, with the 2007 elections in mind, he organized a better strategy for his party so they could win over municipal governments and prepare for the management of the state.

His connection with the president was always cold. Not even as a journalist had Mesa established a relationship with the MAS chief. Evo got along better with ground-level reporters and almost never with editors and media proprietors. In fact, when he assumed the vice presidency, Mesa requested a private dinner with him so the two could get to know each other personally, but Morales turned him down. All of the connections Morales establishes are political. When he goes to eat barbecue, he chooses his *compañeros* or other people within his trust. And he'd always mistrusted Mesa.

The president desperately needed the social peace that Evo could bring him, along with the certainty of the MAS bench's support in parliament. In their first meetings, respectful but distant, Mesa tried to offer him something in exchange. If things went well for him, then Morales would find a favorable setting for his electoral aspirations.

During that same interview in the Palace, Mesa said that he tried to work "with a minimum level of dignity" when it came to the United States. Washington provided $94 million in aid annually, demanding in return a complete eradication of the coca crops. The United States accepted Mesa's coexistence with Morales because the MAS leader had become a protagonist in Bolivian politics. But the U.S. embassy didn't accept him as an interlocutor; they continued to consider him part of the drug-trafficking problem and not the solution.

Mesa struck a balance between both sides. He signed an agreement so that each *cocalero* family remained with a *cato* (2.5 acres) of coca crops.

The accusations of being pro-government made Evo uncomfortable. In an interview, he said:

They called me a llama, a policeman, a trumpet-player. In the White House, they call me a Narcotics-Terrorist. [...] They call me pro-government without understanding that the MAS has a right to support the government in some proposals for the country. What do I think of Mesa? He's a prisoner of the parties of the economic model, of the U.S. embassy, of some social sectors. He wants everyone to like him. He wants to be good with the IMF and the World Bank and the people.

In May 2004, Morales' relationship with Mesa underwent a crisis
when the president approved a law in Congress that gave U.S. troops
immunity to enter Bolivia. It led to the end of Morales' association with
Filemón Escobar, the old Trotskyite leader who spent 14 years politically
and ideologically shaping the *cocaleros* in El Chapare and propping up the
political career of their leader. Neither Filemón nor the MAS senators
attended the session in which the plan was converted into a law. "That
is a betrayal," declared Morales. Afterward, he accused Escobar of having been bought off with $50,000 that he then divvied up among the
bench. He accused him of being a CIA agent and the senators of being
"money-grubbers."

Escobar, a fierce defender of maintaining an understanding with Mesa,
denied the accusations. He argued that he and the senators weren't delib-
erately absent, but that they were meeting with their bench, a circumstance
that the president of the Senate, Hormando Vaca Diez, took advantage of
so he could pass the law. Since then, they haven't stopped attacking and
accusing each other.

Another important difference between Evo and Mesa was the July 2004
Referendum, in which Mesa looked to legitimize his hydrocarbon policies.
Before pronouncing himself in favor of or against the five points of the
policies that he would have to share with the country, he showed them to
Morales, who supported the first three. He was in favor of the abolition
of Sánchez de Lozada's Law of Hydrocarbons, the recovery of the ownership of all the oil and gas in the well heads of the Bolivian state wells, and
the re-founding of the Bolivian State Petroleum Company (YPFB). By
contrast, he didn't accept the strategic use of gas to recover "a useful and
sovereign exit out to the Pacific Ocean" or that the Bolivian state collect
taxes and/or royalties from oil companies, "arriving at 50 percent of the
value of the gas and petroleum production in favor of the country." That
sum seemed low to him. In that meeting with Morales, Mesa tried to gain
Evo's support of the five questions, saying that he was open to making
changes. But to the president's frustration, Evo rushed ahead and made
his position public.

The day that Mesa won the July 18 Referendum—even though the last
two questions received fewer votes than the first three—he called Morales
to discuss the proposal of the hydrocarbons law that he would send to
Congress.

"I am in Cochabamba, I can't...I'll call you back," Evo said.

Later on, the president constructed a theory about Morales' strategy: "He always knew," Mesa would tell me during an interview in 2006, "that he couldn't allow me the breathing room to grow politically and potentially occupy the center and the left-center. He couldn't strangle me until he had the strength to strangle me."

One of the mediators between the two of them, La Paz mayor Juan del Granado, saw that the president's contemptuous attitude and Morales' distrust hindered their relationship. Mesa—the mayor further explained—believed that he could politically transform from transition guarantor to actual transition leader. But Evo wouldn't allow it.

During the discussion of the new hydrocarbons law, their differences grew. Mesa proposed a 32 percent tax and 18 percent of royalties, whereas the MAS were requesting 50 percent of royalties. Evo publicly warned the president that he could end up like Goni, and he ordered him not to export gas until legislation was passed. Susceptible to pressures from the companies, Mesa allowed his great friend and right-hand man, the minister of the presidency, Pepe Galindo, to establish a close relationship with Petrobrás.

The president sought to contain Morales through Hugo Chávez. Intelligence reports indicated the existence of a financing mechanism from Caracas to the MAS that could never be proven. Mesa came to the conclusion that, although Chávez supported Felipe Quispe initially, after 2002 he began to bet on Morales.

Mesa asked Chávez to show the Venezuelan model to Evo and to explain to him why the type of nationalization that the MAS intended wasn't possible. He overestimated the influence of Chávez, while not giving Morales the credit due him.

Evo's blows against Mesa stopped when a worse successor came into view. In November 2004, Morales denounced a conspiracy between powerful Bolivian groups and the U.S. embassy to make Vaca Diez the chief of state. This wasn't the only time Evo chose Mesa as the lesser evil. He also supported the controversial agreement with Argentina, in which Bolivia committed to selling gas at $1 per million BTU. They called it a "solidarity" price, but they should have called it a "throw-away" price. In the next agreement signed by Bolivia and Argentina, with Morales as president, the price went up to $5.

Santa Cruz continued to put on the pressure. The first big mobilization organized by the Pro–Santa Cruz Committee was the June 22, 2004 open council meeting. According to the daily paper *El Deber*, 50,000 people participated. The so-called June agenda included a regional demand, autonomy, and a national one, social pacification. In this way, they tried to counterbalance the October agenda.

"The Santa Cruz elite have a provincial vision," Mesa stated on October 24, 2004, after receiving pressures from the committee to accelerate the process of autonomy. The eastern civic movement responded with a strike, threatened "civil resistance to centralism," and demanded the official announcement of a referendum before the end of the year. The elite saw the president as Morales' puppet. Some of the Santa Cruz media launched an aggressive campaign against him, in which vengeful Goni supporters participated. When the president called Oswaldo Monasterios, the patriarch of a family with great landholdings and owner of the television station Unitel, to seek a truce, he received an unexpected response: "Mr. Monasterios is taking his *siesta*, and nobody is to disturb him." Monasterios never returned the call.

The municipal elections in December 2004 deepened the regionalization of politics, given that the local parties took the main cities. That damaged Morales. Although the MAS party received the most votes, with 17 percent, it was less than they'd expected. Morales interpreted this to mean that coexistence with Mesa had a negative impact on his electoral chances; he took that into account for what was yet to come.

The government's decision to raise the price of diesel on the last day of 2004 resulted in a miracle—the west and east found the same reason to protest. The president said in a speech that the inability to reconcile two extremes were what was keeping him from being able to govern. One "wants to change the economic model, nationalize, and throw foreign companies from the country," whereas the other "wants to preserve the neoliberal order and its private interests."

On January 28, the Pro–Santa Cruz Committee held another council meeting, which it claimed 280,000 people attended (170,000 according to the police). The speech given by Costas, their president, took on a triumphant spirit as he announced that it was "the first day of autonomy." In addition to attacking Morales ("We can't let people outside of Bolivia think that we're just a bunch of *cocaleros*") and the president ("We have the right to a government that governs"), he attempted to establish the idea that autonomy was inevitable.

The United States publicly zeroed in on Morales. On January 20, former army chief of the U.S. Southern Command, General James Hill, had stated that Chávez was financing Morales. Three weeks later, the brand-new secretary of state, Condoleezza Rice, mentioned Bolivia in a hearing before the Senate Committee on Foreign Relations. She said that there was something "strange" going on with the strengthening of a "party of coca cultivators." She concluded, "We're very concerned about that party."

In the beginning of March, Morales, who had requested that Mesa's term of government be shortened, launched a national roadblock that was to last until Congress voted for the hydrocarbons law and called for a Constituent Assembly. He wanted to capitalize on popular dissatisfaction with the president.

Mesa resigned on March 6. In his speech, he justified the decision based on Morales' protests, whom he mentioned 25 times, compared with the seven times he said his own name. In an unusually aggressive manner, Mesa pointed his finger at the MAS boss, as he'd never before done to anyone throughout his entire career as a journalist, historian, and politician.

Evo Morales, with whom I have spoken many times and to whom I've explained this reality in great detail, has a talent for going out and blockading Bolivia. [...] You, sir, come up here and govern, and you'll see what it means to manage the State and just what responsibilities a man of State has. And you, honorable Evo Morales, are now the boss of the opposition, so you can no longer allow yourself the luxury of going out into the streets like a union leader. You're a union leader who sits comfortably in his chair and says: "Blockade, everyone, let's all go out and create a blockade."

At first, the speech benefited Mesa. The opposition refused his resignation in parliament, and he managed to weaken the legitimacy of the blockades and to limit them geographically. A pro-Mesa current emerged in Bolivian society, especially in the middle class, who sealed their support with the so-called March of White Scarves, in which they demanded that the two extremes let the president govern.

Morales was attacked in an airport on the day of the resignation announcement. A group of passengers criticized him for organizing blockades and then eluding them by air travel. He was insulted in the street and even spit at. "This is a war against us," he warned the then-Deputy Antonio Peredo, who had also experienced social rejection. A survey taken after the president's resignation announcement showed that in the four main cities of the country (Santa Cruz, El Alto, La Paz, and Cochabamba), disapproval of Morales rose to 73 percent. His team predicted that Mesa would reaffirm his government and remain in command until 2007.

Evo was battered and bewildered. At that point, someone who would become a key participant in his intimate circle reappeared in 2005, journalist and editor Walter Chávez. Although he worked on the 2002 campaign, he'd distanced himself because he questioned the compromises made with Mesa. "That asshole will always deny the Indians the chance to represent themselves," Chávez said in characteristic frankness. He urged Evo to confront the Mesa movement even further. At that time, another faction of Morales' circle, which included the editor José Antonio Quiroga, advocated a better understanding with the president.

Evo listens more during the biggest crises, such as that of March 6, when he listened to everyone. "I'm going to fight him and bring him down," he told Chávez. To demonstrate the strength of his position, he refused to sign a "national salvation agreement" proposed by Mesa, to be put into effect at times of national crises. He abruptly cut ties with Quiroga, whom he accused of being a traitor. He decided to lean on a camp, consisting of a revitalized and more radical Bolivian Worker's Center (COB) and the ever-intransigent Felipe Quispe, who had once accused him of being progovernment. His future, all of the sudden, loomed uncertain.

The Pro–Santa Cruz Committee didn't realize that this was an opportunity to compromise with the president. In a clear example of its inability to understand the national dimension of the crisis, it proclaimed a "de facto government" if it wasn't granted autonomy. The Santa Cruz elite didn't see any reason for their agenda to take into consideration Mesa's weakness, the demands of the west, or Congress' lack of legitimacy. They continued to believe, despite all evidence to the contrary, that Mesa was Morales' puppet. Facing Mesa's potential fall, ex-president Jorge "Tuto" Quiroga, a Santa Cruz ally, concluded that he would become the victorious electoral option.

On the outside, the hypothesis of an armed conflict or secessionist situation gained momentum. In a private meeting toward the end of March, U.S. Secretary of Defense Donald Rumsfeld remarked to his Argentine colleague José Pampuro that he saw a "disintegration crisis" in Bolivia as imminent—two rebel sides and territorial struggle for power. "Bolivia is the new Haiti," he asserted, suggesting that they should consider a scenario with a multilateral force to prevent the country from being ripped asunder.

After the resignation speech, Hugo Chávez called Mesa to offer his condolences about the situation. While they cut his hair and gave him a shave in the Burned Palace bathroom, the president of Bolivia asked him to mediate: "I can't govern without party or parliament. If Morales doesn't want me to govern, he's going to throw me out. Get him to think about it, Hugo."

"I think I've made a mistake in the way I've been supporting Evo," Chávez replied, according to Mesa's version. "Let me talk to him. I'll call you back."

The Venezuelan never called back. Morales had decided to take more radical steps. In an MAS meeting at the beginning of May, having recently returned from a trip to Cuba, he said that they had to insist on the October agenda. "Evo has decided to be president," determined David Choquehuanca, one of the leaders who knew him best.

La Paz was already blockaded by social organizations demanding that Congress modify the hydrocarbons law and set up the Constituent Assembly. On June 6, after Congress failed in its attempt to call a referendum for autonomy and to organize the Assembly, Mesa resigned for the third and last time.

Hours before recording his message, the president met with U.S. Ambassador David Greenlee in the home of Pepe Galindo. Mesa insisted that the succession should remain in the hands of Eduardo Rodríguez Veltzé, who was the president of the Supreme Court at the time.

"Hormando [Vaca Diez, president of the Senate and first in line for the presidential succession] is the best option," the diplomat answered. "It's insane for it to be Rodríguez Veltzé because he doesn't have any political experience."

Vaca Diez was an astute Santa Cruz senator who represented the country's so-called old politics. He could count on the full support of the Pro–Santa Cruz Committee and had convinced Greenlee that he could put things in order within three days. He assured the ambassador that authority was what the country needed. Greenlee told Mesa, "with the preventative presence of the armed forces, everything [would] calm down." They didn't talk about deaths, but among analysts and commentators, the fear was having to count them by the hundreds.

Morales called Mesa after the resignation message was broadcast.

"Why did you resign?" Morales asked in a friendly tone.

"You're the one who asked for my resignation, Evo," the president answered.

"You're playing the right-wing's game," Morales retorted.

Evo made a toast that night with a 12-year-old rum given to him by Fidel Castro. He said that they had to keep Vaca Diez from coming into power.

The battle for succession grew dramatic. The Bolivian press and the world speculated about the possibility of a civil war. Another president had fallen, there was no successor in sight or any kind of agreement between the east and west, and 90 protests were recorded throughout the country.

After the failure of a church mediation, Mesa asked for a gesture from Vaca Diez and Mario Cossío, the president of the Chamber of Deputies—that they not take over the presidency because of the risks it would entail.

Vaca Diez moved the session dealing with Mesa's resignation to Sucre, given that it wasn't safe for Congress to meet in La Paz. Fourteen thousand soldiers were mobilized to ensure his succession. Vaca Diez guaranteed that the MAS parliament members, led by Evo, would arrive last. Morales wouldn't even deal with him and delegated that task to Antonio Peredo. From the hotel, he coordinated mobilizations heading to Sucre with the objective of impeding the assumption of the president of the Senate.

In those last hours, Vaca Diez deployed his talents as a wily deal maker to promise the reestablishment of order to the U.S. embassy, a nationalization of gas to the radicals, and the implementation of the Santa Cruz agenda to the elites of that region, among other things. He brought his family to Sucre to watch his inauguration. He even committed a gaffe in front of the press: "I am president of the Republic, excuse me, president of Congress."

The death of Juan Carlos Coro Mayta, a mining cooperative leader who was marching toward Sucre, contributed to the erosion of Vaca Diez's plans. He was killed by a bullet in a never-clarified incident. When Vaca Diez heard about Mayta's death, he called Peredo to tell him that he'd move the Congress meeting elsewhere to avoid new marches. But he had to abort the plan. Military leaders cautioned him that the meeting had to be done in Sucre while rumors of a coup d'etat and the pressures for his resignation were rapidly multiplying.

Everything could have changed between 9:00 and 9:30 P.M. that night. Mesa was on the verge of retracting his resignation with the argument that Congress couldn't handle it. The plan consisted of staying on to manage the electoral process and enact great measures by decree. At that prospect, many of Mesa's formal and informal advisors suggested that he close parliament and seek an understanding with the armed forces. Because the president was thinking of his governmental role in terms of the place he would hold in history, he refused. He would have gone down as the chief of state who put a padlock on Congress.

While Mesa was weighing different scenarios and possibilities with his advisors, Vaca Diez made public his resignation from the presidential succession, and Cossío followed suit.

A year after those turbulent days of June 2005, in his Santa Cruz de la Sierra mansion, with the two SUVs that he'd been deprived of in his times as a humble, left-wing journalist, Vaca Diez told me that two deciding factors prevented him from becoming president, his status as a citizen of Santa Cruz and Carlos Mesa. "Someone like me from Santa Cruz had to ask permission to be Bolivian and I am Bolivian without anybody's permission."

The night of Monday, June 6, 2005, I called Rodríguez Veltzé from Buenos Aires.

"Sir, I've been told that you will be the next president."

"That's impossible: You're mistaken," he replied from Sucre.

Almost one year later, in the living room of an Oxford University residence building, he remembered that it had been one of the few calls he received during those hours, and it brought him a certain peace—there had been so few betting on him.

On Thursday, June 9, his young children went off to bed knowing that their father had a long night of work ahead. He awoke them early the next morning and gave them the news of his new title, President of the Republic. He had been sworn in 15 minutes after midnight, but without the presidential sash, a shiny medal, or any kind of ceremony. "I felt," he would recall for the interview, "an initial anxiety." Taking stock of the disorder in the streets was important to him. Furthermore, the internal situation of the armed forces was complicated. According to the information he gathered, several political parties had contacted the military High Command in the weeks before he assumed office looking for some kind of mutual agreement.

His primary objective was to establish a transitional government until the general elections of December 2005.

Morales endeavored to have a friendly relationship with Rodríguez Veltzé. He had dinner with the president a few days after he took control. Evo advised him to put all of Congress up for vote in the election, and he made it clear that the MAS would be part of the transitional government.

Rodríguez Veltzé adopted the same policies with Morales as with the other possible presidential contenders. In moments of turbulence, he would call them to the Palace. "Are we going to make it to the election? What should we do about this situation?" he asked Evo a few times.

The president knew that he had to coexist with what he calls "the U.S. omnipresence in the Bolivian State." But he never imagined that omnipresence would set off the missile scandal. Bolivia possessed 28 Chinese HN-5 anti-aircraft missiles, similar to those used by the Iraqi resistance and the Taliban to bring down U.S. helicopters. The U.S. embassy previously requested that Mesa hand over the arms, but he refused. With Rodríguez Veltzé in the Burned Palace, the missiles were taken from the country and deactivated in a covert operation coordinated by Washington in October 2005, according to what was reported by the weekly magazine *Pulso.*

Despite the missile incident, Veltzé managed to bring Bolivia together for the presidential election. The battle between the east and west was waged yet again, personified this time by Tuto Quiroga and Morales, respectively.

In the summer of 1995, the La Paz daily paper *Hoy* was housed in two floors in the Brasilia Building. It was a gloomy place with fluorescent lights, ancient computers, liquidation furniture, and theater curtains hanging in front of the director's office. Hernán Terrazas was an enthusiastic editor-in-chief. A short guy with frizzy hair and a mustache that he once tried to make into a handlebar, he wore vests, smoked Virginias, and tried to make *Hoy* look like Argentina's *Página/12.* After leaving the paper, Terrazas was called on by Vice President Tuto Quiroga (who would later become president in 2001) to join the government. He ended up becoming the minister of information and Quiroga's right-hand man. In the 2005 election, he felt as if he were once again on the Palace's threshold. So did Walter Chávez.

Chávez worked for *Hoy* as chief editor of culture. He could read up to three books in one day or edit 16 pages in one afternoon. He had come from his native Peru in 1992 as a political refugee and began to make himself known in Bolivian cultural circles. After working for *Hoy* and in the Grafulik family's multimedia organizations, he published *El Juguete Rabioso (Furious Toy),* a biweekly publication that he also was in charge of distributing. *El Juguete Rabioso* was sharp and corrosive. It would do anything from tearing the latest editorial novelty apart to attacking ministers, all the while causing a good many of the people Chávez knew to stop talking to him. He also became the director of the Bolivian edition of *Le monde diplomatique*. But he wasn't planning to travel to summits with the farmer José Bové or sign requests in favor of good causes. Since 2002, when he participated in Morales' campaign, he'd come back to politics.

In their years at *Hoy*, Chávez and Terrazas got along well, and the owner of the paper, Samuel Doria Medina, believed in both of them. In 2005, Doria Medina, a heavy-set guy with a beard, was a millionaire thanks to his cement factory and other more lucrative investments than *Hoy*, and ran for the presidency through National Unity, a party that was run more like a company. During the campaign, he started off leading the polls because, given the Morales-Quiroga polarization, he presented himself as the candidate of a reasonable center.

The world of Bolivian politics was that small and that informal. A decade after 1995, the three men of *Hoy* were in three of the most important positions in the presidential election.

Because Morales didn't specify titles but did assign duties, Chávez became, in essence, his campaign manager. He panicked when he read that 80 percent of campaigns are lost due to bad strategy, and he asked Evo to contract a foreign campaign manager. "We wouldn't be honest," Morales responded, "if we say we are going to nationalize and then we hand the campaign over to a Brazilian or a Gringo."

So Chávez, a Peruvian who lived in La Paz, borrowed from the experiences of an Argentine and a Chilean to carry out a Bolivian campaign. He based his strategy on the five points of the campaign of Salvador Allende and read Miguel Bonasso's book, *El Presidente que no fue* (*The President Who Wasn't*) to learn about Héctor J. Cámpora's rise to his ephemeral government in Argentina in 1973. But Chávez stripped the MAS platform of any type of 1970s radicalism and adapted the ideas of a union leader without university tradition who opts for fiery oratory.

"Instead of five points, like Allende's Popular Unity, we'll have ten commandments," he proposed to Morales.

"That's fine, but make it repeatable so that the people learn it," the candidate demanded.

The ten commandments included hydrocarbon nationalization, gas industrialization, the Constituent Assembly, a law against corruption, a law of state austerity, tariff regulation for public services, and land reform.

Evo gave internal maxims to his team: to dignify the country through the campaign, not to promise anything they couldn't deliver, to keep negotiations public, and that politics should always win over marketing because the campaign would be run by a group of politicians.

Morales would spend nearly the whole day traveling outside of La Paz and host evaluation meetings in his house at night, to which assistants would bring cookies or food because there wasn't anything to eat there. The team made the positioning of the ten commandments the first priority. As in 2002, they had to struggle with the lack of candidates for Congress. The gaps were filled by Morales' intuition to find aspiring candidates among social and independent organizations, and the MAS and its allies.

In June, Evo announced that he would travel to Havana to meet with Castro and Hugo Chávez. Walter Chávez assembled the political team to convince him not to go because it would come at a high cost. In a tense conversation, Morales got up, looked at Chávez, and said to him: "If you think I am going to bury the MAS by traveling, then I won't travel." It was one of the few times in which his team was able to stop an impulse like that. He wouldn't visit Venezuela or Cuba during the entirety of the campaign.

They had yet to find a vice presidential candidate. At first they thought about a candidate from the east due to the minimal MAS presence in that region. Then they looked for a woman—Evo preferred former ombudswoman Ana María Romero—but they finally determined that he needed an intellectual to complement his campaign, which led them to Álvaro García Linera. Morales' offer came as a surprise to him despite the fact that he already figured heavily in his milieu.

"Look for someone a little bit better, brother, someone who might have wider acceptance. If you don't find that person, I'll be your candidate," he answered, determined to act only as a fallback.

The proposal of García Linera for vice president was met with partial rejection in the MAS because of his relationship with Felipe Quispe. García Linera and Quispe had shared membership in the Tupac Katari Guerilla Army (EGTK) and five years in prison together.

Later, when accepting the candidacy, García Linera gathered his friends and colleagues at his house, Chávez among them, and made them promise that the day Evo stopped leading was the day they'd walk away from the project.

In his first speech as a candidate, on August 16, García Linera quoted a phrase from Bolivian President Manuel Isidoro Belzú (1848–1855) to grant meaning to the duo: "Bolivia will have dignity when the poncho and the tie govern together." On the campaign trail, García Linera had the good judgment to accent the indigenous identity of Morales.

Iván Iporre, Evo's private secretary at the time, was in charge of coordinating matters of security and intelligence, and especially the schedules of assistants and secretaries, to ensure that someone was available to the candidate 24 hours a day. Iporre was the subject of several intelligence operations. In 2003, a man who introduced himself as Mr. Hinojosa explained that he was willing to carry out an armed attack in favor of Morales with the military units that he controlled. During the 2005 campaign, a colonel guaranteed him that he had two briefcases of intelligence documents about Evo and García Linera. Following his boss' orders, Iporre responded that they wouldn't negotiate at all.

During the campaign, Morales was given reason to fear that there was a conspiracy against him to bring about a state coup and his assassination. One rumor in particular caused alarm: A group of soldiers would enact a coup if he were to win in the first round of voting. On the way to a rally and in front of the cameras for the documentary *Cocalero*, García Linera advised Evo about what to do if a coup did take place.

"You have to resist from the first moment and not let anything happen to you. [...] You save yourself and lead the resistance and fight for democracy."

Another warning came from Havana. A Cuban agent based in El Salvador reported that there was a plot to assassinate Morales.

At the end of October, an unexpected fear arose, this time in the candidate's dreams. At 2:00 A.M., he called Chávez to his house on Busch Avenue. "Walter, I don't think we're going to win," he said, sitting up in his bed. He'd had a bad dream.

Evo's dreams have a decisive sway over him: They have the power to change how secure he feels about his decisions. If he sees his father in them, he knows he'll have good luck and so is inclined to pursue bolder options. The first time he thought he could rise to a prominent position was after he dreamed about walking through Orinoca when the sky opened up and a bolt of lighting started to lift him higher and higher. But that early October morning, he dreamed of a descent.

"I was walking up a staircase," he told Chávez, "and Tuto was clawing at me from behind. On the top step, he pulled me down."

His campaign chief tried to calm him. "They're just dreams. There's a lot of pressure right now, but we're winning."

But at almost the same hour the next morning, the same thing happened.

"I dreamed that I was constipated. I couldn't do it, I'm not going to be able to," he told Chávez.

They decided to hold a ritual to put an end to the bad dreams. Chávez, who was juggling ads and publicity, the budget, the candidate's speeches, broadcasting the ten commandments, and the coordination of trips to different regions by bus (because they didn't have the budget for plane tickets), encountered a new task—to minimize Morales' dreams. At that point, he was already leading in the polls.

Tuto Quiroga received a troubling message from the U.S. embassy. Washington was making preparations to absorb a MAS victory. Compared with Rocha's direct, head-on approach during the 2002 presidential election, David Greenlee didn't attack Morales, and his primary concern was finding out whether he'd become a satellite of Hugo Chávez.

At the beginning of the campaign, the U.S. embassy stimulated an understanding between Quiroga and Doria Medina. The candidates agreed to have a consultant measure the intended vote, and whoever was furthest behind in the polls would resign his candidacy. But the pact was never actually realized.

Quiroga took refuge in the endorsement of the Santa Cruz elite with a neoliberal and technocratic discourse. He surrounded himself with yuppies and representatives of the old regime. He struggled to connect with the poor. He couldn't summon chemistry, and he wasn't able to demonstrate empathy. He opted for an aggressive campaign against Morales. In addition to installing a fear of his presidency, he accused him, in September, of promoting the "legalization of cocaine" and of being Chávez's puppet. He sought a public debate, but the MAS candidate repeatedly refused.

His team failed to recognize the changes that had been taking place in the country. Luis Fernando Quiroga, Tuto's brother and campaign chief, didn't think that a "union Indian" would be able to beat a University of Texas engineer. Like much of his brother's circle, he laughed at the way Morales spoke.

The Quiroga team committed the biggest blunder of the election, the so-called textile worker spot. A laborer wearing overalls explained that he was worried that during a potential MAS administration thousands of jobs would be lost. That warning, at first, had a significant impact in Quiroga's favor because it expressed the generalized fear about having a *cocalero* leader for president.

But everything changed when Walter Chávez found out that the textile worker wasn't a textile worker at all but rather an employee of Quiroga's campaign headquarters with many roles: waiter, chauffeur, cadet, and whatever else there was to do.

At the beginning of the campaign, two kids asked Chávez to hire them for the MAS campaign.

"And what do you know how to do?" he asked them.

"Put up posters," one of them replied.

"But that's not a profession," the campaign manager concluded. "I'm going to pay you both, but keep on putting up posters for Tuto. At some point you'll be able to help me."

The day after the textile worker spot aired, Chávez was stunned. He had no idea how to respond, and he knew the impact it would have on the campaign. But one of the kids alerted him, "He's not a textile worker. He's the doorman and chauffeur at the Podemos Headquarters." Chávez couldn't believe his luck. He convinced Evo to wait until the spot had done the most possible harm while adding the launch of a counterspot to the agenda. Because they'd need the fake textile worker's papers, they made plans to steal them from the police, but in the end they found them through other means.

The counterspot emphasized all of the lies—such as the identity and profession of the ad's protagonist—and succeeded in having a greater impact than the original ad. Quiroga had deceived the Bolivians.

In addition, the counterspot demoralized his campaign team, who began to look for infiltrators. Their suspicions, mistakenly, fell on Terrazas, Chávez's old colleague from *Hoy*. The team made another decision—that the phony textile worker would shave his mustache and transfer to the Santa Cruz campaign office, where he would live in hiding. When visitors knocked on the door, they could hear the hurried footsteps of someone dashing into the secrecy of a back room.

A Brazilian publicist, Duda Mendonça, also came to Santa Cruz de la Sierra in secrecy. In August of that year, Duda admitted that the Workers Party (PT) had paid his fees with undeclared money for Lula's 2002 campaign. If his presence became known, it might have harmed Quiroga. Duda came in hopes of collecting $2 million from Podemos, but he only managed to get $200,000 in the end.

Tuto's team, his brother in particular, was fascinated by the brain-storming sessions in *Portuñol* (Portuguese and Spanish mixed). Mendonça thought of using the positive idea of "Progress and Peace," which called to mind the Brazilian flag's Order and Progress. Podemos' own flag didn't help. It was a red star with five points, much like that of the pro–Che Guevara People's Revolutionary Army (ERP) in Argentina. Mendonça also suggested highlighting the candidate's authority, but in *Portuñol*: "Authority, Tuto has."

The MAS campaign was launched on October 12 in the Plaza San Francisco in La Paz. Morales went up on stage with a YPFB mining hel-met, a staff, and a whip given to him by indigenous authorities, and he gave a speech that was also broadcast in Quechua and Aymara.

The campaign was characterized by the historic crowds, marches, caravans, speeches, performances by groups who had written propaganda songs, and one-on-one interviews in inhospitable regions. In some ways, it was a repeat of the 2002 campaign, except that Morales was the favorite this time. Yet none of the polls gave him the 51 percent of the votes he'd need to avoid a run-off election in parliament. Since the recovery of dem-ocracy in 1982, Sánchez de Lozada held the record number of votes, 34 percent in 1993.

Evo imposed a severe spending restriction. He didn't want to acquire *a posteriori* commitments, he thought that austerity would strengthen the party members, and he knew how much social consensus he had.

In addition to their $1.4 million share of official publicity, members of congress and other MAS party members who worked in the public sec-tor contributed part of their salaries to the campaign. Union members, along with many other *campesinos*, sold belongings or borrowed money to contribute. Businessmen showed support, such as hotel entrepreneur Juan Valdivia; others paid for flags; one group from Santa Cruz even loaned them a small aircraft. At times, however, Morales could be distrustful, which is why he refused the planes offered to him by Ernesto Asbún, the owner of Lloyd Aéreo Boliviano (LAB) Airlines.

Certain business circles showed their support of Morales, thinking he would put an end to the blockades and because, they presumed, his gov-ernment would fall shortly thereafter anyhow. Perpetuating this cliché, one elegant woman in Santa Cruz told him as much: "You aren't prepared, but you're honest and that's enough for me to vote for you."

In a gathering with the military high command, an officer asked him whether he would respect the hierarchies of the armed forces if he were to win. The candidate responded that he'd learned them during his military service, although he made the mistake of saying "Yes, my commander" to everyone. He also pointed out that if he were to assume the presidency, they—the military leaders—would have to obey him.

On December 18, the day of the election, Morales woke up in a hotel in Villa Tunari, El Chapare. That night's dream had indicated that he would win. He recounted to his spokesperson, Alex Contreras, that he climbed the hill of Cuchi-Cuchi in Orinoca, where sacred rites are performed. From those heights, he looked out over a sublime landscape. In real life, days before, a llama had been sacrificed on the summit of that same hill.

"We're going to get more than 50 percent," he ensured Contreras.

After eating a breakfast of fish soup, he flew to Cochabamba in a small plane so he could get to La Paz by noon. He ate lunch in the home of an ally and mayor of the city, Juan del Granado. He waged a bet that he'd get more than half of the votes. Del Granado thought he'd get 40 percent and that he should already be planning his national mobilization strategy for the second round.

Evo went back to his house in Cochabamba, where he hosted a barbecue for advisors, deputies, and journalists. Despite the auspicious preliminary reports he'd received, he hadn't hired exit pollsters and didn't want to get excited.

He sat on the bed in his room and waited for the television to make him president. The few people present crowded onto the bed with him or sat in available chairs. The exit polls placed him comfortably in first place at 6:15 P.M.; by 7:00, he had about 40 percent of the votes. Even though his phones—two landlines and two cell phones—wouldn't stop ringing with calls of congratulations and those who were there with him were hugging him, he kept his gaze fixed on the television, as if possessed by it. He asked everyone to calm down because they still had to get past 50 percent. When it happened, many of his friends and colleagues began to cry. "Not Evo, though, he'd been through too much," Contreras would say.

At 10:00 P.M., he gave his first speech as president-elect from the headquarters of the Committee of the Six Tropical Federations of Cochabamba. "We have won. For the first time, we the indigenous people are going to govern this country," he said, wearing black pants and a white sweater, not yet knowing that he'd end up with 53.7 percent of the votes. He closed the speech with a *cocalero* cry:

"*Causachun Coca! Wañuchun yanquis!* [Long Live Coca! Death to the Yankees!]"

After hearing that, Walter Chávez cried for the next two hours. That victory put an end to the series of frustrations felt by his generation. For him, it had a personal resonance: Evo's difficulty with reading reminded Chávez of his own father's illiteracy and therefore of everything that his family couldn't be.

Two minutes after finishing his first speech, Morales called him.

"We don't have to be afraid anymore, big boss."

"From now on, nobody is going to spit at you again." Chávez was barely able to say the words as he sobbed with a certain embarrassment.

García Linera shielded himself from the heavily emotional atmosphere. When he found out that they had won, he took a notebook, isolated himself in a room in his apartment, and asked not to be given a single piece of information more. He wrote about what the result meant. "The election expressed something very profound," he told me in an interview. "There was too much historical weight, and it didn't allow for praise, hugs, or celebrating. I also wrote about how to go forward after such a cataclysm."

In the penthouse of a five-star hotel in La Paz, Quiroga was devastated. Morales nearly doubled his votes. Before taking a flight to the United States, he received a consolation from his father: "If these people vote for an ignoramus, let them suffer for it."

Evo ended the night with a toast of beer, champagne, and cake. Then he asked to rest in his room. He wanted to be alone. That was also how he spent his first Christmas Eve as president-elect.

Five days later, the trip that he hadn't been able to make to Cuba during the campaign finally took shape. They received him with the full honors of a chief of state. In a lunch that stretched out until 9:00 P.M., Fidel Castro suggested that he make his imminent international tour (Venezuela, Spain, France, Holland, Belgium, China, and South Africa) in a private plane with guards. "One missed connection will ruin the tour for you," he warned when he found out that Evo had tickets on commercial flights. He insisted on offering a Cuban plane to the point of being a nuisance, but Evo declined. "I think that was the only time he ever got annoyed with me," he recalled a year later.

Back in Bolivia, while visiting Orinoca, he received pressure to fly in a private plane in the form of a phone call from Hugo Chávez: "If I don't convince you, I'm going to have problems with Fidel," he confided.

Finally, Venezuela gave him two small planes: one for the advance patrol and Venezuelan security and another for the small retinue: Morales, Iporre, Contreras, and the economist Carlos Villegas.

One minor detail would alter the outcome of the tour. After he'd already packed his suitcase, Evo grabbed a sweater with a round neck and blue, white, and red stripes that had been given to him as a gift. The rest of the delegation, who hadn't considered the European cold, had to buy coats on their first break from the tour. By that point, Evo's pullover had made news in Bolivia—there was talk of the sweater revolution—and all over the rest of the world. In Germany, the weekly paper Der Spiegel called him President Pullover.

But the sweater didn't keep Morales from arriving in Spain with a cold. Queen Sofia sent him to a doctor. King Juan Carlos had apparently been misinformed about Evo's look. He gave him a tie as a gift. "Are you the real Zapatero?" Evo asked the Spanish prime minister, José Luis Zapatero, because days earlier a Spanish radio show had managed to get him on the air to speak with a Zapatero impostor. In a different tone, the country's businessmen asked him what would happen with private investments in Bolivia. In a majority of the formal meetings, Morales spoke of sovereignty and his willingness to establish a bilateral policy of mutual respect with all countries. He got his listeners' attention with his stories. He said that he'd gone from thousand star hotels—in the nights that he slept out in the open air—to those of five stars, and it made him laugh to think that there were helicopters and boats among his escorts now.

The Venezuelan planes seemed like buses, the way Iporre scheduled the sequence of meetings and explored new routes. They had a setback on the way to China because the fuel froze in the -22 degrees Fahrenheit temperatures at a Russian airport. In Bejing, they were set back by their own exhaustion. "My colleagues are asleep," Evo told Chinese President Hu Jintao.

On the way back to Bolivia, Evo concentrated on designating his government team. But there were other uncertainties: how he would dress and who would be the first lady.

Evo took his brother off the list of potential MAS deputies to avoid nepotism. As a result, Hugo made uncomfortable statements every now and then. He didn't accept his sister, Esther, as first lady either despite the pressures he received. Esther continued tending her butcher shop, which she runs out of the front of her house in Oruro.

Morales' wardrobe for Inauguration Day sparked a national debate. Would he wear a jacket and tie?

A tailor gave him a vicuña wool jacket as a gift, and it was the best option until Beatriz Canedo Patiño, the haute couture designer, gave him a suit. Earlier, in the course of the campaign, as the MAS was attempting to include and excite the middle class and other sectors, it had been proposed that Canedo participate in some events because she had declared her "moral adherence" to the candidate. In addition to having a traditional last name, Canedo flaunted the image of "successful Bolivia." She was educated in Paris, owned a store in New York City, and had introduced alpaca fiber for the first time on the runways of high fashion.

Canedo declined the MAS proposal, arguing that she couldn't make that leap. When they asked her for an overcoat for the candidate, she handed over an estimate of $1,500, which represented far too many posters and flags to accept. But days before the inauguration, she did give Morales a gift: a black jacket made of baby alpaca wool combined with hundred-year-old brown, black, and white knitting, a white shirt without a collar, and pants with suspenders. It didn't look anything like her 2006 collection, and Evo didn't look anything like the mannequins in her catalogs.

Morales refused the pants and the shirt, but he was utterly taken with the jacket. His assistants sent some old black pants to the dry cleaner's, and they bought a shirt, belt, and shoes at Lafayette, a store in La Paz.

The matter of attire settled, they still discussed what Evo would say when he took the presidency. In a meeting with his team, Morales gave ideas of what he wanted to say, made it clear that he wouldn't read, and asked for suggestions. One of the first ideas was to pay tribute to the people who made it possible for him to be there.

"I'm going to do that. Before, the presidents would thank the church, private businesses, their voters. I am going to thank the history that allowed me to become president," Evo suggested.

He asked García Linera who the first Indian to rebel was. He said it was Manco Inca—the Inca chief who has gone down in history as a symbol of Andean resistance to colonialism—and then listed a series of names, including Ernesto "Che" Guevara. Someone objected that he wasn't Bolivian or an Indian.

"He is a blood brother," Evo answered as he stapled together the 16 hand-written pages.

Most of his meetings prior to inauguration took place in his apartment on Busch Avenue. The only way to get to the dining room, decorated with a plastic tablecloth and a few MAS posters, was to pass through the kitchen. Evo observed that he was going to need more chairs for Cabinet meetings.

"But the meetings are held in the Palace," an advisor told him.

"There will also be meetings here," Morales replied.

It was there that he received the Chilean president Ricardo Lagos and the U.S. government envoy, Thomas Shannon, days before his inauguration.

On Saturday, January 21, the indigenous people crowned Morales as their highest representative. The ceremony was held in front of 70,000 people in Tiwanaku, archeological ruins from the height of Andean civilization prior to the Inca Empire.

The ceremony began with the howl of the *pututus* (bull horn instruments). Evo was escorted by *malkus* (indigenous military leaders) with red ponchos and black hats and watched over by the community police. Morales wore a reddish cloak decorated with horizontal stripes as a symbol of the Andean worldview. He carried the staff that represents indigenous authority. He received a sacred command, calling for the end of discrimination, inequality, and unemployment. After being purified with the water of a sacred spring, he addressed the crowd:

> I want to ask all of you, with much respect to the native authorities, to our organizations, to our *amatuas* (Andean ritual specialists): Watch over me and, if I am unable to advance, push me forward, brothers and sisters.

The next day, he assumed the presidency. In the morning, while trying to calm his nerves, García Linera asked Evo whether he should wear a tie, and he answered yes. Héctor Arce, his lawyer, reminded him that on January 22, four years earlier, he had been expelled from parliament. Now he had come back to occupy the most important post of the republic.

He pledged with his left fist raised, and his eyes became misty when his vice president hung the sash and collar on him, thereby turning him into chief of state.

He then delivered one of the best speeches of his life. He began by requesting a minute of silence for his fallen brothers, the *cocaleros* who defended the coca leaf, and those from the high plateau. He named nine people: Manco Inca, Tupac Katari, Tupac Amaru, Bartolina Sisa, Zarate Wilca, Atihuaiqui Tumpa, Che Guevara, Marcelo Quiroga Santa Cruz, and Luis Espinal.

Evo thanked his parents, "certain that they continue on with me, helping me along." He offered a reminder that 50 years ago his ancestors didn't have the right to walk on the sidewalks of Plaza Murillo, and he addressed the indigenous people: "After 500 years of resistance, we now move forward and take power for another 500 years."

Morales combined long- and short-term memory to explain that day. "The battles for water, for coca, for natural gas have brought us to this point, brothers and sisters." He scolded one of his parliament members, "We ask our senator from Cochabamaba not to fall asleep."

Evo was accommodating to the invited guests, and he treated them like the president's older siblings. Among them were Chávez (Venezuela), Lula (Brazil), Kirchner (Argentina), Lagos (Chile), Alejandro Toledo (Peru), and Álvaro Uribe (Colombia). He thanked the U.S. envoy for his presence. He told Kirchner that they had the same noses: "He is a white parrot and I'm a dark parrot," and he emphasized that Lula had given him guidance and taught him.

"Pardon me, *compañeros*, I am not used to talking so much. Don't think that Fidel or Chávez are infecting me," he winked at his primary international allies.

He made some personal remarks about the two ex-presidents of Bolivia, with whom he was angry.

"Last year in March in this same Plaza Murillo, they wanted to hang Evo Morales, they wanted to dismember Evo Morales. [...] Ex-Mr. Presidents, that shouldn't have happened; one shouldn't marginalize another."

He was referring to Mesa. When the ex-president came by to congratulate him a few hours later, Morales responded with his index finger raised: "You wanted to destroy me."

He also recalled Jaime Paz Zamora in his speech.

"We can't let our governments be the runner-up to corruption, can we, Sir Jaime?" he asked in reference to the annual Corruption Perception Index (CPI) published by Transparency International.

Morales offered an alternative: "We want to govern with the law that our ancestors left us, the *ama sua, ama llulla, ama quella*, not to steal, not to lie, and not to be lazy. That is our law."

Evo barely addressed the Santa Cruz elite. Only in passing did he mention Santa Cruz farming, agriculture, and financial sectors. He said that he owed them the guarantee of a referendum on autonomies that he claimed to support. He called for the end of the large rural landholdings.

In gestures and words, he embodied the *campesino* who had come to the most important post in the city. He concluded by thanking the places that had shaped him as a *cocalero* and union leader:

> I salute the place where I come from, Orinoca, which is always with me, my land Orinoca, Sur Carangas in the Oruro Department, which saw my birth and taught me to be honest. [. . .] I salute and thank the Lower San Francisco Syndicate Office of the Villa 14 de Septiembre region, the Federation of the Tropics, the Six Federations of the Tropics of Cochabamba. Cochabamba, which is my place of birth in the union fight and in the political fight, thanks to the Cochabambans for having allowed me to live in Cochabamba and to learn so much from Cochabamba. These two lands taught me about life, and I am confident it will now be Bolivia that teaches me to manage well. I will fulfill my commitment, as Subcomandante Marcos says, to lead by obeying. I will lead Bolivia by obeying the Bolivian people. Thank you so very much.

After the speech, he received the staff of military command. For the first time, the armed forces would have a Captain General of Aymara origin. Then he went up to the balcony of the Palace to watch the military parade.

In his debut as president, he walked five blocks among the crowd. The third swearing in—after Tiwanaku and Congress—was in the Plaza de los Héroes and before "the people," represented by *cocaleros*, miners, *campesinos*, social organizations, and unions. He made a wardrobe change, putting on the leather jacket with a similar trim to that of the jacket he wore when taking his oath. "Evo, Evo, Evo," he heard as he passed by.

After the speeches of Cuban vice president Carlos Laje and García Linera, Evo talked about his future life. He predicted that he would appeal to Andean ritual specialists to get rid of the bad energy left in the Palace by his predecessors. He said that he was afraid of living in the official residence because there were hidden cameras and microphones. Although he didn't say it, he suspected the U.S. government.

Chapter Seven

LIVE IN *GRINGO*-LAND (SEPTEMBER 2007)

At 1:58 P.M. on Sunday, September 23, 2007, the U.S. Secret Service reported to the Bolivian ambassador in the United States, Gustavo Guzman, that it hadn't detected any snipers who would make an attempt against Evo Morales' life.

"We're clean," a secret service agent said.

The U.S. government provides every president who attends the annual inauguration of the General Assembly of the United Nations with security, which they have the option to decline. In a few minutes, the president of Bolivia was scheduled to play a soccer game in New York City on a property alongside the river in southeast Manhattan. This event, for members of the secret service, increased the risk of assassination.

That risk didn't seem to trouble the visiting delegation, which appeared more concerned with the age and physical shape of their opponents, a team made up of Bolivian immigrants living in the United States.

On the way to the game, a new consideration sparked alarm among the agents. If Morales changed in the locker rooms, he would spend too many minutes in a location without an emergency exit. They suggested to Ambassador Guzmán that he not change there, and the president responded: "Do they want to know everything?"

Five minutes later, the secret service experienced their first live crisis. When the delegation arrived on the field, some 2,000 Bolivians rushed on Morales to touch him, take photos with him, or talk to him. Ten huge men attempted to hold them back without success.

"This is a mob. This isn't how we do things here," one of the men said.

The secret service would spend the next four days of Morales' visit to New York doing things in ways they don't usually do them.

His arrival to the city hardly appeared auspicious. The Venezuelan Boeing that brought him received an order to avoid New York's JFK Airport and to change course to Newark Airport in New Jersey. Because the flight wasn't previously on the list of landings, the delegation had to wait three hours for approval to land the plane. According to the State Department, the detour was a misunderstanding. The Venezuelan pilots claimed they had sent two flight plans from the last layover in Santo Domingo, but an airport change was decided from JFK.

Morales was convinced it was all part of a series of mistreatments that, he believes, the U.S. government lays on whenever it can. That incident, seemingly small, contributed to the greatest escalation of conflict between Washington and La Paz since he assumed government.

The delay caused the delegation—triple its regular number, with seven guards instead of the one they usually have—to have to run by the hotel to drop off their suitcases, only to rush out again to play the game.

"Evo, if you were president 25 years ago, we wouldn't be here," read the biggest banner waiting on the soccer field. From the steps where he gave his first speech, he could see the bridges of New York City, the silhouettes of Queens and Brooklyn, a helicopter combing the area for snipers, and some young people dancing a *tinku* (an Andean form of ritual conflict) with athletic fervor.

In the locker room, he gestured for his assistant to give me a T-shirt so that I could make my debut on his team. The only jersey left had a number ten with the word "Evo" written across the back, just like the president's. He was concerned about my socks.

"Boss, those are Abimael Guzmán socks. You look like Abimael Guzmán, and we're in *Gringo*-land. Don't you have any others?"

The black and white stripes reminded Evo of the images of the leader of Shining Path (the Peruvian guerilla group), dressed in his convict's uniform inside the cell where he was judged and condemned.

With the Bolivian and Wiphala flags, the team walked to the middle of the field and stood facing the fans gathered on the bleachers and the track surrounding the field. Half of them sang the Bolivian national anthem the way Morales usually requests, right hand on the heart and left fist up in the air. The right wing in Bolivia, whose mouthpiece is the TV station Unitel, responded by saying that there was an "Evo style" of singing it and another "Bolivian style." The guards, not authorized to break from police traditions, opted for the second style. The opponents did as well. Those two options reflect the tension between the symbols that came with Morales and those that were already established.

While I waited for my turn on the subs bench, a little girl came by to scold me: "You have Evo's jersey, but you're not Evo. You're an impostor."

The president's team was twice the age of their rivals, who were winning 2 to 0. Besides the guards, Minister of the Presidency Juan Ramón Quintana and Chancellor David Choquehuanca were playing the best. Morales kicked a penalty over the crossbar. "I've missed a lot of penalties in my life, but this was only the second time over the crossbar," he would later say at dinner.

At halftime, he was exhausted and dehydrated by a heat made stronger by the 3:00 P.M. sun and the turf rubber. The secret service kept the spectators from approaching him while the Bolivian security team discussed some tactical changes for the second half of the game.

I replaced Quintana. The president dribbled past two players in one of the first plays and then passed me the ball through a wide opening. I received the ball and with a weak, left-footed shot scored our first goal. Because somebody on the field shouted "Nice, Argentina," a journalist asked an official whether there were foreigners playing in the Bolivian jersey. "Are there any Venezuelans?" he also inquired. The president didn't even hear this, but in the middle of the field, he ran up to me and said, "We'll nationalize you."

Morales has a quiet presence on the field. He doesn't argue with the referee, talk to his opponents, or even give instructions to his own team, but he always asks for the ball. The president's team was poorly positioned on the field, so the immigrant team was advancing easily, but they couldn't score. After 35 minutes, the score was 2 to 2, and just 30 seconds before the end, one of the president's guards made the victory goal.

"Watch how this game will put him in a good mood," another guard said in the locker room.

I asked Evo about the enormous scar on his stomach. "My appendix, it burst on me in 1992."

Dinner consisted of a fixed menu at a second-rate Italian restaurant in midtown. The other patrons, young locals, some of them Latinos, didn't know anything about Bolivia and its president. With his chancellor, whom

he calls Davicho, by his side, Morales sat enthusiastically eating an arti-
choke salad, pasta Bolognese, and chicken marsala.

They talked about llamas. "They're smarter than humans," Choquehuanca
asserted. He explained how they walk in circles and also defecate in a tidy
way and at the exact same hour each day. "They're like Swiss watches," he
added. Evo recalled that when he was ten years old and a llama wasn't giving milk to her offspring, he put saliva on the teat so that they would have
something to suckle.

The chancellor had been led to think about llamas' remarkable sense
of direction a few days earlier when he got lost in New York. Because he
couldn't find his point of reference—the Empire State Building—he went
in circles in a cab until the meter read $98. That sum frightened him even
more than the prospect of wandering around the city.

At 9:00 A.M. on Monday morning, Morales entered the UN headquarters to participate in a global warming seminar. Part of his delegation was
still struggling with the difference between primary authorization cards
and those that only allowed them to enter certain events: The violet was
worth more than the red but less than the green. The cards classify, open
doors, and can even avoid metal detectors, which presidents don't have to
go through.

Evo walked quickly down the high-ceilinged, carpeted corridors until he
arrived at room number four, a conference space without any natural light
and decorated with blank, plasma screen televisions. Once there, he found
out that he could only enter the global warming seminar accompanied by
one other person. In the jargon of diplomacy, it is a "president + 1" situation.
Those who stayed outside saw Secretary of State Condoleeza Rice pass by.
"The war lady," Quintana said.

Morales delivered a speech about global warming.

The world has a fever from climatic change, and the illness is today's model of capitalist development. [. . .] We're living through the
sixth extinction of living species in the history of planet Earth, and
this time the rate of extinction is a hundred times more accelerated
than in geological times. [. . .] Transnational interests propose that
we go on as before and just paint the machine green, that is to say, to
continue with the irrational and unequal growth and consumerism
generating more and more profit without taking into account that in
one year we're consuming what the planet produces in one year and

three months. [...] I read the World Bank reports that say we must put a stop to subsidies on hydrocarbons, put a price on water, and promote private investment in the clean energy sectors. They want to apply the prescriptions of market and privatization to create businesses with the very same illness [...]. Heavy taxes should be applied to the super-concentration of wealth, and effective mechanisms should be adopted for its equitable distribution.

Since the UN places participants in alphabetical order, the Belarusian representative was able to congratulate and hug Evo due to his proximity of initial letters.

"And now what do we do?" Evo asked once he left the "president + 1" situation and headed off with the delegation to rest in a room with green carpet, white leather chairs, and 16-foot-tall curtains. Beside him were the leftovers of meals eaten there, three Japanese people with two authorizations, and an African woman who was crying and talking on her cell phone.

It was time for another lunch, another "president + 1," in which Al Gore would deliver a speech. "Are we eating like birds again?" Evo worried. An advisor tried to uplift him by saying that they would serve a good fish. He listened to the ex–vice president of the United States without hiding his fury. From his perspective, Gore had left out the reasons behind global warming and contamination. "He doesn't explain anything. I'm going to crush him," he later said to me about his then-competitor for the Nobel Peace Prize. At that point, an international campaign in support of his candidacy had already been launched. Three weeks later, it was announced that Gore would receive the prize.

There wasn't time at the lunch to debate with Gore, but for every president visiting the UN, there was time to discuss the final arrangements for bilateral meetings. Often these short meetings prove to have a greater significance for the internal politics of the countries than the speeches delivered in the General Assembly.

For this tour, Morales asked his foreign ministry to set up meetings with European leaders. He had neglected to make that continent a priority since taking office, and an outstanding topic from the European perspective continued to be the hydrocarbons nationalization decree. Nicolas Sarkozy cited scheduling conflicts during his first visit as premier, but Evo was able to converse with the president of the European Commission (EC) and the highest representatives of Italy, Spain, and Holland.

The EC president, José Manuel Durão Barroso, a Portuguese Maoist activist in the 1970s, didn't seem to remember his previous faith in the *campesinos* when he had a *campesino* president union leader in front of him. On the contrary, Barroso decided to advise Evo that changes should be made through democratic means.

"What rules did I break?" Morales asked him. "Tell me. Your ambassadors should keep you better informed. We haven't done anything against democracy."

The meeting with Romano Prodi, the prime minister of Italy, didn't turn out any better. In the world headquarters of presidents, bilateral meetings take place in uncomfortable cubicles separated by carpeted partitions, without bathrooms. The Dunkin Donuts coffee that an assistant of Evo's tried to bring in was prohibited. Women dressed like flight attendants time the meetings to ensure that they don't exceed 30 minutes. They're like blind dates held in small spaces to contribute to the rapprochement of the participants and within limited time frames as other presidents await their turn.

That bilateral meeting took place in a corner balcony overlooking the main hall. The delegations chose to separate themselves on either side of a wood and glass coffee table. With his legs crossed, reclining backward, and closing his eyes to listen to Morales, Prodi spoke in English with a pronounced Italian accent while a Bolivian government advisor, Tom Kruse, translated.

Evo was leaning on his left elbow with his right hand free while he listened to him. From this position, he looked out on green-, yellow-, and violet-stained glass windows and circles of balconies.

Three young advisors accompanied Prodi, a Christian Democrat who likes to think of himself as an arbitrator. One of the advisors answered Prodi's phone in the middle of the bilateral meeting. Another one made a bigger mistake. He allowed the Bolivian delegation to see a memorandum prepared for his premier, which reported that Morales had just reopened relations with Iran and the battle between the Bolivian east and west could lead to the country's division.

Prodi's main interest did not appear in the memo.

"I do think that social demands are very important, and I believe you are doing good things for Bolivia. Your process could have influence in the region. But I also think it's important that you not do anything that could affect cooperation," he stated.

Prodi was referring to the announcement of the La Paz government that it would buy shares of Telecom amid its nationalizing policies. "I'm not a part of it since I'm not from Telecom. But I believe it's important that everyone come to an agreement to avoid any conflicts."

Morales didn't react. They said their goodbyes cordially, with promises of future encounters.

Evo went down one floor to an even smaller and more poorly lit box to meet with José Luis Rodríguez Zapatero. They shook hands in the entrance in front of photographers. "Fortunately, Zapatero is to my left," he said. The surprised Spaniard smiled at the joke as the flashes whitened their faces.

Thirty-two feet away, Iranian president Mahmoud Ahmadinejad was arriving from a conference at Columbia University, where he had announced that there weren't any homosexuals in his country. It was his response to a question about death sentences by hanging in the last year. At that time, the United States was applying pressure to obtain sanctions against Iran for its nuclear development plan. They classified Iran as the number one ally to terrorism, and they gave its president a visa that didn't allow him to go farther than 25 miles from UN headquarters. Washington and La Paz were therefore positioned as opposing extremes: Morales would receive Ahmadinejad in Bolivia just after leaving the United States.

"We've spoken with Lula," Zapatero said to Morales in the meeting, "in pursuit of a way to cooperate with Brazil to help Bolivia."

"Look, thank you very much, but with Brazil and Petrobrás, the relationship is complicated, and we'd prefer to talk to them one on one," Morales replied.

They didn't talk about Repsol. Actually, despite the fact that the Spanish government had pressured more than others to keep the company from earning the least possible in the nationalization process, both chiefs of state managed to maintain a certain level of sympathy for one another.

Zapatero asked Morales about relations with the United States.

"They're financing my rivals. Since there isn't opposition, they're trying to create it in order to destabilize me," he said.

The Spaniard promised to ask Condoleezza Rice what was going on.

A UN official with bleach-damaged hair came in to say there were only two minutes left for the meeting.

The next event listed on Morales' agenda was his speech at Cooper Union. It was in the main hall of this university, founded in the mid-nineteenth century, that Abraham Lincoln gave a speech against slavery, decisive for his presidential nomination.

The organizers of the event waited for Evo in a room with fruit, cheese, and cans of soda. Surrounded by quotes of Martin Luther King, Jr., Thomas Jefferson, and Lincoln, they informed him that tickets to listen to him speak had sold out two days ago.

An activist from the Bronx with the last name of Carter, almost exploding in her green dress, broke down upon introducing him. "He is the first indigenous president...." The audience cheered.

Before a like-minded audience, Morales gave his longest speech of the tour:

> Pardon me, brothers and sisters of the United States, but in the 1980s U.S. officials and soldiers were operating on our national territory. In my country, the United States no longer installs and removes ministers like they did before. [...] The internal problem was with the trio of priests, lawyers, and the military. First they tried with the law, then with God, and if that didn't work, with wooden clubs.

By 9:00 p.m., the president had lost his voice. He tried to recover it in the hotel restaurant with a double tea with a lot of honey and Propolis lozenges.

"You're just tired," Ambassador Guzmán told him.

"No, because here I hardly do anything except go to conferences and then back to the hotel. Maybe it's the air conditioning," he replied.

Morales already had four points for his UN speech: Bolivia, climate change, indigenous rights, and the Iraq War. He took the minister of the presidency's hand, telling him, "We'll work on it tomorrow."

While eating salmon and mashed potatoes, Evo spoke of his childhood and adolescence. He didn't really pay attention to women until one of them gave him a thrashing: "'He thinks he's a big shot because he owns a lot of llamas,' she said about me."

Evo was 19 or 20 years old, and since then, he said, he began to pay attention.

He remembered that his younger brother, Hugo, would beat him in fights because Hugo was chubby. When Hugo started to grow a beard, a malicious rumor spread through Orinoca because their father was beardless. Because Hugo started drinking alcohol at age 13, they gave him a bass guitar so that he'd have other interests. His father sent him to do military service, hoping that it would get him to lose weight and quit drinking.

While Morales was reminiscing, one of his guards told him that the secret service had challenged the team to a soccer game. "We'll play them for Bush's airplane," somebody answered.

Communication between the Bolivian guards and their U.S. peers didn't improve. In addition to the language problems—there were few Latinos among the secret service—the agents couldn't understand why most of Morales' security was sleeping in New Jersey, 40 minutes from the hotel. "How can they not have enough budget?" one of them asked. Another sought the friendship of one of the Bolivians and gave him a CIA pin without knowing his name—Fidel.

After dinner, Evo went up to his room to go to bed. On the way, he said that we had to talk.

"What are you going to call your book?" he asked.

"Jefazo [Big Boss, the original title of the Spanish edition]," I replied.

"Big Boss? [laughing]. No, it should be Sub-big Boss," he answered.

"Please don't say anything," I requested.

"Relax, boss, it's a state secret from now on."

Evo slept poorly that night. He woke up sweating and feared that the fever would mean that he'd have to stay in the United States. At 5:00 A.M., his room smelled like Propolis, and the carpet was covered in wide-open lemon peels.

After a press breakfast in the hotel basement, he walked to the UN Mission of Bolivia for the only meeting he had scheduled with a U.S. official, John J. Danilovich, chief executive officer of the Millennium Challenge Corporation, a special fund that "finances initiatives to improve the economies and quality of life in developing countries." He was waiting for Evo with a couple of good jokes, a smile that never faded, and a "but": "We want to help Bolivia, *but* it's Congress that determines if there will be money."

"I can help you with that. Leave it to me," Evo replied.

Morales decided to go back to the UN to listen to Lula's and Bush's speeches.

The chief of secret service, with a goatee and big hips, was giving high fives to some of his colleagues while Morales made his way through the presidents of the world and their foreign ministers. He saw BlackBerrys and spouses wearing long dresses, and he heard the pleasantries: "See you next year" and "Come and visit me sometime."

Evo sat in one of the three seats designated for Bolivia and asked for a notebook to write down Bush's words. When he wasn't writing, he leaned back and his head crossed through the borders of Cape Verde and Bhutan. After the speech, he looked for the Cuban delegation to express his solidarity because the U.S. president had said there was a "cruel dictatorship" on the island.

During the recess, Michelle Bachelet approached Morales.

"How are you, boss?" Evo asked.

The Chilean president wanted to guarantee his presence in the Ibero-American Summit in November 2007, which she would host.

When he was leaving the floor, Morales bumped into Colombian president Álvaro Uribe. "How are you, boss? If there's a reason for it, let's meet," Evo said. He exchanged raised eyebrows with Chancellor Celso Amorín in a show of the cold status of Bolivia's relations with Brazil. The Argentine minister of labor, Carlos Tomada, told him: "We love you very much, Evo." Chancellor Jorge Taiana kissed him.

Out in the street, where some of the police paid him attention but pedestrians didn't seem to recognize Morales, I asked him about Bush's speech.

He replied, "That bastard. He spoke as if he were the master of the world. Against Cuba. Against Iran. Tomorrow I'm going to say that there shouldn't be any more world masters. And that access to energy should be universal."

"Does nuclear energy in Iran worry you?" I asked.

"Of course," Evo answered.

"And why have you decided to reestablish relations?" I inquired.

"They're cooperative agreements. There are investments in gas, petrochemistry, milk processing, and mining," he stated.

A short while later, he met with social leaders in the UN Church Center. A Moroccan described how he lost 58 friends on September 11, and that he put together a cooperative. A woman explained what it's like to work on the fringe of traditional unionism in the United States. Another leader proposed categorical action against global warming.

"Our government," said Evo, "is a government of social movements. Before, I would debate alongside the social movements, and now many of them, since I became president, have relaxed too much and stopped debating [...]."

When he got to the UN Mission of Bolivia, he asked to eat.

"Hi, big boss. Here I am, in *Gringo*-land," he answered a call from Víctor Orduna, his press advisor. He asked him how much coverage there was in the Bolivian press about the tour.

He ate chicken with potatoes and salad.

"Why don't potatoes have any taste here?" he asked as they poured his Coca-Cola.

When they told Evo that Cuban minister Felipe Pérez Roque wasn't staying in a hotel, he said they would imitate him next time. "We'll sleep here."

Evo was troubled by a protest marching toward La Paz, whose goal was, in his opinion, to request positions in public office. "They want to talk to me and negotiate. I've told them to give up the march and that we will talk when I get back to Bolivia. They can't be protesting the day that the president of Iran arrives."

That afternoon Evo was interviewed on *The Daily Show* with Jon Stewart. When he got to the studio, they took him to a dressing room without windows but filled with sweets, iced coffees, and other drinks. He asked to watch Ahmadinejad's UN speech.

Stewart, an Emmy-award winner and Oscar host, welcomed him. "I really appreciate that you're here. Thank you so much. Do you have any questions?"

"No, everything's okay," he answered, recently made up.

"Would you like something to drink?" Stewart asked.

"Coffee," Evo requested.

"We don't have any," Stewart replied.

Stewart was trying to make a joke, but it created an awkward silence. The hot coffee arrived with an assistant who also brought the interview contract. Tom Kruse, Morales' advisor, didn't accept the article that would allow the program to retain the contents of the interview for their disposal. He requested—and obtained—the right to veto.

Walking around the studio, Morales seemed surprised by all the dogs wandering around entertaining the program's creators, the M&M candy machines, the giant mangos, the young creative-looking people, the editing rooms, and the hallway leading to a studio with loud dance music. That same week, Bill Clinton would also pass through the studio, along with Alan Greenspan, former chairman of the Federal Reserve. Inside, the most significant eight-and-a-half minutes of the tour for the U.S. public would occur.

Biting his lips and appearing timid, he was placed on a television set that wasn't at all familiar to him. The only familiar thing was behind him, and he couldn't see it, a map of South America that highlighted Bolivia's geography. He distrusts everything, but Stewart welcomed him with a comment that set the tone for their chat:

"Your story is remarkable. A poor farmer without a high school education becomes the first indigenous president."

Stewart said that, in the United States, everything seemed a little rigged so that an indigenous person couldn't become president.

"So if it's rigged, then something needs to be done to change that," Evo answered, and he heard the "woos" and "woo-hoos" from the studio audience.

"In North America, we have a tendency to get scared when a leader visits Chávez or Fidel Castro," Stewart said.

"Please don't consider me to be a part of the axis of evil [laughter]," Evo replied.

In subsequent shows, Stewart continued talking about that interview, which was discussed in several U.S. daily papers. He also asked for the sincerity of his audience:

"In this country, do we even know what Bolivia is?"

Bolivia was the last South American country to receive a diplomat from the United States.

In the early summer of 1848, Secretary of State James Buchanan warned the first envoy about the presence of the enemies of free government who encouraged anarchy, confusion, and civil war. "When faced with the Bolivian authorities..., present our country as an example, where all controversies are decided at the ballot box." U.S. official John Appleton's first report didn't contain anything very encouraging. Only two North Americans resided in the whole country, roads were nonexistent, the climate was so hostile that he wanted to return as quickly as he could, and, perhaps most problematic, there wasn't any government to which he could present his credentials. For weeks, he couldn't explain the ballot box solution to them.

Communications improved over the next hundred years, although U.S. policies in Latin America hardly involved Bolivia at all.

Toward the end of the nineteenth century, a new interest arose in Washington—tin. The United States, which dominated the world market, had bought more than half of Bolivia's "devil's metal" in the mid-1940s. By that time, the dispute over another natural resource—oil—had already sparked the first significant conflict between Bolivia and a U.S.

company. In March 1937, David Toro, the personification of a military socialist government, decided to confiscate Standard Oil's holdings and rescind their concession. It was the first Bolivian nationalization of the twentieth century.

The April 1952 Revolution, amid the tensions of the Cold War, marked a breaking point in the bilateral relationship between the two countries. In much the same way it had done to Peronism, the State Department characterized the MNR as a pro-Nazi party. During the events of that April, it requested that its embassy investigate the level of communist influence. It also asked whether the nationalization plans would lead the country to become another Iran, in reference to the oil nationalization project led by Prime Minister Mohammed Mosaddeq, later overthrown in 1953 by a coup in which the CIA played a central role.

In contrast to Iran and Guatemala, where Washington had decided to take down Jacobo Arbenz, the new Bolivian government received great economic support and political protection. The objective was to deradicalize the MNR government and move it away from any type of Soviet influence.

During that same period, Washington financed and encouraged the re-founding of the Bolivian Army, which had been decimated by the Revolution. U.S. plans to stabilize the country and the growing importance of multilateral credit organizations commenced a 50-year era of enormous U.S. influence in Bolivia. In an essay published in 1969, British scholar Laurence Whitehead conceptualized the bilateral relationship as a case of neocolonialism. In *Requiem for a Republic*, Sergio Almaraz, a Bolivian nationalist, wrote:

> If the spectacle of the bourgeois squeezing himself tightly around the ambassador and smiling obsequiously in order to obtain credit is repulsive, then it is painful to watch a *campesino* laying out arches of flowers to demonstrate his gratitude for the little school or the well of water donated as a gift. Extreme poverty facilitates colonization. The men in Bolivia have a lower price. There is a certain level at which poverty destroys dignity; the North Americans have discovered that level and use it to their advantage. From the North American's eyes to his pockets, a Bolivian costs less than an Argentine or a Chilean.

With the militarizing turn that U.S. foreign policy took in Latin America after the Cuban Revolution, Washington emphatically supported the military governments of René Barrientos and Hugo Banzer, the most decidedly anti-communist and pro-U.S. leaders of the military interregnum (1964–1982).

The 1985 neoliberal reforms relied on the decisive backing of the United States with Jeffrey Sachs as celebrity advisor in the time before he began his global fight against poverty. That year, the fight against drug trafficking was already Washington's new priority in Bolivia, at least in its public discourse.

Washington's influence on the makeup of public policies increased in this setting. It could impose—or veto—ministers and state secretaries in certain sensitive positions, such as the minister of defense and internal affairs, and finance or definance the country according to the results of the fight against drug trafficking. In short, the country's economy was led into foreign hands with capitalizations, the dependence on organizations controlled by Washington was deepened, and security and defense policies were de-Bolivianized.

By 1989, the U.S. embassy in La Paz had become the second most important in Latin America, according to Eduardo Gamarra, making the Bolivian government a secure ally in the war on drugs. In turn, the embassy served as a central institution for Bolivian economy and politics.

Certain ambassadors contributed to fomenting the public perception of neocolonialism. In 1988, Robert Gelbard assumed the position, probably the most important official to occupy that role given that Bolivia was functioning as a test lab for the design of the antinarcotic policies of the Bush Sr. administration. In public declarations, Gelbard gave his opinion on partisan issues, recommended policies to the government, accused officials or ex-officials of links to cocaine trafficking, and even took the liberty of accusing Jorge Crespo, the La Paz ambassador in the White House, of interfering in U.S. internal matters.

The granting—or denial—of visas was a key element of U.S. influence on local politics. The so-called *desvisados* (those without visas) suffered a severe stigmatization. But not only the *desvisados*. In 1999, Ambassador Donna Hrinak stated that Bolivia didn't have "the balls" to fight against the so-called narcotics judges.

Nobody was further off than Manuel Rocha when he classified the *cocaleros* as potential Taliban members and called on Bolivians to vote against Morales in 2002. The "War on Terror," which was rejected by the majority of Latin American governments, didn't have any better reception in Bolivian society, which ultimately reacted against Rocha's interference in that year's presidential elections.

The embassy decided not to become involved in the 2005 campaign for fear that their participation would benefit Morales. They made their concern known to the MAS campaign team: If Evo were to win, would Bolivia become a satellite of Venezuela? Not even the "No" that they received would temper the worst political defeat of the United States in Bolivia since 1848.

Hours before Morales assumed office, Assistant Secretary of State for Western Hemisphere Affairs Thomas Shannon implied to García Linera that he didn't see this as such a radical change. "There are serious people who are working with the president," he said by way of praise.

At that point, the embassy was pressuring Bolivia to sign a Free Trade Area of the Americas (FTAA) agreement. "One way to come to a quick agreement and have good relations is by signing the FTAA," a U.S. official explained to Pablo Solón, one of the architects of Morales' foreign policy who had been staunchly anti-FTAA from the start.

The decision not to sign the FTAA opened up a long debate about the Andean Trade Promotion and Drug Eradication Act (ATPDEA), tariff preferences that the United States grants products from Andean countries in exchange for antidrug policies.

Here, as in other areas, Washington and La Paz studied one another during the first seven months of government.

In their first meeting in the Burned Palace, Ambassador David Greenlee stated his discomfort with Morales' designation of two officials in particular—Minister of the Presidency Juan Ramón Quintana, who had played a central role in the denunciation of the U.S. government's alleged dismantling of Bolivia's Chinese missiles, and Alex Contreras, the president's spokesperson. Greenlee attempted to find out whether the vetoes his country had been accustomed to would continue to hold.

Morales didn't even respond to Greenlee's objections, which only served to establish both of the mentioned officials more firmly in their roles and deepen his respect for them. During that meeting, Morales secretly delighted in seating the ambassador beneath a painting of Che Guevara, made from coca leaves, and then called in the photographers.

The appointment of a *cocalero* in the role of antidrug czar didn't sit well with the embassy either. Felipe Cáceres took over to coordinate the supervision of coca leaf production in the *campesino* unions. A few weeks later, the United States revealed that it would cut back military support for that year by 96 percent (from $1.7 million to $70,000) in response to the Bolivian Congress' refusal to grant immunity to U.S. soldiers arriving in the country.

The next traumatic appointment was the chief of F-10, a Bolivian military group that up to that point had been financed and supported by the embassy. Again, U.S. officials tried to veto the appointment. "Tell them that they're not going to be selecting any officials and that they shouldn't meddle in El Chapare because I will take them out," Morales ordered to García Linera. The F-10 became a group within his trust.

The government debated what tone to take with the United States. More prone to confrontation, Evo cited two events to reinforce his approach. First, in March 2006, an incident in which a U.S. citizen set off a bomb, killing two people, sparked a presidential reaction: "Is the U.S. government in a fight against terrorism or are they sending North Americans here to create terrorism in Bolivia?" The embassy had known about that citizen's entry and didn't notify Morales, although they did apologize afterward. The government also denounced a group of Marines that entered Bolivia in the guise of students to perform covert operations.

The president tried his best to contain himself when dealing with the United States because Bolivia was trying to get an extension of the ATPDEA. García Linera had assumed the role of liaison with the embassy and Greenlee since the campaign.

"There are old wounds, ambassador. The president was persecuted by U.S. intelligence organizations, and many of his friends and colleagues were assassinated," García Linera explained in light of Morales' first hostile declarations.

"It's time to turn the page," Greenlee proposed.

During internal debates, the vice president didn't encourage the confrontation with the United States for both practical and theoretical reasons—he doesn't believe in imperialism as an explanatory category. According to his perception, the interferences, manipulations, and subordinations that other countries exercise over Bolivia are due, in part, to the local intermediaries who should be removed.

Hoping to reach a rapprochement, García Linera organized a trip to the United States with the salient objective of obtaining the expansion of the ATPDEA and to refuse, once again, a commercial relationship with the United States based on the FTAA. But when he arrived at the American Airlines counter in the El Alto airport, they informed him that he wasn't permitted to enter U.S. territory. "This is an unnecessary provocation," he said. A few minutes later, a U.S. official arrived dressed in something looking like pajamas. It wasn't even 6:00 A.M. Although they had given him a visa, Linera remained on a "terrorist" watch list, a classification made by the State Department because of his previous involvement with the Tupac Katari Guerrilla Army (EGTK).

In Washington, local officials requested specifics as to Bolivia's relations with Venezuela and Cuba and wanted to know how the Bolivian government perceived the United States.

"While some countries have decided to embrace us, like Venezuela, the United States has decided not to embrace us, and that has shaped the bilateral relationship," the vice president explained a half-dozen times.

Under Secretary of State for Political Affairs Nicholas Burns reproached him, reminding him that Morales' first speech as president-elect had ended with "death to the Yankees."

"No declaration of President Bush could compare," Burns asserted.

Dan Fisk, the senior director of Western Hemisphere Affairs, employed a Cold War tone throughout the meeting. However, in reference to another subject, he said, "In the United States, all businesses are offered the same opportunities, but we are given the impression that in Bolivia private ownership is at risk."

The airports continued to treat the vice president poorly. In Los Angeles, they made him take off his shoes so they could inspect them. He had traveled there, among other reasons, to support Desirée Durán, Miss Bolivia, in the Miss World competition. Gloria Limpias, proprietress of Bolivian beauty pageants, guaranteed him that he could become Mister Bolivia.

The Bolivian embassy in Washington remained vacant, causing the government to delay one of its goals on U.S. soil: to obtain the extradition of Sánchez de Lozada.

In September 2006, Gustavo Guzmán, a journalist and editor, took charge of the embassy. Evo had called him to the Burned Palace because he had "a little something" to propose to him.

"But I'm just a journalist," was Guzmán's first reaction.

"And how do you think I ended up president?" he asked and then explained that he'd begin an intensive course in English.

George Bush received Guzmán with a gracious comment: "It was from that very telephone that I called your president to congratulate him when he first assumed office." He continued with an uncomfortable question.

"Do I have to worry about Bolivia?"

A club for corduroy wearers in New York, by contrast, paid him tribute for being one of the few ambassadors to dress in that fabric, in addition to keeping his hair long and refusing to wear a tie.

Guzmán immediately understood that Morales' anti-U.S. rhetoric—his use of the word *empire*, for instance—was Washington's primary grievance. In La Paz, North American officials often pass that complaint along to their local colleagues. A common phrase is, "The words of your president don't help any."

Another complaint reiterated by the embassy regards their economic assistance to Bolivia not being recognized despite it going on for more than half a century. Meanwhile, Venezuela and Cuba's cooperation is praised.

Far from resigning itself to Chávez's influence, Washington has tried to reduce it. When Bush visited Uruguay in February 2007, Washington arranged things so as to prevent Morales from attending an event in Buenos Aires where Chávez had prepared an anti-American rally. "Ambassador, it would be best if you could keep that event from becoming a problem," a U.S. official said to Guzmán as part of the constant game of suggestions. The Bolivian government reported that a technical problem with the plane during a return trip from Japan kept the president from attending.

In September 2006, Evo visited the United States for the first time to attend the inauguration of the UN General Assembly. Until then, he had appeared on a list of terrorists not allowed to enter the country.

Presidents, ex-presidents, lobbyists, academics, and politicians received him with surprise and even a certain admiration. Bill Clinton was one of them.

Walking down the line of people waiting to enter his foundation's event, Clinton rubbed shoulders with personalities such as Vicente Fox, Javier Solana, Bill Gates, and Madeleine Albright. He stopped at Morales.

"I am honored by your presence, Mr. President," he thanked him, to the surprise of everyone watching.

They would have a meeting in a penthouse in the Sheraton Hotel shortly thereafter. Three advisors and a businessman friend accompanied the ex-president.

"You aren't Chàvez. If you have oil, you can flaunt it. It is imperative to the Bolivian democracy that things go well for you. If it goes well for you, it means that there is democracy," he said, touching Evo's arm in his usual warm way.

Morales spoke to him about the 500 years of colonial domination, but that subject didn't seem to interest the ex-president all that much.

While drinking black coffee, Clinton referred to the Republican administration. "Don't worry too much about the problems you are having with this government. The ones I've had have been worse."

Clinton closed with a final gesture. "If I were a Bolivian miner, I would have voted for you."

When leaving, Clinton said to a Morales advisor: "Is that guy for real? Listen, I want to help him, and I'm not bullshitting."

Like Clinton, Evo also managed to surprise his entourage. In his first meeting with a group of Native Americans, he asked all the attendees to introduce themselves. "I am Evo Morales, an Aymara from Ayllu...." They went around until it was a tall redhead's turn, and the president indicated for him to participate as well. "I am John, from the secret service," the man stated.

He also surprised the audience at Columbia University by saying, "I've always wanted to speak at Harvard." He made its president, Lee C. Bollinger, uncomfortable with the question, "Is this university public?" Nervously, Bollinger answered that it wasn't, but that there was plenty of room for minorities.

Evo set the tone for his UN speech by holding up a coca leaf:

Coca is green, not white like cocaine. It doesn't make sense for it to be legal for Coca-Cola and illegal for traditional and medicinal consumption. [...] The seizure of drugs has increased 300 percent in Bolivia, but the U.S. government doesn't accept that there are limitations on how to modify our laws. I want to say with utmost respect to the U.S. government: We're not going to change a thing. We don't need blackmail or threats. The so-called certification or decertification [a controversial legislation that offers Bolivia trade benefits in exchange for drug-war cooperation] of the fight against drug trafficking is an instrument for the colonization of Andean countries.

Washington would give Bolivia certification during the first year of Evo's administration but under careful observation. In December 2006, it announced that it would cut back antidrug assistance by 25 percent, meaning that 2007 aid would go down to $33.8 million, more than

$100 million less than the $173 million that was given to the Banzer presidency in 2001. Although the State Department publicly attributed this cutback to "internal adjustments," in private it was attributed to Morales' permissive increase in coca cultivation, which for Washington signified a laxness with regard to cocaine. Around that time, the Bolivian government decided to extend the number of allowed coca acres from 30,000 to 50,000.

Morales began to explore different ways to counteract the veto that the embassy continued to exercise through the approval or denial of visas. García Linera wasn't the only one having problems entering the United States during the first year of government. Coca farmer and Senator Leonilda Zurita, for example, was one of the "de-visads."

Evo and his Cabinet spent New Year's Eve working together at the palace. Among various announcements and decrees, the one that stood out established a visa for U.S. citizens. "It's the principal of reciprocity," he said. His chancellor, Choquehuanca, had suggested that idea based on the principles of the Aymara communities.

Choquehuanca and Morales treat each other like brothers. The chancellor has ties to various nongovernmental organizations and strong influence in the highland communities. Choquehuanca constructed his view of the world from various trips he made with Evo before coming to the presidency and through denying or ignoring the canon of international relations. He made waves in the government and became the butt of the opponents' jokes when speaking about the internal matters of the country. He said that he'd gone 20 years without reading an entire book, but that he could read the wrinkles of the elderly, that his ancestors had lived to be 200 years old, and that coca could replace a child's daily glass of milk. His shortcomings in international politics were supplemented by a group of advisors led by Pablo Solón.

In a long interview in the Palace in December 2006, he told me that he wasn't there:

> For me the strategy is that of not being. Being there is the Bolivian flag and not being there is the Wiphala flag; being there is the man and not being there is nature; being is the University and not being is the natural universities; being there is knowledge, not being is intuition; being there is human rights, and not being there is cosmic rights. For me the important thing is the not being. I am not here in front of you.

Morales manages his government's foreign relations and is often in touch directly with the foreign ambassadors in La Paz. One afternoon he called the ambassador of Brazil, Federico Cézar de Araujo.

"Who is this?"

"Evo," he answered.

"If you're Evo, I'm the King of Spain," he replied and hung up.

He's also almost solely in charge of one of the most important subjects in foreign affairs, Bolivia's relationship with Chile. During the War of the Pacific with Chile (1879–1884), Bolivia lost its access to the sea and part of its territory. Since the swearing in of Morales and Bachelet—in January and March 2006, respectively—a notable rapprochement with the Chilean president took place thanks to frequent bilateral meetings. Morales and Bachelet agreed not to discuss the maritime question through the press, and the Bolivian president has been careful not to voice any statements that might make his peer uncomfortable. The 13 points of the bilateral agenda include maritime and energy topics.

Coco Pinelo, an experienced leader of social organizations, assumed the role of consul in Santiago. He attempted to put the chancellorship's document into practice, Plan Chile, which called for continuous and guaranteed access to the Pacific coasts. Choquehuanca described it to him as an "exclusion-free agenda."

After various meetings with Chilean officials in October 2006, Pinelo revealed to the president and three ministers Chile's true demands to advance the maritime question: "Chile demands security from Bolivia. Your government should never drop below 53 percent approval or lose internal support. There can't be governability problems. Venezuela shouldn't be on the border between Chile and Bolivia."

Bachelet was bothered by Chávez' paternalistic treatment of her as well as of Evo. One of the examples she gave was the way that he hugs them.

In November 2006, the government relieved Pinelo for reasons never clarified, and his successor, Enrique Finot, was also asked to step down after stating that Bolivia and Chile were "close" to coming to an agreement to resolve the issue of Bolivian coastal access, and that the resumption of relations at the ambassador level appeared imminent. "We don't talk about Chile through the press," was the Bolivian government's response.

In the Palace, Morales' inner circle envisions middle ground that would include a port with relative sovereignty (for a period of 99 years) and a transformation of the energy agenda. They also see a total collapse in relations with Chile as a possibility.

As it is—for many more reasons—with the United States. La Paz doesn't want to provoke an unnecessary rupture. García Linera maintains that the government needs time to strengthen itself and that the internal position shouldn't be reinforced externally.

The arrival of Philip Goldberg in September 2006 provoked a slight change. The government perceived him as a more dangerous and astute man than Greenlee, and he came with a troubling resumé. He'd worked in Kosovo, Bosnia, and Colombia; countries with strong internal conflicts were his expertise.

"We should chew coca together [a Bolivian ritual of sharing]," Evo said to Goldberg in one of their meetings.

"No, Coca-Cola only," the ambassador answered.

The minister of the presidency formulated a hypothesis about Goldberg's plan. In his assessment, the plan consisted of eroding the government by stimulating left-wing groups critical of the administration, on the one hand, and by influencing two internal factions, on the other hand: one inside the MAS and another inside the armed forces.

Two declassified documents from the State Department illustrate part of the strategy. One, dated February 2007, says: "The United States' primary challenge in Bolivia is to support democracy actively in a country with a history of political unrest. . . . To help meet these challenges, partnerships will be developed with regional and local governments and non-governmental organizations [NGO], the private sector, and other non-executive branch entities to prevent further erosion of democracy. . . ." "Nonexecutive" means without the national government. Another declassified document pointed out that USAID, a U.S. cooperative agency, "is focusing its assistance to Bolivia in programs that will strengthen vibrant and effective democracies, including the support of counterweights to one-party control." That "one party" would be the MAS.

In July, as a result of that document, other sources, and their own political assessment, the Bolivian government began to brandish the argument that Morales would deploy in New York that September—that the United States was financing the opposition.

A few weeks later, Bolivia announced that it would resume relations with Iran. Alarmed, Goldberg requested an emergency audience with the president. A few days before flying to New York, he arranged to meet at the Palace at 5:00 A.M.

"Ambassador, make the financing transparent and relations will improve," Evo demanded.

On September 26, 2007, Morales began the last 24 hours of his U.S. tour by eating unusual flavors of ice cream. He didn't like spicy chocolate, but he loved vanilla with M&Ms—which he called "peas"—and ginger with raisins. His advisors were leaving to buy the ice cream at Blue Pig when a hotel employee told them that they'd be charged $3 for each cup and little spoon, so they picked up plastic containers at a deli. "That's good, *compañeros*, austerity," Evo congratulated them. His face changed when they told him that ice cream is fattening.

For such a big name, the presidential suite turned out to be pretty small. Wearing a baggy white sweater and no shoes, Morales continued eating spoonfuls enthusiastically.

"I'll talk about decolonizing the United Nations. Pass me the one with peas. The speech is almost done," he said.

At 9:00 P.M., he ate dinner with the Cuban chancellor in the hotel restaurant. The first floor was filled with Cuban guards who were resentful of the secret service's presence. They scrutinized each other, not paying much attention to Nicaraguan president Daniel Ortega, who had just come back from a run through Central Park. The old guerrilla leader's return to the UN for the first time during his second presidency went almost unnoticed. He walked past wearing blue jogging pants and had sweaty, jet-black hair. He didn't go in to greet Morales.

Evo woke up at 5:50 A.M. on Wednesday. They gave him the cover of the Hispanic daily paper, *La Prensa*, in which he shared headlines with President Bush and the president of Iran. The paper advertised that a video of Evo's missed penalty kick from the Sunday game was now available on its website.

He had breakfast with members of the Council of the Americas. Founded in 1965 by David Rockefeller, the Council aims to promote free trade, free market, and democracy in the Americas. Membership is comprised of more than 200 businesses, law firms, and lobbyists who invite presidents, officials, and celebrities to find out, first hand, what's happening in a given region and, also first hand, to try to influence their decisions.

The connection between politics and the members is made through Susan Segal, the organization's president. There is a Botero painting hanging just outside her office, and beige carpeting and white walls cover the inside. On her desk, she has vacation photos of her family at the beach and in the snow. She has flat-ironed hair, a smile that couldn't withstand a lie detector, and a few tricks to make her guests feel more comfortable.

She asked Morales whether he'd been playing soccer. Evo, who had already yawned a few times, became more animated with the story of Sunday's game. He went on to the story of a previous game. "We played with some youngsters not too long ago, and they bet me 2,000 bolivianos [$300] for the game. I told them, sure, even though of course I wasn't going to make them pay, but when the game ended, they just took off running and didn't even wave goodbye." To Segal, everything sounded so exotic.

Sitting by her side was another member of the Council of the Americas, Christopher Sabatini, who anticipated that attending members would ask about relations with Chile, as well as Lula, Brazil, and Petrobrás, at the breakfast. "With Petrobrás it's not so good," Evo answered.

All of the guests were reading a pamphlet while they waited in the second-floor dining room. "Since 1983, President Morales has been very committed to unions, staying at the forefront of social activism for most of his life." Noteworthy representatives included those from banks such as Citi and Credit Suisse, risk consulting agencies such as Standard & Poor's, law firms such as Ferrere, companies such as Telefónica and Microsoft, and lobbying firms such as Kissinger McLacarty (chaired by founder Henry Kissinger).

Beside the large mirror and fireplace, Evo didn't tell them what they hoped to hear. He wouldn't say that Bolivia was a safe place for investments, he wouldn't guarantee legal protection, nor did he venerate the Council of the Americas for its contributions to the continent.

"When I came to the presidency, I didn't know that the circulation of a lot of money would bring about inflation," Morales said.

Evo enumerated the macroeconomic successes of his administration: "And they call us ignorant." He softened his harsh tone by making jokes that the attendees didn't take all that well.

"The laws of the neoliberals are...[did not complete the phrase]... Forgive me if the neoliberals are your colleagues."

Some of them laughed. Many of them had odd looks on their faces when Morales told about how his father had extracted his molars with a knife and a rock and when he said he wanted healthcare for all Bolivians.

After Evo's speech, an agro exporter from Cali, Colombia, asked whether Morales supported the decriminalization of drugs as he did. "I don't understand that subject," Evo answered. A German banker asked about his dependence on Chávez. "He doesn't ask us for anything in exchange. They say that he demeans me with how he hugs me, but I don't think it's like that. Now you're not going to go off advising Podemos [the opposing party], are you?" Morales asked.

Susan Segal announced that there wouldn't be any more questions. They didn't applaud him.

Evo went up to greet Thomas Shannon and ask him a question: "When are you going to come and visit my country?" During Morales' talk, he'd said: "The U.S. ambassador used to come and give the Bolivian government $10 million to help contain social conflicts. Now he serves as a counterweight to our government."

Back at the UN, General Secretary Ban Ki-moon asked for Evo's cooperation in Haiti. Evo declared that he would arm a union of ambassadors, and the Korean hesitated: Ki-moon didn't know he was making a joke. But in the end he realized and laughed.

The president was waiting for the particularly uncomfortable question from the UN that his ambassador had anticipated.

"Could the conflict with the east of your country intensify?" Ki-moon inquired.

He responded that he wanted to engage in a dialogue with the opposition.

When Evo got back to the hotel, he spoke with Cochabamba leaders to get the details for Sunday's event, in which an under-18 soccer tournament would take place. I asked him whether it was true that he wasn't going to prepare any notes for his UN speech.

"I've never read my speeches, and I'm not going to do it now. I use little bullets. But since here there isn't applause or any pauses in the middle, it's harder. But I put down little issues. Five little issues. Where's a good place to eat?" he asked.

Ten minutes later, he was chatting with Jimmy Carter, who was accompanied by his bodyguard and an advisor.

"How are your peanut plantations?" Morales asked.

"Very good. And yours?" the ex-president responded.

"No, I don't have any time for my little plot," Evo said.

They moved on to the subject of heads of state. Carter told him that he'd called Condoleezza Rice after last year's meeting to ask her how relations were between Washington and La Paz. Then Carter asked about the Bolivian press.

"My main opposition," Morales responded.

After each response, the Nobel Peace Prize recipient repeated, "Sounds good."

Carter consulted Morales about Fidel's health. Evo reported that he was getting better. Carter said that he and Castro were two years apart in age. And "Sounds good."

At 1:30 P.M., after saying goodbye to Carter, Evo started eating chocolate cookies. They informed him that they'd gone through the delegation's budget and there was only enough lunch money left for him, ministers, and ambassadors.

"Alejandra [his personal assistant] has a little bit of money. We all get to eat, bosses. What are we having?"

The food would take an hour and a half to arrive. A consulate secretary had ordered from a Bolivian place in Queens, about 40 minutes away. They decided to buy him a hamburger at Wendy's during the wait.

"I dreamt about Chávez again," he told me.

"When?" I asked.

"I went to look at my notes for the speech and fell asleep. Then I dreamt about him. What are those dreams trying to tell me?" he wondered.

That morning he took a pill of Maca supplement because he still hadn't fully recovered from the first night's fever. He walked to the UN and, when he sat down, the Iranian president came by to greet him. "I'll see you tomorrow in La Paz," he said. That encounter became the photo of the day.

Morales delivered a speech that lasted a little more than 20 minutes.

My delegation had a lot of trouble coming out here due to visa problems; our parliament members can't obtain visas. When I come over here, I'm blockaded from the airport, my ministers who come, my indigenous brothers, are subjected to hours and hours of inspection, and some of us countries come here only to be threatened by our hosts, by President Bush [he pronounced it "Booch"] [...] we should think about changing the headquarters of the United Nations, I personally do not agree to come here and be subjected to certain investigations. [...] I also feel that we should begin with the decolonization of the United Nations and that we all respect one another whether we're small or large countries, whether we have problems or don't have problems. [...] Other accusations, other distortions, include those accused of being cruel, of being dictators like I heard

President Bush say yesterday directed at the president and commander of Cuba. A salute to all of the revolutionaries, especially
President Fidel, for whom I have a great deal of respect because Fidel
also sends troops to many countries, but troops to save lives, unlike
the president of the United States who sends troops to end lives.
[...] I want to say to you all, in closing, though sometimes the red
light makes us nervous [the red light is the signal that the speaker's
time is up] what's important is to change those economic models and
to eradicate capitalism.

A line of officials, chancellors, and even presidents waited for him in
the area designated by the UN for congratulations. He asked whether their
salutations implied support for his request to change the headquarters. He
then went down to the CNN truck outside for a live interview. Drops of
perspiration rolled down his face. He answered questions about his relationship with Iran and Libya, knowing that he would be giving explana-
tions for them for a long time to come.

From there, Evo traveled straight to the airport. I joined him in the
sedan for our last chat. Only the chauffeur and secret service chief of security who traveled in front could hear us.

"I didn't see the red light when I was giving the speech," he said.

"What were you reading from?" I asked.

"You're not going to understand what it says," he said, and he took out
the hotel notepad with the words he had jotted down: *Bolivia, Constituent
Assembly, colonialism, natural resources, ONU, bio, War, indigenous people,
basic services, energy without accomplices, basic services, capitalism the worst
enemy to humanity, New millennium, life, living well, living in harmony with
the mother of the earth.*

I turned on the tape recorder.

"I left this interview for the end, so that you'd have to follow me the
whole time in *Gringo*-land," he explained, while resting his elbow on the
cream-colored armrest complete with cup holders.

"When you assumed the presidency, did you think that you would have
better relations with the United States?" I asked.

"I knew that the United States wasn't going to be an ally. They accused
me of narcotics trafficking, of murder, of being an Andean Bin Laden, and
they organized persecution teams from the State Department. So we made
an alliance with countries not subjected to the empire's dictations."

"Do you think that you'll eventually dispense with U.S. assistance altogether?" I asked.

"One hundred and fifty million dollars doesn't define the country's destiny, but it'd be preferable for that aid to make its way to the people. The problem is that they use the money to empower the opponents. We don't need help attached to blackmail and conditions," he said.

"How was your stay here?" I inquired.

"I never thought I'd be in the United States, and I never had any desire to come, but out of respect to my country and to the United Nations…"

"Aside from the potatoes, what didn't you like?"

"Everything from the hotel to the UN headquarters and from the UN to the meetings and from the meetings to the airport. The food gave me diarrhea. Otherwise, I don't know," Evo responded.

"Where would you like to change the UN headquarters to?"

"I didn't think about another headquarters," he replied.

"This time they gave you a visa for the whole year, more than last year," I noted.

"Last year they only gave me one for a few days because they thought they were going to take me right out of the presidency; now maybe they know that I'm going stick around for longer," Morales answered.

After listening to Evo's speech at the UN, Goldberg, in La Paz, stated that he wouldn't be surprised if the Bolivian government asked to change the headquarters of Disney World, too, because the UN seemed to be right on par with the amusement park. The ambassador's words were meant to demonstrate his disapproval of the Iranian president's visit to La Paz, during which Morales would refer to him as a "revolutionary *compañero*." Evo was less pleasant to Goldberg. In the days that followed, he proclaimed that he was no longer a suitable interlocutor, and he prohibited his entrance into the Burned Palace. On October 12, during an event with indigenous organizations, he concluded his speech with a cry that he hadn't delivered since taking office: "*Causachun Coca! Wañuchun yanquis*! (Long live Coca! Death to the yankees!)"

When the vehicle driving him to the airport abruptly slammed on its breaks, he told me to ask the chauffeur whether they were trying to behead the president. The secret service official didn't understand the joke. "It's just that the car in front slammed on his brakes."

"Next time we're going to go to a Karaoke bar, boss," Morales said.

"Karaoke? Well, maybe, sure," the secret service agent answered, somewhat surprised.

"You know? When Fidel compliments me, it's really nice. I really feel it [bringing his hand to his chest]. One time, when I ended up quarreling with [Álvaro] Uribe in Rio de Janeiro, Fidel called to tell me that I was brave, intelligent, and brilliant," he recounted.

"And you never compliment him?" I asked.

"No, I never do that," Evo responded.

"Why not?"

"Because if I compliment him, it's like I'm telling him that there are some things that he does well and others that he's doing wrong," he explained.

Because the trip had already taken 45 minutes, he asked whether they'd moved the airport somewhere else.

"We'll be there in 15 minutes," the chauffeur responded.

After that much time passed, he asked whether they were hiding the plane from him. The chief of security explained that it would only be a little longer and that his arrival to Newark had just been a misunderstanding, that they hadn't done it on purpose. This remark seemed to be in response to his UN speech.

"We're just going around and around, what's going on, boss? I have to get back to my country," Evo demanded.

On the roads inside the airport, he was surprised that some of the planes only carried mail.

"Around and around, it's a carousel, boss," Evo complained.

"Is this your last time in the United States?" I asked.

"Maybe one more little trip. I don't know," he said.

Two Venezuelan officials with red berets were awaiting his arrival, and they bowed to him on the plane stairs.

Chapter Eight

THE PRESIDENT (2006–2007)

On January 31, 2006, the Burned Palace smelled of alcohol and burnt sugar because of the Andean ko'a ritual that the president arranged to expel bad energy from the building. The *amautas* (Andean ritual specialists) set two tables—one with a white cloth and the other with a colorful one—and presented him with the incense. They asked for his health, for a good governmental administration, and for him to find a wife soon. Morales ordered that the ritual be repeated in each corner of Plaza Murillo. The bad vibes, he maintained, had passed through the Palace walls.

That ko'a and other indigenous rituals served as counterpoints to the cocktail party ten days earlier on inauguration day. It was perhaps the last social occurrence of its kind. Previously, the Palace lounges would have been bursting with ladies and gentleman: the proprietors of the country, the well-off professionals, and the diplomats who were accustomed to that era's Bolivian cultural protocol.

The existing Palace personnel were the children of that tradition. In the past, the male employees, for example, were required to wear suits. "Let them come dressed however they want," Morales declared in the first week.

He also requested that they cook for all of the employees because in previous administrations that benefit only reached the officials at the top of the hierarchy. Despite the Palace manager's complaints, expenses tripled in that area. Bolivian dishes—especially soups—replaced the international cuisine. The president began to ask for his first meal before 10:00 A.M.

The building felt alien to Evo. Many previous chiefs of state planned to make alterations to turn it into their own space before assuming office. But the new inhabitants, apart from minor details, neglected even the possibility of such changes.

During the first days, Morales was made uncomfortable by the lack of privacy—there were people around him constantly—and by the bureaucratic slowness. He began to miss the syndical decision-making mechanism immediately.

No member of his intimate circle had ever been a civil servant before. One of them, his spokesperson, Alex Contreras, took a picture of himself stepping into the Palace for the first time. This way he'd be able to see, at the end of his administration, the marks left on his body by the passage of time. He didn't have long to wait: Within a few months, he had to be hospitalized due to the intensity of the work schedule.

There were obstacles with some old Palace employees. They fired an employee because she described the president's secretaries, Janet and Eva, as "two Indians in need of refining." Both of them were less than 25 years old and activists loyal to Evo, and they made up for their lack of experience with a volunteerism that turned the Palace into their home.

The position of personal assistant was not an easy job to hold. The first one appointed was asked to leave after insulting employees, the second because Morales didn't trust her. Before appointing the third one, Paola Zapata, who lasted until mid-2007, Evo commanded her to treat everyone respectfully, never to lie or keep anything from him, and never to use his name to help anyone else. Zapata found out what presidential ire was when Evo asked her whether she'd sorted out a funeral flower delivery with Javier—his chauffeur—and she answered that she had. Morales confirmed her falsity and unloaded his fury: "Don't ever lie." His fits of rage are a source of panic among the men and women of the Palace.

Evo's distrust and his intervention in every detail—such as asking to change the letterhead on official papers—were two traits of his administration that would not change. The tools available to the state were often minimal or inadequate. Shortly after taking office, his team discovered that one official was photocopying files. But the investigation couldn't advance because they would have needed phone taps, and the U.S. embassy supervised the two police divisions dedicated to that function.

During the first few days, Cuba participated in matters of intelligence and security. The Cubans suggested changing the entire Palace personnel, but the president wouldn't agree to it. He did allow them to look for micro-phones, but they didn't find anything. A good friend from Havana, Iván Iporre, who came to the Palace as a private secretary and left in less than two months, took charge of both intelligence and security. A group of civil-ians under his command were given training in Cuba and shared the task of guarding the president with the police and the army. Morales' love affair with that group of civil guards ended when a letter disappeared.

Although the president didn't re-create the Palace as his own space, he did take control of its schedule, which became a way of exercising his authority over less like-minded visitors. In his first meeting with the Episcopal Confederation, at 5:00 A.M., a pair of bishops began to nod off. "Don't fall asleep on me!" he requested. At that same hour on another day, he scheduled an appointment with a group of U.S. representatives. At first they declined but the president wouldn't accept any changes, so Ambassador David Greenlee had to convince them. The new routine also affected his own people. During the first month, some of them got sick, others fainted, and a few ended up in the hospital.

In one of his first measures, he reduced the president's salary by 57 percent, to $1,875 per month. Ministers and officials stopped receiving their "supplementary wages" with the elimination of reserve spending.

To elect his ministers, he welcomed suggestions from an extensive list of people and organizations. There were some predictable placements, such as David Choquehuanca for the chancellorship or his economist, Carlos Villegas, for developmental planning. Some of them he didn't know at all, such as the minister of the treasury, and others were placed as part of agreements made with different social sectors during the electoral campaign, such as the minister of mining. He placed the labor union chief of domestic employees at the head of the ministry of justice, and he surprised everyone with the appointment of another woman in the ministry of government in charge of the police. Minister of hydrocarbons went to a representative of the National Left, and the ministry of water was given to a radical from El Alto. A Santa Cruz millionaire, who didn't align himself with his depart-ment's elite, ended up in the ministry of public works. Education was under the command of an Aymara intellectual. No one expected the naming of Juan Ramón Quintana as minister of the presidency because he had only recently arrived to Morales' milieu.

After occupying the Cabinet, the searches for the 700 hierarchical posi-tions and the remainder of the government workers began. To fill in the chart, García Linera went around with an enormous list. The president named candidates and decided on hierarchical appointments from the top to the bottom. The leakage of appointments to the press became commonplace. Every time one was published, Evo suspended it and demanded to know how the leak had happened.

Party members and leaders began to present themselves at the Palace, claiming that they were carrying out mandates to assume certain positions. "The assembly of my syndicate has elected me to..." became a repeated phrase. It foretold something that would become more noticeable in coming months, the hunt for "gigs" (*pegas*), as government positions are sometimes called in Bolivia. The petitions also came in the form of letters to the president. An elderly MAS party member used three pages to ask for her son-in-law to be appointed as a consul in India, but she explained that he could just as well work as a gardener in the San Jorge residence.

Quintana, an ex-army captain, sociologist, and specialist in security and defense affairs, became a liaison to the armed forces. Morales wanted to undo his incrimination as narcotics *cocalero*, and he was eager to know what place the armed forces would come to occupy within the country's power structure. When Quintana first suggested that Morales skip over a couple of promotions in the appointment of a new High Command, Morales was skeptical. He thought his minister was attempting to instate officials of his own choice. He later became excited about the idea of imposing authority as a first step, aiming to initiate the call for restitution of national sovereignty in the armed forces. Twenty-four generals were skipped over, according to Quintana, the greatest purge since 1952.

The day of the appointment of the High Command—48 hours after inauguration—was the most difficult moment of García Linera's first 18 months in office.

"Some of those who were dismissed are gathering on the second floor," the president was informed on January 24. He wasn't quite sure what was going on with the police and the army. The ministers proposed a dialogue with the rebels. Morales responded that his authority would not be negotiated in military terms. He requested a contingency plan from the chief of police and asked him whether he had tear gas. He refused to change the location of the High Command assumption ceremony. When he was going down from the third floor to the central hall with García Linera, the elevator got stuck, but it wasn't a rebel trap.

During the military swearing in, the wife and daughter of a discharged general shouted at Morales that he was committing an injustice. "We said that we were going to respect the established institution, and we are doing so," Evo reminded his audience in his speech. "I am very sorry that some generals drew the attention of the previous government. They aren't being punished, but they do have to surrender themselves to an investigation."

One of the president's weaknesses was his lack of information, as evidenced by another crisis at the beginning of his administration—the bankruptcy of LAB, Bolivia's primary airline. Without concrete data about the company's situation, the government sought help from the Kirchner administration in a peculiar way: Two Palace officials rang the doorbell of the Argentine embassy. The Casa Rosada (Argentine house of government) sent a delegation via the minister of federal planning, Julio de Vido.

Evo wouldn't accept a LAB rescue plan financed by the state. He began to consider founding a new airline, Abya Yala, the name that certain indigenous groups had given to the continent that would come to be known as America after 1492. Because he was skeptical of the pilots' proposals, he decided on a company takeover.

There were repeated requests for foreign assistance during the first weeks of the new government, especially during the floods, which resulted in the deaths of at least 20 people. Cuba and Venezuela stood out among the countries that offered their help.

The management of social conflicts was left under the control of a member of the president's inner circle, Alfredo Rada. He was a former member of a Trotskyite party and director of the Center for Judicial Studies and Social Investigation (CEJIS), one of the many nongovernmental organizations that provided the executive branch with public servants.

Rada assumed the role of vice minister of coordination with social movements, formerly known as the vice ministry of strategic matters. Under the previous governments, that division ensured law and order based on the discretional use of reserve funds and, failing that, force. During the first months, Rada received intelligence reports detailing marches, rallies, and roadblocks and their respective risks, but they didn't explain the reasons for the protests. To change his department's modus operandi, the vice minister organized a group to analyze the proposals and demands of the protestors, and he began to better monitor any agreements made between the government and social organizations.

That new vice minister's approach, in conjunction with the conviction that the administration would never suppress the protesters, led Morales to believe that there would never be a death under his administration. On June 9, 2006, however, after a judge ordered the evacuation of shelters organized by Sin Techo (homeless), a confrontation arose in which an off-duty police officer lost his life.

Morales found out through the radio. He called Minister of Government Alicia Muñoz.

"What have you done? How can you dirty us with blood!?" he asked her, almost desperately.

The president and his team believed that previous governments had always given orders to kill. They didn't consider that the police, or even sometimes the army, exercised a certain degree of autonomy or that some deaths might have been involuntary or the result of a lack of skill. Morales wasn't prepared to bury a Bolivian as the consequence of a social protest.

That first death under his government also called attention to the demands and urgencies of those same groups that his government believed itself to represent. Evo quickly realized that they wouldn't have much patience with the government even if they did see them as honest and nearly their own.

On September 29, the same day as the arrival of the new U.S. ambassador Goldberg, two *cocaleros* died in a clash with both the army and police. The minister of government sounded like her predecessors in her initial reaction. Muñoz declared that "they were planters who were working in drug trafficking." Devastated, Morales shared his sorrows with his intimate circle.

Paradoxically, in a case involving even more deaths, he didn't feel any responsibility. During the first week of October, the unified cooperative miners—to whom Evo had handed over the ministry of mining—disputed over gunshots and dynamite with the salaried miners of Posokoni Hill, which possessed 948,000 tons of tin valued at approximately $580 million. Sixteen people died. Prior to the confrontation, the government had held 20 meetings with the two groups. "As a *campesino* who is now president and as your brother," he pleaded, "tell me what I have to do." But the stubbornness of both sides, a certain degree of state incompetence, and ministry inefficiency prevented a way out. "What should have been a blessing became a curse," García Linera stated in reference to the boom of mineral exports, which went from $287 million during the first ten months of 2005 to $642 million in the same period of the following year.

Although alarming intelligence reports were arriving from the mining region, the president decided not to militarize the conflict. There was the risk of further confrontations to consider, this time between security forces and the miners. He unloaded his fury against Minister Walter Villarroel in what was perhaps one of the greatest peaks of his rage in 2006 before dismissing him. The new minister, Guillermo Dalence, didn't last in the position either. He was asked to leave in March 2007 after he had signed agreements without authorization on a trip to Cuba.

Andrés Soliz Rada, attorney, journalist, and former member of the CONDEPA (Consciousness of Fatherland) party, is a nationalist obsessed with the natural resources of his country. At 67 years old, Morales appointed him as minister of hydrocarbons. His presence brought echoes of the national left that participated in the governments of generals Alfredo Ovando and Juan José Torres (1969–1971), when the Gulf Oil Company was nationalized. Soliz Rada worked on fostering understanding between the syndicates, the partisan left and the anti-U.S. sectors of the army.

The nationalization of the hydrocarbons industry—the primary promise of the MAS campaign—could count on vast social consensus. Since taking office, the president and a small group, in which Soliz participated, worked on the 22 drafts of the nationalizing decree before arriving at the final one. Evo entrusted them with his strictest confidence and was even careful not to notify certain people within his inner circle.

Attentive to symbols, he had the team reverse a number. Because the oil companies gave 18 percent of their production profits to the country through taxes and prerogatives, keeping 82 percent for themselves, the decree would force them to pay up to 82 percent and keep the 18. "They need to make a little something," Morales clarified.

Soliz Rada believed that if the government didn't nationalize in a reasonable amount of time, and with a solid presidential decree, the protests would continue with such force that they'd be able to topple the new administration. For weeks the team discussed how to ensure that the decree read as a nationalization, although it wasn't in the classic sense. They wouldn't be expropriating or expelling any of the companies.

In the debate over where to stage the measure, Soliz Rada proposed mounting a big event in El Alto because that was where the War of Gas against Sánchez de Lozada had begun. Walter Chávez, an influential presidential advisor, suggested the San Alberto megafield, run by Petrobrás, and he presented a plan complete with military participation.

The military command responsible for nationalization worked out of the offices of the vice presidency. Dressed for the job, the officials unfurled their maps and became excited talking about the theatrics of the operation. In this way, the armed forces reclaimed a nationalist tradition, which had apparently been forgotten for years.

At sunrise on May 1, the Cabinet approved the nationalization decree and sang the national anthem a cappella: "In glorious splendor let us preserve the lofty name of our native land. And on its altars we pledge anew, To die before living as slaves!"

In a Hercules plane, alongside the high command of the military and police, Evo flew to the San Alberto field, following the script. "This is the beginning of the *Jacha Uru* [the big day]," Morales announced as he piloted the plane for a few minutes.

In San Alberto, the people who should have been awaiting the delegation weren't there because it was a holiday (Latin American Labor Day). Instead, Petrobrás emergency personnel were left in charge of showing the president around the plant, completely unaware of what would happen next. They found out just a few minutes later.

Flanked by ministers and soldiers, with the megaphone in hand and wearing the Bolivian State Petroleum Company (YPFB) helmet, Morales read Supreme Decree 28.701: Chaco Heroes. The image had a notable national and international impact. By decree, the state recovered the "property, possession, and absolute control" of the country's hydrocarbon natural resources. As Morales commanded, in the case of the big fields, it permitted the state to collect up to 82 percent of the companies' profits before the signing of the contracts. The decree gave the companies until October 28 to renegotiate contracts with the state. The rules had changed.

Evo's popularity climbed to 81 percent: He had fulfilled his primary campaign promise.

"Evo's Bad Manners," headlined Spain's *El País* in an editorial about the Bolivian on May 1: "By decree [...], with the direct confiscation of shares [...] without previous negotiation, and sending in military troops including troops of engineers [...] as if such force were necessary and all this happening beyond any kind of reason." It shared the objections of YPF-Repsol.

In Brazilian circles of power, the military presence was interpreted as an invasion. The event changed the paternal relationship between Brazilia and La Paz. "It was unilateral and not amicable," described Petrobrás president José Gabrielli. Half of the gas that Brazil received came from Bolivia.

"If we didn't guarantee the provision, Brazil would have invaded," Soliz Rada told me in June 2006.

The oil companies objected to the decree and threatened to turn to the international courts or even leave the country. They applied pressure through chambers of businesses, the press, and the opposing parties. Soliz Rada decided not to negotiate through the Bolivian Chamber of Hydrocarbons but instead on an individual basis. "Every oil company comes in here and speaks badly of the rest," the minister explained in his office. A few weeks earlier, a delegation from Repsol had arrived from Spain to speak with him in a plane that had double the capacity of the Bolivian presidency's aircraft. The differences didn't end there: The Repsol executive's secretaries earned double what Soliz Rada made, who in turn was arguing for $300 billion, the approximate value of his country's gas and petroleum reserves.

Soliz Rada's differences with Morales and García Linera led to the first schism in hydrocarbon politics. The president selected vice ministers and several officials for his ministry. García Linera's negotiations with Argentina and Brazil over the increase of gas prices diminished Soliz Rada's power. Furthermore, before taking office, he had written that Kirchner was a "representative of YPF-Repsol."

Soliz Rada called for firmness with Brazil given that they were paying a derisory sum. Moreover, he argued that Brazil's urgent need for gas permitted them to increase the price: For the importation of gas going to the Brazilian state of Mato Grosso, they paid $1.09 per million BTU (a package of 1,200,000 cubic meters daily) and $4.30 (for a package of 26,000,000 cubic meters daily) for that going to São Pablo. The Bolivian Workers' Center called for the even more radical expulsion of the companies altogether.

At times, the president shared Soliz Rada's position about the necessity of recovering Bolivia's two principal refineries, both in the hands of Petrobrás, but he was afraid that it would work in favor of the Brazilian right wing during a year in which Lula was seeking reelection. Mainstream media in that country had already made fun of his supposed softness on Bolivia.

"Evo," said Hugo Chávez, "you have to consider what would happen if Lula lost."

In fact, the Brazilian president was falling in the polls, less because of his attitude toward La Paz and more because of accusations of corruption against his Worker's Party, specifically allegations that they had purchased votes in Congress.

The fears in the Burned Palace took the form of questions: What would happen if Brazil cut off its purchases? What would happen if the ducts were covered? What would happen if the country ended up without fuel? Soliz Rada flew to Caracas and came back with an answer to reinforce his position. If it came to that, Venezuela would be the one to answer these questions in practical terms. Their government and its state oil company, PDVSA, had already assisted in the nationalizing process with advice, expert help, and money. According to Manuel Morales Olivera, the future president of YPFB, they'd contracted a New York law firm.

Soliz Rada resigned on September 15 after the president suspended Ministerial Resolution 207/2006, which enforced the state monopoly on the commercialization of oil and oil by-products. The resolution therefore excluded Petrobrás, the owner of the refineries. Lula described it as a "dirty trick." The more conciliatory position with Brazil, represented by García Linera, prevailed.

His strategy was to first come to an agreement with Argentina, which paid a record sum for a bordering country of $5 per million BTU. "That agreement both curbed the companies and broke the spirit of the oil companies who had been determined not to negotiate," the vice president explained to journalist Pablo Stefanoni.

Lula didn't take the news well. He thought that Argentina should have had to agree on the price with Brazil first. On September 21, he said something publicly to the Bolivian chief of state: "You can't hold a sword over the head of Brazil just because you sell us gas [...]. We can also hold a sword over your heads [...]. If you don't sell [the gas] to us, I can see to it that it becomes very difficult for you to sell to anyone else." It sounded like a poker game between two ex-union leaders turned presidents.

By the time Carlos Villegas replaced Soliz Rada, the oil company negotiations had advanced little, and the deadline to sign was set to expire in a mere 40 days. That wasn't the only problem: Villegas wasn't able to draft renegotiation plans for individual companies because of an interior conflict in YPFB and accusations against its ex-president, Jorge Alvarado, which had damaged the state oil company's credibility.

Until October 28, Villegas lived in YPFB. He worked with a group of Bolivian attorneys and with the New York firm hired by PDVSA.

Pressures mounted in a variety of ways. The vice president of the Spanish government, María Teresa Fernández de la Vega, was in communication with the Burned Palace almost daily to demonstrate her interest in the subject. It was evident to the Bolivian negotiators that, in contrast to other European countries, YPF-Repsol acts in tandem with the Spanish government. On October 28, Bernardino León, the Spanish government's secretary of foreign affairs, introduced himself to Villegas. "I am here to ensure that we come to excellent agreements," he said. The minister took it as a new (and unpleasant) form of pressure.

If the companies didn't sign the contracts before midnight on October 28, the armed forces would occupy the fields. "I was certain that we would have to take the fields in Gran Chaco," Minister Villegas told me in an interview in December 2006.

That day, shortly after 11:00 P.M. on October 28, Morales confirmed that every single company would sign the contracts. YPF-Repsol was the last to agree. The 20- or 30-year contracts implied a significant increase in tax revenue for Bolivia. In fact, according to official data, Bolivia went from collecting $173 million in oil and gas revenue in 2002 to $1.3 billion in 2006.

Despite their threats to leave the country, the companies stayed because even after the considerable increase in taxes, they would continue to earn huge profits.

The government needed a firm YPFB to maximize the benefits of the nationalizing decree. It had to confront several obtsacles—the migrations of experts to the private sector, the limitations of hiring staff that wouldn't balk at the salary cap ordered by Morales, and the company's internal quarrels.

The difficulties continued. The government sent Congress nondefinitive contracts, and the opposition took advantage of their sloppiness. After long negotiations, they were approved and put into effect on May 2, 2007.

The president knew that nationalization had become the hallmark of his government, and he began to use that word in reference to different projects. On June 20, 2006, he announced that they would also nationalize mining, electricity, telephones, and railroads. One time he said, with laughter, that he would nationalize *La Razón*, the daily paper of the Spanish group Prisa, which he considered in the opposition's camp.

He began to worry about how to translate the nationalization decree into government action that would benefit the people. First, he created a scholastic voucher (Juancito Pinto) of $25 per student. The money came from the decree that had forced Petrobrás, Andina, and Total to pay $32 million more per month for their additional holdings, 50 to 82 percent of the income in the San Alberto and Sábalo megafields. Because the voucher had to make its way to remote places, the armed forces participated in its distribution, accentuating their presence in the process. The same thing was done with the "dignity income," a voucher extended to anyone more than 60 years of age.

In February 2007, the government nationalized the Vinto metallurgic plant. It took control of the Swiss company Glencore and, maintaining that there were illegalities in the way it had originally been sold, announced that it wouldn't compensate the company. "We condemn the violation of private property," claimed the company's spokesperson after army troops stormed the plant.

While the president and his vice president waited for the nationalization ceremony, the barracks commander told them that he'd put an Andean folk dance together for them. One of the dancers invited Morales and García Linera onto the stage.

"You'd better watch that girl because the vice president is very smooth," Evo warned the soldiers.

"Yes, I know, but this girl is my daughter," the colonel answered, drawing his sword.

Amid the laughter, Morales concluded with a shout: "To nationalize, bosses."

At that point, not all of these radical changes seemed possible: neither widespread nationalizations in the classic sense (with the exception of Vinto), the educational revolution, the hoped-for Constituent Assembly, the definitive defeat of the Santa Cruz elite, nor an extreme economic program. Government programs that would make clean breaks with the past did accompany the president's radical discourse—especially during the first six months—but not on the same scale that he had once ventured. As part of his presidential education, he needed to negotiate and give in.

In a speech emphasizing the idea of decolonization, Minister Félix Patzi declared education to be secular, so that no belief—referring particularly to the Catholic Church—could be imposed and also to stop Spanish from being the dominant, central language, around which all of the education system was organized. Allying itself with the majority of the press, the Church launched a relentless campaign against him. During a Cabinet meeting, Evo asked his minister to back down, although he maintained his firmness against the Church.

In a private meeting with its leaders in November 2006, Evo reproached the Church for its opposing position.

"If you want war, there will be war," he warned. "I will defeat you. I have not forgotten that you were accomplices to a genocide [referring to the conquest of America]."

"We have changed, Mr. President," Cardinal Julio Terrazas responded.

"If you go on like this, I am going to renounce my religious practices," Morales concluded.

In January 2007, Patzi left the Cabinet.

The economic plan was also limited. The person in charge, Carlos Villegas, had been a consulting economist for Morales since 2002. Villegas would give him lessons on the Bolivian economy and always received the same request from his pupil: "Concrete examples, big boss."

During the 2005 campaign, they'd met with the delegations of multi-lateral credit organizations, which were concerned about nationalizations and "populist" measures. They encountered new concerns after the election, such as the deficit and inflation. They warned the government that it would lose control of the economy. Villegas showed that he was capable of gratitude—those sent from the IMF and the World Bank ended up being friendly with him—but he informed them that under the new administration it would be the ministry of treasury and the Central Bank that would formulate the economic plan. Advising and "standing by" wouldn't be necessary. The World Bank forgave the debt and lowered the annual allowance from $75 to $35 million. At the government's request, the IMF stopped lending money altogether.

In June 2006, Villegas presented his economic plan in PowerPoint to the president, the Cabinet, and the High Command in the Palace hall. The gradualist spirit of the administration could be seen through certain objectives. Moderate poverty would go from 58.9 percent in 2005 to 49 percent in 2011; extreme poverty and indigence from 35.3 percent to 27.2 percent;

the GDP growth rate from 1.84 percent to 4.31 percent; the Gini coefficient (which measures inequality) from 0.59 to 0.58.

"If they don't kill me, they're idiots, was what I was thinking at the time, and I was right about that," García Linera told me. "They gave me a second chance, and now I am the vice president. When I was being tortured, all I was thinking about was how to escape from there, developing an attack plan, hiding things, digging a tunnel. It was a battle of intelligence. How could I possibly betray and demolish my own project? The physical hardship was nothing. What concerned me was the project, how to preserve it."

During a long conversation in Morales' office, while acting as interim president in Evo's absence, García Linera recounted the years during the 1990s that he spent being tortured and held prisoner for belonging to the Tupac Katari Guerilla Army (EGTK). A captain, who had been his jailer at the time, and his guard were resting in a small office a few feet away. When he came to the vice presidency, he ignored his torturers. When he found out that one of them was seeking a promotion, he didn't do anything to prevent it or to help him.

Born in Cochabamba, his primary objective since the age of 17, as both an activist and an intellectual, had been to see an indigenous person become president. When that moment materialized, "when the sash was hung on Evo," all he remembers is trying to guess what thoughts were going through his running mate's mind.

His relationship with his old army and prison companion, Felipe Quispe, ended badly. Unlike the vice president, Quispe made the dispute public. He said that Álvaro had betrayed him with Morales, airing private matters and providing the right with a homophobic plotline during the 2005 presidential campaign. The vice president never responded, as he makes a point of denying claims of the right hemisphere, or emotional side, of his brain in public matters.

With a degree in mathematics, he has turned cold calculation into an art. He understands that as vice president he is playing at least seven chess games and that they all require dispassionate objectivity. He also applies this technique during negotiations. He concerns himself with knowing what the other person is looking for, what his interests and objectives are, and he even makes an effort to guess what he's thinking. "I do it diplomatically. Mine is a rationalist pragmatism."

Described as an "encyclopedist"—social science and Bolivian history dominate his library of more than 15,000 books—he hopes to become a vice president of everything. His primary limitation—or his greatest weakness—is the budget. It's difficult for him to have a generalized out-look and to decipher the best interests hiding in so many numbers. His days in academia have come to an end: "In the Palace, one must take action on the spot, often without any time to get into the details."

His relationship with Morales has become one of the biggest topics of discussion surrounding the administration. They laughed when the first article came out referring to supposed disputes between them. They were where they usually are: at the two heads of the rectangular table in the president's office. Their mutual trust has been constructed through the day-to-day.

From the start, Morales resolved to make him part of the majority of the decisions. He perceived that his vice president was of his same disposition. Some powerful actors in Bolivian politics, especially the U.S. embassy, thought that García Linera could be the Trojan Horse who would allow them access to influence the president. But the vice president heads off any misunderstandings, telling his boss about every single meeting and meeting request.

On the whiteboard located to the side of the rectangular table, García Linera usually articulates or translates the president's ideas and initia-tives. He develops a discourse and gives it meaning. In public, he some-times serves as the explainer. In a complementary role, he also embodies the reconciler. That is what happened in gas negotiations with Brazil and Argentina, with the United States, and with some internal interlocutors such as the Santa Cruz elite, at first.

Although they exhibit a stonelike unity on the outside, the vice president will argue with Morales in the privacy of the office. They disagreed about relations with Washington. The vice president always supported depart-mental autonomy and the approval of the new Constitution by two-thirds; Morales prioritizes public investment in roads and public works, García Linera in more productive projects; and the vice president has a more criti-cal view of the Cuban and Venezuelan governments.

Those discrepancies have provoked some disputes. When the vice president signed a declaration supporting Chile's entrance into the Andean Community of Nations (CAN), Morales speculated that Santiago would join the "neoliberal" bloc of Peru and Colombia, thereby weakening

Bolivia in CAN since Venezuela had already withdrawn. The president also requested that García Linera publicly criticize the idea of autonomy and got upset when he took a long time to do so. But afterward, as with everything, García Linera fell in line.

A lot of power is concentrated in the Burned Palace. This is due, in part, to Morales' decisionism and the centralization of his government, but also to the lack of devotion at the secondary levels of the state bureaucracy. "If I were to call a vice minister or director right now," García Linera explained to me one Sunday in the Palace, "their cell phone would be turned off. And that happens all the time." The presidential duo is faced with that lack of commitment—and initiative—among deputies, senators, and representatives of the Constituent Assembly.

Morales never created a School of Civil Service when he came to the Palace or any kind of school for future government employees as was suggested to him in 2002. Consequently, new officials and leaders are trained on the job. Some of them didn't get there in the best of ways. A group of MAS leaders and parliament members bought recommendations (endorsements) to obtain state jobs. It became a public scandal. During the twelfth anniversary celebration of the MAS in March 2007, some of those present demanded employment from García Linera, and others shouted "racist" at him when he denied their requests.

The government relies on fewer indigenous officials than it originally planned. They attribute this to the internal power dispute among different MAS sectors that sparked discussion about the supposed "white" cabinet (*entorno blancoide*) that had captured the president. The magazine *Willka* published a photo of him on its cover with a provocative headline: "Evo Morales: amidst cracker cabinet, restoration of the oligarchy and indigenous movements."

The president denies the existence of the so-called cracker cabinet. The vice president attributes it to displaced MAS members and certain Indianists who, he says, suffer from the infantile disorder of Indianism, in reference to *Left-Wing Communism: An Infantile Disorder* by Lenin, one of the authors he has re-read the most since coming to the Palace.

Morales has surrounded himself with different groups he trusts. One of them, at the center of governmental management, is Juan Ramón Quintana, the minister of the presidency and one of those most resisted by the MAS regime and the ministers of the treasury, hydrocarbons, and mining. According to the minister of the presidency, he earned

Evo's trust with a strong work ethic, physical capacity, attendance, and discipline.

Another group connects the president with social organizations. Choquehuanca, Santos Ramírez, and Sacha Llorenti, the second vice minister of coordination with social movements, handle that area with little intervention from García Linera. Morales is in direct contact with those groups, with whom he has discussed the biggest issues: hydrocarbons, land reform, and the Constituent Assembly. "He has a lot of patience with the leaders and their supporters," Llorenti says. "He tells them what he can do and what he can't. On top of meeting all of the time, he keeps them informed about what else he's doing as if that were among the president's duties."

Two people served as spokesmen for the administration during the first year. One of them was the president's spokesperson, Alex Contreras, one of his most loyal officials. The other, Walter Chávez, was responsible for propaganda and campaigning, in addition to being a figure in Evo's inner circle. Chávez had to leave the government at the beginning of 2007 when the press reported that the Peruvian justice system would request his capture and extradition over an alleged case of extortion during his affiliation with the Tupac Amaru Revolutionary Movement (MRTA), the group that took the Japanese embassy in Lima in 1996. It was the opposition, some of the press, and even some MAS party members who staged the political lynching of Chávez. The journalist, Víctor Orduna, took his place in the second year of government.

Another branch of Evo's administration is the group of attorneys responsible for supervising the legality of governmental actions and, most important, the decrees. Morales refers to this group of lawyers as "bananas" because he insists that all bananas are crooked. He describes Héctor Arce, the vice minister of governmental coordination, as "a banana for export (the best bananas are always exported)."

To handle international relations, Morales brought David Choquehuanca and Pablo Solón to his team. The chancellor, in an interview for this book, said that he wasn't as concerned about the so-called cracker cabinet as he was about the leftist one: "They want to divert attention from the indigenous process and make a leftist government; the leftists have always betrayed us."

For these various branches, Morales is the incarnation of the "process of change," which is how the government defines itself. In this context,

"Evolatry" was born. Some of its hallmarks include the decree that made his house in Orinoca into a national historic patrimony, the declaration made by a group of indigenous people who announced they would found Evo Morales City in a town near the Brazilian border, and the mayor that called him God Evo.

García Linera and Walter Chávez came up with a response to that Evolatry in the conceptualization of "Evoism." According to them, Morales' widespread support represents the strength of the process, and that type of leadership has an indisputable forcefulness within Bolivia and outside. In the article "Evoism: The National-Popular in Action," the vice president wrote:

> Evoism is a form of state-political self-representation of the plebe-ian society. [...] The Indianism that Morales proposes is cultural more than anything else, and therefore it can call together more ex-pansive sectors of the nation [...] With traces of Indianism, of the national and the popular, of syndicalism and Marxism, Evo Morales has turned the MAS into a power structure that now controls the state and dares, from this point forward, to undertake the construc-tion of a post-neoliberal model, perhaps the only serious one in Latin America.

Evolatrats and Evoists began to envision reelection during the first year of government. One Evolatrat publicly went too far. In April 2007, the vice president of the MAS, Gerardo García, declared that many of his friends and colleagues wanted Evo at the helm of the presidency for 50 years or more. That discussion moved into the Constituent Assembly.

The Santa Cruz elite, through some of its mouthpieces, announced that his reelection implied the beginning of a civil dictatorship.

The Bolivian east remained a complex problem for the president.

As part of the ten commandments of the MAS campaign, Walter Chávez asked for an autonomy proposal from attorney Juan Carlos Urenda—linked with the Santa Cruz elite—as a demonstration of their willingness to have a dialogue. But in the final ten commandments, the indigenous understanding of the autonomy proposal prevailed. The party of government postulated a plurinational state, which would include both ideas for autonomy.

Although at the beginning of his term the president declared himself in favor of autonomy, in May 2006 he began to change his position. The then-president of the senate, Santos Ramírez, was the only one of his intimate circle to support Evo in that regard. In addition to his own political experience and instinct, Morales took into account other voices to reaffirm his new position, such as social leaders, polls, MAS factions in Santa Cruz, and the racist sentiments from the Santa Cruz elite. In June, he stated that he no longer wanted departmental autonomy "for the bourgeoisie—it's a weapon to conserve their privileges."

The Pro–Santa Cruz Committee responded with a rally that, according to data collected by the local paper, *El Deber*, joined together half a million people. They called for departmental autonomy with a government that could sanction its own laws and make use of its own resources.

In the July 2, 2006, election, the government received 137 of the 250 votes, which is to say 53.7 percent of the members of the Constituent Assembly were responsible for reforming the Constitution. MAS won in Santa Cruz, where 20 of the 44 elected representatives were from the ruling party. As for the autonomic referendum, 57.6 percent voted No, whereas 42.4 percent voted Yes. In the Bolivian east, Yes won in four departments: Tarija, Beni, Pando, and Santa Cruz (in the latter, Yes obtained 71.11 percent). For its part, the west demonstrated a preference for No: the five departments (La Paz, Oruro, Potosí, Cochabamba, and Chuquisaca) averaged out to 69.46 percent.

The results generated two possible interpretations. The Pro–Santa Cruz Committee, to ensure that Santa Cruz obtained its autonomy, insisted that the referendum results should be binding for each respective department, making any discussions about it in the Constituent Assembly moot. For its part, the government held that the referendum was binding on the national level. In other words, the Committee wanted the Santa Cruz results to apply to that department. But for the government, the national results applied to the whole country, including Santa Cruz.

The Constituent Assembly had to resolve Santa Cruz's argument for autonomy. Originally demanded by indigenous groups in 1990, the Assembly became a banner of social organizations in the new millennium, given that it could serve as a platform for the country's refounding.

On August 6, 1825, the day of Bolivia's birth, the indigenous people, who represented about 80 percent of the population, weren't able to participate in the foundation of the republic. The Assembly's deputies had to be able to read and write, have an income, and be either employed or teachers.

On August 6, 2006, approximately 14,000 people from 30 of the 36 native nations inaugurated the Constituent Assembly and paraded through the streets of Sucre. The Bolivian national anthem was sung in Spanish, Quechua, Aymara, and Guaraní. One *cocalera* leader—Silvia Lazarte—assumed the presidency of the Assembly. Morales said that he would make himself subordinate to the Assembly and proclaimed that it should stand above the government. In practice, however, the government stood above the Assembly.

The Assembly had significant problems enacting legislation. Its tenure was only anticipated to take a year, but at the end of that period only one article had been approved. The opposition's demand—protected by the Convocation Law—that new articles be approved by two-thirds instead of the simple majority proposed by Morales impeded the Assembly's effective operation.

Autonomy and the two-thirds majority became the banner of an opposition that reinvented itself as a regional movement after the electoral failure of December 2005. On September 9, 2006, Santa Cruz civic leadership, in alliance with its peers in the departments of Beni, Pando, and Tarija, as well as other oppositional parties, made the first civic strike against the government with those two demands. MAS activists tried to break up the urban pickets that members of Santa Cruz Unified Youth had organized in the popular neighborhood of Plan Tres Mil and other spots in Santa Cruz. Both groups threw stones and exchanged blows until the police arrived, somewhat surprised at what was happening. MAS activists had done something that didn't figure into their repertory of protests—breaking down a roadblock instead of setting one up—and those from Santa Cruz used the pickets that they'd always condemned, considering them part of the country's backwardness.

By the end of November, Morales had accepted that declaring himself against autonomy had been a mistake. Yet he couldn't avoid what Alfredo Rada recollects as being one of the worst moments in his first year of government. Santa Cruz, Beni, Pando, and Tarija held four simultaneous councils on December 15, 2006. They declared that without the two-thirds they wouldn't comply with the new Constitution. The Santa Cruz elite announced that they had managed to assemble a council of one million even though they'd only convened about 300,000 people. Twenty people marched in New York, among them the soccer player "El Diablo" Echeverri, who carried the sign "No to Communism in Bolivia." Instead of launching a counterattack, Morales praised the councils for demanding the country's unity.

The regional conflicts continued into 2007. In January, a group from the MAS went out into the streets calling for the resignation of Cochabamba governor Manfred Reyes Villa. When they confronted members from his party, two people died, one from each side.

In July, Sucre's demand to recover its full status as the country's capital had already made it to the national level (the judicial power is run from there, but not the executive and legislative), where it had received incitement from Santa Cruz and the rest of the eastern departments, hoping to erode Morales' power in the west. Meanwhile, La Paz mobilized en masse to refuse the transfer and reaffirm itself as the political capital.

For the August 7 military parade, Morales arranged a march that was intended to reinforce the relationship between the armed forces and indigenous people of Santa Cruz. Both marched together. At the head of the indigenous people were Los Ponchos Rojos, an Aymara militia with a territorial base in the Bolivian west. Some voices of the Santa Cruz elite described the parade as terrorist. But the harshest words came from the commander in chief of the armed forces, Wilfredo Vargas. He said that the country was threatened by "abominable enemies" who put "national security, integrity, and dignity" at risk. He was speaking about the Santa Cruz elite without naming them.

The breach between the west and east persisted.

The Constitution was initially approved in the last week of November. Without the opposition's presence, MAS constituents held the vote in a military school. Outside, in the streets of Sucre, local marchers demanded the full powers of a capital and rejected the Constitution because it excluded that subject. Three people died during the police suppression, two of them from the shots of firearms. After the confrontations, Governor David Sánchez went into hiding and later exiled himself to Peru. The police withdrew to neighboring Potosí, allowing a hundred prisoners to escape from the San Roque Prison, although a few hours later, 30 of the prisioners repented and returned.

The first article of the new Constitution proclaimed Bolivia to be a "plurinational communal and social unified State." With nationalist and state spirit, it omits references to socialism in a clear differentiation from the Chávez rhetoric. It considers the "alienation of natural resources in favor of foreign powers, companies, or persons" to be treasonous to the homeland (an offense punishable by 30 years in prison). It establishes a separation between church and state, guarantees regional departmental autonomy with limited powers, includes "indigenous autonomies," allows one presidential reelection (a sector of the government pushed for unlimited reelection), and forbids the installation of foreign military bases.

On December 15, the day in which the president of the Constituent Assembly, Silvia Lazarte, submitted the new Magna Carta, the opposing crescent reasserted at a rally in Santa Cruz that they would ignore it and declared, once again, full autonomy. "They promote communism," shouted Branco Marinkovic, president of the Pro–Santa Cruz Committee. He swore to *Globus*, a Croatian magazine, that Morales admired Stalin.

Bolivia frequently undergoes periods of tension, conflict, and deaths, but it has an astonishing capability to begin a cycle of calm again. The incendiary language—and a certain frivolity of the foreign press—contributed to the mistaken prediction of civil war.

"If you want to get me out, you'll have to take me out of the Palace dead," Morales stated, hours before Christmas Eve. It was reported that there was a conspiracy against him involving the United States, José María Aznar, and the Santa Cruz oligarchy. "They're banging on the door to the barracks."

On January 7, 2008, the president and opposing governors sat down in the Burned Palace to negotiate. The dialogue table sought to come to an understanding through an agenda that touched on a variety of subjects, but the two main ones were the oppositional regions' approval of the new Constitution and the national government's recognition of regional autonomy. Unofficially, both sides confirmed their intention of moving forward with an electoral timeline that included a vote to approve the new Constitution, making decisions about the large rural estates (if 12,500 or 25,000 acres should be the maximum area allotted for farming and livestock estates), and autonomous referendums. However, the negotiations didn't work out.

In his first two years as president, Evo relied on the construction of opposing identities. He was nationalist and anti-imperialist; popular and plebeian against the elites and oligarchies; an Indian defiant of internal and external colonialism; anti-neoliberal, but careful not to call himself a socialist.

In the Burned Palace, those identities coexist with the political gymnastics of giving and asking. It's how he's been his whole life, against the eradication of coca and in the roadblocks. He negotiates by calling for sacrifice, putting aside sectarian attitudes, and coming together. Then he demonstrates his own commitment. If that fails, he accuses the interlocutor of being an accomplice to the old order or an activist against change. If all of that fails, he'll begin to negotiate.

Evo is a machine of assimilating and processing information and ideas. A sponge. He puts a lot of stock in his dreams but more still in his political instinct and intuition. For instance, he said, for no apparent reason, that he didn't want to attend the event at the René Moreno University of Santa Cruz in November 2006. He ended up going, someone tried to assault him, and the police threw tear gas. He got angry with the ministers who encouraged the trip. He asked them not to contradict his intuition.

Practically, he has no life beyond politics. He didn't have one as a union leader and now even less so as president. He is ignorant of each and every one of the familial customs. His children, Álvaro and Eva, born from different mothers, live far from the Palace. One of their mothers denounced Morales, in his time as a parliament member, for not giving her monthly alimony. When a European diplomat was told that the president's children are the same age, he asked whether he had twins. "I'm not selfish, and I wanted each of them to have their own mother," he replied. He sometimes refers to the unknown older women who salute him in the streets as mothers-in-law or ex-mothers-in-law.

The stories of those mothers-in-law's daughters have multiplied since he assumed the presidency. On March 11, 2006, *La Razón* reported that the president had an "intimate friend," referring to Nieves Soto, a 25-year-old *cocalera*. "She is," the column detailed, "a woman who wears a traditional indigenous skirt, possesses a slender figure, a precocious smile, and a pair of braids that are always well kept." The writer, Elena Poniatowska, revealed Evo's relationship with the Mexican María Luisa Reséndiz in 2006. Taking into account the intermittence of distance, they saw each other for 12 years. Poniatowska had accessed their photos and correspondence. "I read over the letters," wrote the author of *Massacre in Mexico*, "that now feel like shrouds from being read so much and that speak more than anything about struggle and of encounters in Vienna, in Paris, in Liege, in

Berlin. Every time I exclaim: 'What a very handsome man!' María fluffs up with pride."

After assuming the presidency, Evo declared that he owned one car, his plot in El Chapare that he's neglected due to lack of time, and two small properties. He only allows himself a few material pleasures, such as that carnival when he bought a Nautica jacket. He likes to dress well and wear brand-name sneakers. He takes care of them and is careful not to ruin his presidential pairs playing soccer.

Evo likes to show the few people who enter into the privacy of one of his rooms the photos of the public man. The story of his life—the one that he tells—is a succession of portraits; he saves few video and audio records. He can remember the photos from a march at the end of the 1980s, and he'll notice the absence of an assistant in the pictures from a bilateral meeting. That memory gives him a tremendous power over others. He can reproach them with inconsequential or inopportune facts from the past that they do not even remember.

Morales considers trust to be a supreme value. He divides the world between the people he can trust and those he can't. Walter Chávez—who developed a science of how to understand him and knew when his corporal movements meant that he felt like going to the bathroom or eating fruit—concluded that his eyes narrow when he distrusts or dislikes someone. But when the opposite occurs with someone, he makes jokes about women—if it's a man—or he invites that person to travel with him, although he might not talk to him later on.

Evo's distrust can be explained through his history and because some leaders that he respected sold themselves out. A detail can earn his mistrust. If a leader promises to bring truckloads of people to a rally and doesn't follow through—as has happened—he or she will have problems. The president will remember and even look for those demonstrators in the crowd. He retains the description of social organizations and their members in his head.

Evo hears details about conspiracies against him almost once a week. He has made many of them public—such as the coup broadcast by a German journalist or the supposed assassination attempt that would have involved Santa Cruz soldiers—provoking a negative social perception of him: that he sees conspiracies on every corner. Some of the conspiracies, however, he doesn't report. Once, a group of officials brought him gossip and rumors of a coup with the objective of showing themselves to be useful informants. Evo saw through to their ulterior motives and broke with them.

In general, his ministers are submissive and fearful of him. Once in a Cabinet meeting, Morales asked them to criticize him. Nila Heredia, in charge of the health sector, told Evo that he is often hasty to make statements, and she demanded that he consider what his ministers have to say more. Although Morales responded angrily to her, Heredia went up in his esteem. He is aware that he often decides what to say without thinking. Evo thinks of his statements in terms of their impact. Perhaps it's an echo of his old union days—he knows how to win an assembly.

The more docile of the ministers feel obligated to implement Morales' ideas even if they don't always agree with them. Some initiatives, however, are not realized because execution is impossible. In truth, many measures are initiated, but few are consolidated.

The president becomes angry with officials when he sees them as depoliticized, idle, or lacking commitment. He doesn't always promote discussion. In an evaluation meeting, Morales concluded that Venezuela and Cuba had done more than many of the ministers.

Evo reproaches officials for their pasts. "You supported Goni," he threw at one. "You're not a revolutionary," he fired at another. When someone suggested that Evo marry, he responded by saying, "You have two mistresses." To another he listed the number of divorces he had had. He went even further with an ex-advisor, calling him "*witsu*"—twisted—for having a mistress.

Like a child eager to learn, Morales listens to the experts, but he can quickly become argumentative, which happened with a group of Spanish advisors who were showing him an electoral system to select the Constituent Assembly in PowerPoint. He grabbed a marker and drew on the screen, proposing just the opposite.

Morales has a historic mistrust of the middle class. He always saw it as moody and fickle. He maintains that he has included them in his political project, that they have benefited from his measures, and that he has given them half of the Cabinet. However, in the first year and a half, the government did not demonstrate a consistent strategy to secure its support.

Evo understands some of the challenges facing him. The social organizations sometimes lack historic vision and clientelism tends to erode their foundations. He lacks political anchoring in the east of the country. He fears that the transformative momentum is wasting away or wearing down and that the government will end up as a mere administrator of the status quo.

At times he governs in an astoundingly unstructured environment. The MAS refuses to have possessions or any offices beyond the many syndicates where they have already organized. Morales doesn't enjoy even the most minimal comforts; he encourages ascetism and surrounds himself with like-minded people, without material ambitions.

The precariousness is material; it appears in the state bureaucracy, in the training of his officials, in the chaos of governmental organization, and in the institutional weakness of the country. But the strength is in the rupture with the past and in the ambitious transformation of Bolivia that he has proposed.

Evo is the son of that precariousness and, simultaneously, the embodiment of change.

La Paz, February 5, 2008

AFTERWORD

Between May 2008 and January 2010, Bolivia underwent dramatic transformations. Even the name changed, and the Republic of Bolivia turned into the Plurinational State of Bolivia. The new denomination was promoted by the new Constitution, the first in the history of the former Republic to be approved by popular vote.

The January 2009 constitutional referendum was seen as a temporary conclusion to a political and regional conflict that harassed the country, and especially the government, during the preceding year. A majority of the international press warned of the imminence of civil war. According to this foreign correspondent gospel, the Republic of Bolivia was heading toward territorial secession because of a forceful clash between the central government and the regional leaders in the east of the country.

During the same period, as a president, Evo Morales endured hardships in his political life that would have been unforeseeable years and even months before. After failing in his attempt to visit several eastern cities and eventually losing territorial control of those regions in August 2008, he won his reelection as president in a landslide in December 2009. He obtained 64.4 percent of the popular vote—nearly 40 percent more than his main challenger, the ex-Cochabamba mayor, Manfred Reyes Villa. His party won two thirds of the seats in Congress, which ensured him absolute majority. Bolivian voters turned him into the most popular president ever; he enjoyed the widest support of any public servant who took office during a democratic period.

Beginning on May 4, 2008, the eastern departments convened to vote on a series of popular proposals regarding their autonomic institutions and especially drafts of future state constitutions. With these proclamations, the regional leaders aspired to further the process of establishing departmental autonomies. The legality of these drafts was questioned by the central government every bit as much as the voting process set up to legitimize the claim to broader autonomy. In Santa Cruz, the biggest, richest, and most populated of the eastern departments, 85 percent voted in favor of autonomy status.

The night of the election, as thousands of people from the city of Santa Cruz were already honking their horns and unfurling Santa Cruz's green and white departmental flags, Morales lost his composure in front of the cameras. He angrily emphasized the low turnout—39 percent—and the general illegality of the election. These manners were proof of his weakness in the east and of his resolve to take on its leaders. In the following weeks, the departments of Beni, Pando, and Tarija carried out their own autonomic plebiscites. The results were similar to those in Santa Cruz. The Party of the Crescent was born. The name evoked the shape of the conflation of those four departments on the map of the Bolivian east.

The Crescent was the only opposition during Morales' first term to acquire a notoriety and significance of its own. Claimed by a socially transversal alliance, *autonomy* was the catchword of an ever-growing regional identity. This identity strived to conceal the greatest fear of the region's elite: loss of control over the exploitation of natural resources. Many land property titles were relatively recent and dated from the years of Hugo Banzer Suárez' dictatorship—a military man from Santa Cruz. "Autonomy now," the prevailing slogan in the Crescent departments, also unveiled a peculiar weakness, the Party's inviability on the national level.

The Party of the Crescent gained a precarious ally when the city authorities of Sucre, host in the middle of the country of the troubled Constituent Assembly, adhered to demands for autonomy. Eastern spin doctors skillfully reminded people in Sucre of their own territorial objective: restoring this historical urban center of colonial times that had proclaimed independence in 1809 to its former status as a capital city. The emergence of that regionalist movement, coupled with the unwillingness of the government to incorporate autonomies into its own political agenda and find a common ground with regional leaders, strengthened the idea of Morales' vulnerability.

The parliamentary brigade of Jorge "Tuto" Quiroga, leader of the political opposition, thought they had come to see the definitive decline of the president. As a result, they accepted Morales' challenge to hold a recall referendum for the offices of chief of state and the governors (technically, *prefectos*) in the nine Bolivian departments. If he were to lose, the chief of state would have to resign and hold general elections.

In the week before the recall referendum, due to road and airport blockades, Morales was unable to attend the Sucre Independence Day Celebration and an event in Tarija, where he would have met with Cristina Fernández de Kirchner and Hugo Chávez. The oppositional groups thus revealed what they had learned from the tactics of indigenous and social movements. The referendum resulted as an affirmation of Morales' command over the general will of his country. On August 10, Morales was ratified with 67.4 percent of the vote. The opposing eastern governors also managed to keep their positions. Santa Cruz governor Rubén Costas obtained 64.4 percent of the vote. In his victory speech, he accused the national government of being a dictatorship and of practicing state terrorism and Aymara fundamentalism. His sympathizers shouted, "Independence, independence."

Morales received me alone in the presidential residence during his first post-election dinner. He narrated how, in the weekend before the referendum, he fell back into the habit of speeding around in his car listening to Andean and wind instrumental music as a sort of soundtrack. He cast his vote accompanied by his children. "I have always been in favor of dialogue. I don't know why there's so much surprise about my speech," he said in reference to what he'd said from the Burned Palace balcony when he called for national unity, congratulated the ratified governors, and proposed an agenda to harmonize the new Constitution with departmental autonomy. The media's harsh handling of Morales was spotlighted during election night. Unitel, which is owned by one of the wealthiest eastern landowning families, stood out in particular. "Ninety percent of the media is against me, but two-thirds of the country supports this process of change." While eating a bowl of quinoa soup, one of his two cell phones rang with news from Pando, the eastern department where the central government had directed the greatest effort to recall Governor Leopoldo Fernández. They fell less than 2,000 votes short.

After the referendum, radical voices from the east argued that the president had been recalled in Santa Cruz (he lost 59 percent to 41 percent) and no longer exercised the presidency in those territories. According to that interpretation a dual power was then in effect in Bolivia, one in La Paz and the other in Santa Cruz.

The regional opposition radicalized. The oil region of Chaco declared an indefinite blockade, demanding a refund of oil revenues allotted by the government for a universal pension for those more than 60 years old. In the east, autonomist groups occupied the offices of the central government, eventually destroying some of them. Organizations sympathetic to the central government initiated a siege of Santa Cruz de la Sierra. The opposition responded with more blockades of roads and airport runways. They also obstructed the delivery of food to the western departments.

September 11 gave rise to the so-called Pando Massacre. According to a UN report based on the investigations of the Bolivian judiciary, the governorship of Pando and other like-minded groups were responsible for the deaths of nine *campesinos* who supported Morales' government. Two members of the opposition also died in the confrontations. The investigation motivated a long debate. A report by UNASUR (Union of South American Nations, an organization that reunites South American nations) recorded at least 20 deaths, although at least two victims turned up alive in Brazil.

That same September 11, Morales expelled the U.S. ambassador in Bolivia, Philip Goldberg. He accused him of conspiring against democracy and promoting Bolivia's division. "Like he did in Yugoslavia," the president summed up, in reference to the diplomat's previous position in the Balkans. "Without fear of the empire, today I declare Philip Goldberg persona non grata, and I ask that our chancellor [...] be sent to the ambassador today to inform him of the decision of the national government and its president so that he may return to his country immediately," he stated at an event in the government Palace. He also expelled the DEA.

Hours later, the state-run Bolivian State Petroleum Company (YPFB) reduced gas delivery to Brazil by 10 percent due to a pipeline explosion in the Chaco region. The company held the autonomist groups responsible for the "terrorist attack."

The possibility of civil war picked up enthusiastic headlines in the international press.

The crisis resulted in an urgent and extraordinary meeting of the UNASUR members. Most of the South American presidents traveled to Santiago, Chile. In a statement showing full support of Morales, they announced that they would not react kindly to any incidents involving an attempted coup, institutional rupture, or any other action that could affect the territorial integrity of the country. Morales had come to Santiago denouncing a civil-military coup with U.S. participation. He asked UNASUR to be harder on Washington, but his request was not heard.

A long negotiation began in Bolivia between the central government and regional leaderships. At first no visible progress was seen. Resolving the conflict would involve an agreement in Congress and a new consensual Constitution approved by referendum. Negotiations moved into parliament.

To put pressure on the opposition, progovernment groups launched a massive march in support of the Constitution. In one week, *campesinos*, miners, coca workers, farmers, and other sectors affiliated with the MAS walked the 120 miles that separate the village of Caracollo from La Paz. Morales joined the march on October 20, the last day. The next morning, the president was in downtown La Paz calming down supporters, who, tired of listening to a congressional debate that had lasted for more than 18 uninterrupted hours, were threatening to take the legislative Palace by storm. Later, to further express their impatience, they exploded sticks of dynamite.

The government and parliamentary opposition agreed to change 100 of the 411 articles of the Constitution. The concessions made by the government were considerable, especially when concerning land ownership and indigenous rights. They gave up the original idea of enforcing a retroactive limit on landholdings. Certain peculiarities of the indigenous autonomies and their legal system were limited, and the number of their direct representatives in the legislative body was reduced. Departmental autonomy was incorporated into the constitutional text, although with less powers than the east had desired. The possibility of just one reelection for the executive branch limited the prospect of an indefinite number of terms. In this consensual Constitution, the government saw the deepening of a nationalist state model, as well as the consolidation of an inclusive agenda unprecedented in the country's history.

The eastern governors refused the parliamentary agreement. One of them did so from prison—Leopoldo Fernández had been arrested on the grounds that he was responsible for the Pando Massacre. Also dissatisfied with the consensual text were certain Indianist and leftist groups that had hoped for a more radical Constitution.

When he learned of the agreement in Congress, the president broke down in public with relief. The officials accompanying him in Plaza Murillo were visibly moved by his response. He'd been up all night with the aid of 13 cups of black coffee. "Now I can die in peace," he said. The new Constitution was approved in January by 61.4 percent of Bolivians; 80 percent voted to limit the quantity of acres that one single citizen can posses to 12,500.

Days after the referendum, a great scandal of government corruption was made public as Morales dismissed one of his most trusted men, the president of the YPFB, Santos Ramírez. The move was made after the discovery that

businessman Jorge O'Connor D'Arlach had been murdered during a trans-
action involving the delivery of a bribe of $450,000. His company, Catler
Uniservices, had obtained a contract for the installation of a gas processing
plant.

In the beginning of February, the president named the sixth YPFB
president in three years of government. This company, the government's
flagship, had showed serious difficulties industrializing hydrocarbons, ful-
filling the gas supply, and exercising administrative transparency.

In April 2009, regional opposition carried out its last great self-coup. A
group of special police agents killed three "foreign mercenaries" in a Santa
Cruz hotel, among them the Bolivian-Croatian Eduardo Rosza Flores. In
an interview that he'd requested be published in case "something should
happen to him," Rosza Flores told of how his objective was to found a
"new country in Santa Cruz" and that "he had been called" for the mission.
According to the prosecutor in the case, his cell received financing from
members of the Santa Cruz elite. Part of the arsenal was found in Cotas, a
telephone company that stands as a symbol of Santa Cruzism. One of the
cell's plans appeared to have been to assassinate Morales. The Rosza Flores
case helped the government to prove the existence of destabilizing plans
against it and to hold certain sectors of the Santa Cruz elite accountable.

In September 2009, Morales traveled to New York to attend the annual
inauguration of the UN General Assembly. It was the first time he'd told
me it was now appropriate to evaluate that term of his presidency.

On his way to Central Park, where he would go jogging between 5:45
and 6:45 A.M., he explained that the fate of his government had been
defined precisely between August and October 2008.

"There have been defining moments in my presidency. The recall in
August, the attempted coup and the Pando Massacre in September, and
the march in defense of the Constitution in October. Anyone who wants to
fully understand my government should study in detail what happened on
each one of those days."

The conversation was interrupted when the president heard the call,
"Evoooooo," by José Luis Rodríguez Zapatero. He continued his exercise
flanked by the Spanish prime minister.

Later on in the suite, with a very North American breakfast of eggs,
sausage, and potatoes before him, he talked about his decision to expel the
U.S. ambassador. "I wanted to throw him out earlier, but they told me not
to, until I said enough, I'll do it anyway."

At his side, Chancellor Choquehuanca explained that he had been in the middle of a meeting with Goldberg in his office when Morales made the announcement. Within a few minutes, he was interrupted by an urgent call from the president.

"I just fired Goldberg."

"I'm with him now."

"Tell him."

Choquehuanca went back into his office and informed the ambassador of the president's decision.

Goldberg said that it couldn't be true, but he came out of his shock when he received a text message confirming the news.

"Chancellor, I ask that you reconsider the decision. I ask that you speak with your president."

Goldberg left the room and returned shortly thereafter.

"I ask that you reconsider."

Morales did not reconsider.

While peeling a hard-boiled egg, the president asserted that the coup against him was broken up once he'd let go of Goldberg. He compared it to the overthrowing of Manuel Zelaya in June 2009. "What they couldn't do in Bolivia happened in Honduras."

Morales was already beginning to lower his expectations of Barack Obama's policies in Latin America. "He's surrounded by hawks," he said of the new U.S. president he'd met during the Summit of the Americas in Trinidad and Tobago.

In May 2009, Secretary of State Hillary Clinton had criticized the Bush administration's policy regarding Morales and Chávez. "The prior administration tried to isolate them, tried to support opposition to them, tried to turn them into international pariahs. It didn't work." According to Clinton, that policy had allowed China, Iran, and Russia to increase their presence in the hemisphere. "If you look at the gains particularly in Latin America that Iran is making and China is making, it is quite disturbing. They are building very strong economic and political connections with a lot of these leaders."

The first significant decision made by the Democratic administration in relation to Bolivia was to decertify the Bolivian government in the fight against drug trafficking, along with the governments of other countries such as Venezuela. The measure prevents Bolivian goods from enjoying tariff preferences in the United States, turning China into a favorite destination for the country's exports. Decertification is a continuation of

Bush administration policies. "Narcotizing" the bilateral relationship with Bolivia had already tested its limits in the last quarter of the century.

In U.S. power circles, the predominant interpretation of the phenomenon of Bolivia is to present a leader emotionally connected with the indigenous and poor majority and influenced and financed by Chávez. The notion of a mentor relationship underestimates Morales more than it overestimates Chávez. That portrayal, glossed with the vilifying labels of populism and authoritarianism, proves insufficient to explain the results of the presidential election of December 6, 2009.

Morales obtained 64.2 percent of the votes and took two-thirds of the seats of the brand-new Plurinational Legislative Assembly. The opposition, which had centered its campaign attacks on labeling the government authoritarian, was hit hard by the 38 percent MAS lead. The right-wing candidacy made up of Manfred Reyes Villa and Leopoldo Fernández only bolstered Morales' strategy of dividing the political sphere between the old and the new. While Manfred Reyes Villa faced the court on various charges of corruption, Fernández had to campaign from jail because of his role in the Pando Massacre. Morales' supporters repeated that one candidate was using the election to avoid prison while the other was using it to get out.

The regional opposition of the east did not present its own candidate nor did it involve itself definitively with any party in the opposition. It attempted to preserve itself for the departmental elections of 2010. But the surprising number of votes for Morales in the east (he won Tarija and rose above 40 percent in Santa Cruz and Pando) and the internal divisions of the opposition leadership called into doubt the effectiveness of their strategy.

The election results fueled the fervor of political analysts. In an editorial, British daily paper *The Guardian* compared Morales to former South African president Nelson Mandela:

> Mr. Morales has gone a long way to making the social transformation inside Bolivia irreversible. The Indian majority is getting back the voice denied to it for centuries. South Africa remembers Nelson Mandela and Eastern Europe the fall of the Berlin Wall. What a former herder of llamas has achieved in one of the world's poorest nations may be no less momentous.

At the regional level, Brazil has strengthened itself as a world power and player. But Bolivia is the inevitable point of reference in understanding the radical liberal turn in South America. The nationalizations, the rise of state control over the administration of natural resources, and the approval of a new Constitution have become deeply rooted in Bolivian society. A more rational regime in the hydrocarbons sector—run with the belief that benefits should be received by the whole of society—and a Constitution that improves representation in a country marked by exclusion help to elucidate Morales' popularity in the first place.

This support may be explained by both symbolic and concrete elements. It is undeniable that Morales' situation as the first indigenous president has had a noteworthy impact. But that change of zeitgeist is not limited to the presence of *campesinos* and indigenous people in government, nor to the effective slogan, "We are all presidents." New aspirations appear on those horizons: the possibility of living well and occupying spaces previously banned to them. For the first time in history, Indians can walk through parts of cities they had previously been forbidden to enter.

Among the concrete elements are the social programs designed for school children, seniors, and young mothers (the Juancito Pinto, Dignity Income, and Juana Azurduy vouchers). The literacy program has been a major success in a country with high levels of illiteracy, leading UNESCO to declare Bolivia free of illiteracy in 2009. These universal plans have had an even more significant impact in rural areas.

The economy's good performance has been accumulative and remarkable. During the years of the Morales administration, the reserves in the Central Bank have increased from $1.7 million in 2005 to $8.58 million, there has been fiscal surplus and a low deficit, the peso has risen in value against the dollar, and inflation has been restrained. In a country familiar with the traumatic experience of hyperinflation, such stability and confidence are crucial to understanding the support of the lower and middle classes.

Two final reasons explain Morales' popularity. He managed to reappropriate the idea of autonomy. He stopped calling it "a tool" of the oligarchy and turned it into part of his agenda. He has also succeeded in installing the idea of a new sovereignty when faced with Washington, and in so doing he has strengthened the nationalist vein of his government program. In the most anti–North American of the South American countries, this new relationship with the United States is popular.

The 2006 inauguration ritual was repeated.

Morales was named the spiritual leader of the indigenous people of America in the ruins of Tiwanaku on January 21, 2010. He was presented with two indigenous ruling staffs in the entryway to Kalasasaya Temple. He took the crowd by surprise by speaking in Quechua and Aymara for a few minutes. In Spanish, he said that his government is run by the Inca laws of *"ama sua, ama quella, ama llulla"* (not to steal, not to be lazy, and not to lie). "Over the last four years, I have been the first to rise and the last to go to bed; they've accused me of many things, but no adversary could ever say that I'm lazy."

He assumed the presidency the next day, inaugurating the Plurinational State that buried the liberal Republic that had governed the country for 180 years. Certain native symbols were substituted in the ceremony. The José Antonio de Sucre medal worn by the vice presidents, which had read "Republic of Bolivia," now said "Plurinational State of Bolivia." The new presidential sash includes the *Wiphala* flag. Until the year before, there had only been one painting of Simón Bolívar and another of Sucre (considered the standard "founding fathers") in the Congress building, now home of the brand-new Assembly. A painting of Túpac Katari and his consort, Bartolina Sisa, those responsible for the indigenous insurrection of 1781, has now been added to highlight plurinationality.

Morales did not swear by God but instead by the "national heroes who gave their lives for the nation, the Bolivian people, and the equality of all human beings." He observed the assemblage before him of hats, Andean caps, ponchos, and mining helmets on the members of the new Assembly. He was surprised by the presence of so few neckties. "The colonial State is dead. The new plurinational, autonomic, and communal State is being born," he said in a long speech, in which he enumerated the achievements of his presidency, without omitting even the slightest details, such as the quantity of low-cost light bulbs distributed.

He appointed a cabinet with 50 percent female ministers (another unprecedented occurrence in Bolivia) and with a relatively small indigenous presence. He said that he would govern them until 2015 toward a new horizon, the horizon of "communitarian socialism." The present was already another time.

New York, January 23, 2010

ACKNOWLEDGMENTS

Alfredo Grieco y Bavio's contribution was indispensable. Ariel Magnus, Sinclair Thompson, Manuel Trancón, Ernesto Semán, Gabriela Esquivada, and Pablo Stefanoni read chapters and/or full drafts, emending errors and making good suggestions.

Documentary filmmaker Sean Langan, with whom I shared a long journey from Buenos Aires to Tijuana and a few weeks in 2002 with Evo Morales, suggested that I write this story down. I began an outline as a graduate student at the University of London. Historian James Dunkerley supervised my thesis on regional conflict in Bolivia and always gave me sound advice. My gratitude also goes to my professors, Colin Lewis and Caterina Pizzigoni, and to my fellow graduate students, Eleonor Murphy, Andressa Caldas, Pablo Uchoa, Guillaume Long, Natalia Gavazzo, Tom Feldberg, and Julián Miglierini.

I received much help in Bolivia. Maggy Talavera was generous in Santa Cruz. Cecilia Illanes of CEDIB and Liliana Aguirre of *La Razón* assisted with the archives. Andrés Soliz Rada and Pedro Susz have been gracious with their ideas and time. José Antonio Quiroga and I argued about the Bolivian process in various tones of voice. Cayetano Llobet, Juan Carlos Rocha, and Fernando Molina provided their critical perspectives.

Many people in the Burned Palace contributed in various ways. At the risk of forgetting some names, I mention Maya Nemtala, Sacha Llorenti, Juan Ramón Quintana, Eva, Janet, Lucía Suárez, Álvaro García Linera, Alex Contreras, Víctor Orduna, Tom Kruse, Olivier Fontan, Gustavo Guzmán, Carlos Villegas, and Patricia Costas. I thank Noah Friedman-Rudovsky, the official photographer for this book.

My gratitude to Jin Auh, from the Wylie Agency, for her staunch support in securing the English edition, as well as Florencia Ure and Paula Viale from Random House Argentina.

I shared material and discussions, among other things, with a group of Bolivianized foreigners, among them Hernán Pruden, Pablo Stefanoni, Bruno Fornillo, Hervé Do Alto, Gloria Beretevide, Pedro Brieger, Hinde Pomenariec, and Salvador Schavelzon. I was able to see an unedited interview with Manuel Rocha thanks to Julia Solomonoff and the Cocalero crew.

Guillermo (Antonioni Wilson) Cruces transported research material for the book from Buenos Aires to New York thanks to pilots Franco Rinaldi and Philip Kitzberger. Dorián, Silvina, Manuel, Ariel, Esteban, Gabriela, Nicolás, María José-Josefina, Natalia, Horacio, Ernesto, and Julián were the best company in the dog days of that summer when I began to draft this text.

Finally, two special acknowledgments: to Walter Chávez, a protagonist of this book, for his friendship over so many years and for that chat in a Plaza Murillo café; and to Maxine Swann, for all this time: twice, of course.

SOURCES

Interviewees Who Agreed to Be Mentioned

Evo Morales, Álvaro García Linera, Juan Ramón Quintana, Alex Contreras, Sacha Llorenti, Filemón Escobar, Héctor Arce, Walter Chávez, Alfredo Rada, Carlos Villegas, Andrés Solitz Rada, David Choquehuanca, Pablo Solón, Gustavo Guzmán, Pablo Guzmán, Iván Iporre, Maya Nemtala, Paola Zapata, Antonio Peredo, José Antonio Quiroga, Carlos Mesa, Ricardo Paz, Jaime Paz Zamora, Oscar Eid, Felipe Quispe, Hormando Vaca Diez, Germán Antelo, Sergio Antelo, Carlos Dabdoud, Rubén Costas, Osvaldo "Chato" Peredo, Carlos Hugo Molina, Pedro Rivero, Eduardo Rodríguez Veltzé, Juan del Granado, Coco Pinelo, Cayetano Llobet

Archives

Pro–Santa Cruz Committee
La Razón
Center for Documentation and Information (CEDIB)
Library of the Higher University of San Andrés (UMSA)
Ministry of Foreign Relations and Culture of Bolivia
George Washington University

Newspapers and Magazines

Bolivia

Hoy, La Razón, El Diario, Presencia, Útima Hora, Los Tiempos, Opinión, El Deber, La Prensa, Nuevo Día, Estrella del Oriente, Extra, Enfoques, Pulso, El Juguete Rabioso

Foreign

Clarín, La Nación, Ámbito Financiero, Página/12, Perfil Veintitrés, Txt, Noticias, O Globo, Istoé, Veja, The New York Times, The Washington Post, The Guardian, The Economist, The Financial Times, Le Monde, Brecha, Nueva Sociedad, El Nacional, Granma, El País (España), El Mundo, La Jornada

Documentaries

Travels with a Gringo, Sean Langan (2003)
Our Brand is Crisis, Rachel Boynton (2005)
El estado de la cosas (*The State of Things*), Marcos Loayza (2007)
Cocalero, Alejandro Landes (2007)
Looking for the Revolution, Rodrigo Vazquez (2007)

BIBLIOGRAPHY

Albó, X. (2002) *Pueblos indios en política*. La Paz: Plural, Cipca.

Almaraz Paz, S. (1985) *Réquiem para una república*. La Paz: Los Amigos, del Libro.

Añez Ribera, L. (2003) *Breve historia del Comité Pro Santa Cruz*. In La sociedad de Estudios geográficos e históricos en su centenario, Libo homenaje. Santa Cruz.

Ardaya Salinas, G. and L. Verdesoto. (1993) *Entre la presión y el consenso: escenarios y previsions para la relación Bolivia-Estados Unidos*. La Paz: Upadex, Ildis.

Assies, A. and T. Salman. (2003) *Crisis in Bolivia: The elections of 2002 and their aftermath*. Institute of Latin American Studies, Research Papers No. 56.

Baldivia, J., F. Molina, and H. Oporto. (2007) *Buscando el porvenir en el pasado. Radiografía de la ideología del gobierno*. La Paz: Eureka.

Barrios Marón, R. (1989) *Bolivia y Estados Unidos. Democracia, Derechos Humanos y Narcotráfico (1980–1982)*. La Paz: Flacso, Hisbol.

Barrios, Suvelza, F. X. (2005) *Propuesta autonómica de Santa Cruz*. Balance de fortalezas y debilidades. La Paz: Plural.

Bascopé Aspiazu, R. (1982) *La veta Blanca. Coca y Cocaína en Bolivia*. La Paz: Aquí.

Blaiser, C. (1971) "The United States and the Revolution." In Malloy, J. and R. Thorn, eds. *Beyond the Revolution. Bolivia since 1952*. University of Pittsburgh Press.

Calderón, F. and A. Szmukler. (2000) *La política en las calles*. La Paz: Ceres, Plural, Usab.

Caparrós, M. (1992) *Larga distancia*. Buenos Aires: Planeta.

Chávez Zamorano, O. and S. Peñaranda del Granado. (1997) *Jaime Paz Zamora: Un política de raza*. La Paz.

Comité Pro Santa Cruz. (2005) *Gestión Rubén Costas Aguilera 2003–2005*. Santa Cruz.

Contreras Baspineiro, A. (1994) *La marcha histórica*. Cochabamba: CEDIB.

———. (2005) *Evo, una historia de dignidad*. Cochabamba.

Corte Nacional Electoral. (2006) *Asamblea Constituyente Referéndum Autonómica*, Documento de Información Pública No. 3. La Paz.

Curia, W. (2006) *El último peronista. La cara oculta de Kirchner*. Buenos Aires: Sudamericana.

Dunkerley, J. (1984) *Rebellion in the Veins: Political Struggle in Bolivia, 1952–82*. London: Verso.

———. (1998) *The 1997 Bolivian election in historical perspective*. Londres: University of London, Institute of Latin American Studies, Ocassional Papers No. 16.

Dunkerley, J. (2000) "The United States and Latin America in the Long Run (1800—1945)." In J. Dunkerley, *Warriors and Scribes*. Londres: Verso.

———. (2003) "The Origins of The Bolivian Revolution in the Twentieth Century: Some Reflections." In M. Grindle and P. Domingo, *Proclaiming Revolution. Bolivian in comparative perspective*. David Rockefeller Center of Latin American Studies, Harvard University and Institute of Latin American Studies, University of London.

———. (2007) "Evo Morales, 'The Two Bolivias' and the Third Bolivian Revolution." In *Journal of Latin American Studies, University of London* No. 39. Cambridge University Press.

Gamarra, E. (1994) *Entre la droga y la democracia. La cooperación entre Estados Unidos-Bolivia y la lucha contra el narcotráfico*. La Paz: Ildis.

García Linera, A. (2006) *El evismo: lo nacional y popular en acción*. In Observatorio Social de América Latina No. 19. Buenos Aires: Revista del Observatorio Social de América Latina.

García Linera, A., R. Gutiérrez, R. Prada, and L. Tapia. (2000) *El retorno de la Bolivia plebeya*. La Paz: Muela de Diablo.

García Linera, A., R. Gutiérrez, R. Prada, F. Quispe, and L. Tapia. (2001) *Tiempos de rebelión*. La Paz: Muela de diablo, Comuna.

García Linera, A., R. Prada, and L. Tapia. (2004) *Memorias de octubre*. La Paz: Muela del diablo.

García Linera, A. (coord.), M. Chávez León, and P. Costas Monje. (2005) *Sociología de los movimientos sociales en Bolivia. Estructuras de movilización, repertorios culturales y acción política*. La Paz: Diakonia, Oxfam.

García Vespa, H. (2004) *Fundación del Comité Pro Santa Cruz (documentos)*. Santa Cruz: Editorial e Imprenta Universitaria.

Grandin, G. (2006) *Empire's Workshop. Latin America, the United States, and the Rise of the New Imperialism*. New York: Metropolitan Books.

Gómez, L. (2004) *El Alto de pie. Una insurrectión aymara en Bolivia*. La Paz: Preguntas Urgentes.

Gumucio Baptista, M. (1986) *Historia contemporánea de Bolivia*. México: Fondo de Cultura Económica.

Gumucio Granier, J. (2005) *Estados Unidos y el mar boliviano*. La Paz: Plural.

Hylton, F. and S. Thomson. (2007) *Revolutionary Horizons: Past and Present in Bolivian Politics*. New York and London: Verso.

Klein, H. (1992) *Bolivia: The Evolution of a Multi-Ethnic Society*. New York: Oxford University Press.

———. (2003) *A Concise History of Bolivia*. New York: Cambridge University Press.

La sociedad de Estudios geográficos e históricos en su centenario. (2003) *Libro homenaje*. Santa Cruz.

Lazar, S. (2006) *El Alto, Ciudad Rebelde: Organisational bases of revolt*. In *Bulletin of Latin American Research*, Vol. 25, No. 2. Londres: Blackwell Publishing.

Lavaud, J. P. (1998) *El embrollo boliviano (turbulencias sociales y desplazamientos políticos) 1952–1982*. La Paz: IFEA-UMSS-HISBOL.

Lehman, K. (1999) *Bolivia and the United States: A Limited Partnership*. Londres: The University of Georgia Press.

Llobet, C. (2005) *Sobremesa*. La Paz: El Observador.

Llorenti, S. (1999) *El silencio es cómplice*. La Paz.

Marcano, C. and A. Barrera Tyszka. (2007) *Hugo Chávez: The Definitive Biography of Venezuela's Controversial President*. New York: Random House.

Mesa, C. (1983) *Presidentes de Bolivia: entre urnas y fusiles*. La Paz: Gisbert CIA.

———. (1993) *De cerca, una década de conversaciones en democracia*. La Paz: PAT.

———. (2005) *Santa Cruz*. La Paz: Dirección de Informaciones de la Presidencia de la República.

Mesa, J., T. Gisbert, and C. Mesa. (2001) *Historia de Bolivia*. La Paz: Gisbert.

Ministerio de Hidrocarburos y Energía. (2007) *Nacionalización en el siglo XXI. 111 años de historia petrolera en Bolivia*. La Paz: Multimac.

Molina, F. (2006) *Bajo el signo del cambio. Análisis de tres procesos electorales (2002, 2005, 2006)*. La Paz: Eureka.

———. (2006) *Evo Morales y el retorno de la izquierda nacionalista*. La Paz: Eureka.

Navia, R. and D. Pinto. (2006) *Un tal Evo. Biografía no autorizada*. Santa Cruz: El País.

Orgáz García, M. (2003) *La guerra de gas. Nación versus estado trasnacional en Bolivia*. La Paz.

Peña, P. (2003) *La permanente construcción de lo cruceño. Un estudio sobre la identidad en Santa Cruz de la Sierra*. La Paz: PIEB.

Peña Claros, C. and N. Jordán Bazán. (2006) *Ser cruceño en octubre*. La Paz: PIEB.

Pineda Zamorano, F. (2007) *Evo Morales. El cambio empezó en Bolivia*. Córdoba (España): Almuzara.

PNUD Bolivia. (2004) *Informe de Desarrollo Humano en Santa Cruz*. La Paz: Plural.

———. (2007) *Informe Nacional sobre Desarrollo Humano. El estado del estado en Bolivia*. La Paz.

Presidencia de la Nación. (2004) *El libro azul. La demanda marítima boliviana*. La Paz.

Ramonet, I. (2008) *Fidel Castro: My Life: A Spoken Autobiography*. New York: Scribner.

Rivera Cusicanqui, Silvia. (1986) *Oprimidos pero no vencidos. Luchas del campesinado aymara y qhechwa 1900–1980*. La Paz: Hisbol.

———. (1993) *La Raíz: Colonizadores y colonizados en Violencias encubiertas en Bolivia Tomo (1)*. La Paz: CIPCA, Aruwiyiri.

Roca, J. L. (2001) *Economía y Sociedad en el Oriente Boliviano (Siglos XVI-XX)*. Santa Cruz: Costas.

———. (1999) *Fisonomía del regionalismo boliviano*. La Paz: Plural.

Rodas, H. (1996) *Huanchaca, modelo empresarial de la cocaína en Bolivia*, La Paz: Plural.

Sandoval, C. (2003) *Santa Cruz: Economía y Poder (1952–1993)*. La Paz: PIEB.

Sandoval, Rodríguez, I. (1979) *Culminación y ruptura del modelo nacional revolucionario. Torres en el scenario político boliviano*. La Paz: Urquiza.

Seleme, S. M. Arrieta, and A. Abrego. (1985) *Mito ideológico y democracia en Santa Cruz*. La Paz: PIEB (serie Realidad Regional).

Sierra, M., Subercaseaux, E. (2007) *Evo Morales. Primer indígena que gobierna en América del Sur*. Santa Cruz: El País.

Sivak, M. (2001) *El dictador elegido. Biografía no autorizada de Hugo Banzer Suárez.* La Paz: Plural.

———. (2007) *Santa Cruz: una tesis. El conflicto regional en Bolivia 2003–2006.* La Paz: Plural.

Soliz Rada, A. (1996) *La fortuna del presidente.* La Paz: La tarde informativa.

Stefanoni, P. (2007) *Siete preguntas y siete respuestas sobre la Bolivia de Evo Morales.* In Nueva Sociedad, No. 209. Buenos Aires.

Stefanoni, P., Do Alto, H. (2006) *Evo Morales de la coca al Palacio. Una oportunidad para la izquierda indígena.* La Paz: Malatesta.

Suárez, H. (2003) *Una semana fundamental.10 a 18 de octubre de 2003.* La Paz: Muela del Diablo.

Taboada Terán, N. (2006) *Tierra mártir. Del socialismo de David Toro al socialismo de Evo Morales.* La Paz.

Tapia, L. (2002) *La condición multisocietal, multiculturalidad, pluralismo, modernidad.* La Paz: Muela del diablo.

Thomson, S. (2003) *We Alone Will Rule: Native Andean Politics in the Age of Insurgency.* Madison: University of Wisconsin Press.

Torrez García, C. (2003) "La revolución de los Domingos en el contexto nacional e internacional." In I. Loza and I. Calmotti Crevani, *Investigaciones Históricas sobre el Oriente Boliviano. Santa Cruz*: UPSA Santa Cruz.

Urenda, J. C. (2005) *Cambio de Epoca. ¿Bolivia autonómica?* Fundación La Paz: FBDM, CAF.

Urioste, M. (2001) *Bolivia: Reform and Resistance in the Countryside (1982–2000).* Institute of Latin American Studies, Ocassional Papers No. 23.

Valverde, C. (1996) *La nación en la llanura. Santa Cruz, Beni, Pando, Tarija y su derecho a ser independiente.* Santa Cruz: Landívar.

Villegas Quiroga, C. (2002) *Privatización de la industria petrolera en Bolivia. Trayectoria y efectos tributarios.* La Paz: Cides-UMSA, Plural.

Whitehead, L. (1969) *The United States and Bolivia: A Case of Neocolonialism.* Londres: Haslemere Groups.

———. (1973) "National Power and Local Power: The Case of Santa Cruz de la Sierra, Bolivia." In F. Rabinowitz and Trueblood, eds. *Latin American Urban Research*, Vol. III, Beverly Hills: Seige.

Zalles, A. (2006) *Una pieza más en el rompecabezas boliviano. El proyecto autonomista de Santa Cruz.* In Nueva Sociedad No. 201.

Zavaleta Mercado, R. (1986) *Lo nacional popular en Bolivia.* Mexico: Siglo XXI.

———. (1987) *El poder dual.* La Paz: Los Amigos del Libro.

———. (1992) *50 años de Historia.* La Paz: Los Amigos del Libro.

INDEX